中國古代貿易瓷特展
——大英博物館館藏——

ANCIENT CHINESE TRADE CERAMICS
From
The British Museum, London

By
Regina Krahl and Jessica Harrison - Hall

國立歷史博物館
NATIONAL MUSEUM OF HISTORY
REPUBLIC OF CHINA

ANCIENT CHINESE TRADE CERAMICS
From
The British Museum, London

Publisher	Chen Kang-Shuen
Commissioners	National Museum of History
	#49, Nan-Hai Rd. Taipei, Taiwan, Tel：(02) 361-0270
Association	The British Museum, London
Editor	Committee of Edition, National Museum of History, Taipei
Writer of entries	Regina Krahl and Jessica Harrison-Hall, Dept. of Oriental Antiquities, British Museum
Translator	Cassandra Lin Tsai、Sung Kee-In, National Museum of History, Taipei
Collator	Lin Shwu-Shin、Hwang Yong-Chuan, National Museum of History, Taipei
Chief Editor	Sung Kee-In、Yang Shih-Chao, National Museum of History, Taipei
Art Editor	Wang Hsing-Kung
Printing	Sheńs Art Printing Co.
Computer Editor	Wen Hong Enterprise Co.
Publication Date	May, 1994
ISBN	957-00-3623-0

目錄
Contents

序

中國文化源遠流長，陶瓷藝術更是遠播世界，直至今日，西方人仍以china作爲陶瓷的代名詞，中國陶瓷得到世界性的肯定，自不待言。自唐代始，近千年來，貿易瓷除從陸路外傳，主要由南方遠銷至東北亞、東南亞、中東、非洲東岸以及歐洲各地，銷售有年逾百萬之紀錄，由此可見中國陶瓷文化如何風靡世界。至今世界各國博物館無不保存了很多精美絕倫的中國貿易瓷器，便是當時貿易瓷對世界行銷盛況之最好說法。

國立歷史博物館近年來致力於國際文化交流工作，成績斐然，先後舉辦多項國際合作展覽，也能獲得各界好評，尤以提倡陶瓷藝術，連續舉辦我國第一屆至第五屆陶藝雙年展，發揮了鼓勵青年陶藝創作，增加陶藝欣賞人口重要的影響。兩年前歷史博物館與歐、亞、美、非等八國合作舉辦「中國古代貿易瓷國際邀請特展」，開創了我國與世界知名博物館合作先例，尤足稱道。

今年國立歷史博物館再次與大英博物館合作，展出大英博物館所典藏中國明清時代貿易瓷珍品一六一件，並共同出版特展圖錄一鉅冊，兩館貿易瓷之合作展出與出版乃爲中英兩國博物館二百多年來首度合作，確屬難能可貴。大英博物館爲舉世聞名歷史悠久的博物館，不僅藏品豐碩，各項文物研究水準也爲學術界所推崇。今日樂見兩館進行文物以及學術合作之交流，相信對於我國博物館之發展，必能獲益，十分值得欣慰，茲以特展目錄問世在即，用綴數言，以誌紀念。

一九九四年五月二十日
教育部　部長

郭為藩

謹誌

Preface

Chinese culture has distant origins and a long history of continuity. Its ceramic art in particular is known far and wide around the globe, and today Westerners still use the word 'china' to refer to porcelain. It goes without saying that Chinese porcelain has received world-wide recognition. For almost 1,000 years commencing from the T'ang period, in addition to overland transportation, Chinese trade ceramics were mainly shipped by sea from South China to Northeast Asia, Southeast Asia, the Middle East , East Africa and Europe. Records attest to in excess of 1 million pieces being sold annually. Clearly Chinese ceramic culture at one stage took the world by storm. The fact that today museums in different countries possess so many exquisite examples of Chinese trade ceramics speaks volumes for the extent to which Chinese porcelain was marketed throughout the world in centuries past.

In recent years the National Museum of History has done remarkably well in the field of international cultural exchange, sponsoring a number of international collaborative exhibitions which have received widespread acclaim. As part of its drive to encourage ceramic art, it has also sponsored the first five Chinese ceramics biennial exhibitions, which have done so much to encourage creative work from young ceramic artists, as well as increasing the public's appreciation of ceramic art. Two years ago, the National Museum of History joined museums from Europe, Asia, America and Africa in an eight-nation collaborative effort to sponsor the "Special International Invitational Exhibition of Ancient Chinese Trade Ceramics," which deserves praise for opening up a new chapter in cooperation between the ROC and famous museums around the world.

This year, the National Museum of History is again working alongside the British Museum to mount an exhibition of 161 fine examples from the British Museum's collection of Chinese trade ceramics of the Ming and Ch'ing periods, as well as jointly publishing a large-format illustrated catalogue of the special exhibition. This joint effort between the two museums in the field of trade ceramics marks the first collaboration between Chinese and British museums in over 200 years, making it a particularly memorable event. The world-famous British Museum has a long and venerable history. Besides possessing a rich and extensive collection, the standard of British Museum research is also held in high esteem among the academic community. Today I am delighted to see these two museums engaging in an exchange of cultural artifacts and academic collaboration. I believe that this is bound to be beneficial to museum development in the ROC, and as such is well worth our appreciation. As the special exhibition catalogue goes to press, it is my privilege to mark the occasion with these few words by way of a preface.

Dr. Wei-fan Kou,
Minister of Education
May, 1994

序

　　對於此次倫敦大英博物館與台北國立歷史博物館二館密切合作舉辦此項展覽並出版展覽圖錄，本人深感欣慰！這是貴我兩館之間第二次的合作，在一九九二年，本館曾提供展品參加了國立歷史博物館舉辦之中國古代貿易瓷國際邀請展，此次再次提供的一百六十一件瓷器舉辦特展，可謂再度合作。展品內容包括早期十六世紀的青花瓷到十八世紀的彩瓷，都是當年特別為歐洲貿易市場而訂製的瓷器，因此不論在風格和形制上均與中國一般的內銷瓷器品有很大的不同。

　　在描繪方面，除了裝飾貴族豪門的徽章紋餐具、茶具以外，尚有引人入勝，從西方版畫臨摹的一些歐洲填彩完成的瓷器，上面的歐洲景象融入彩瓷作品，內容也明顯地反映出當時的政治、歷史背景，例如：描繪政治人物John Wilkes的肖像，他是主張自由主義的英國政治家，其他有的描繪英法兩國政治緊張關係，有的是顯示反法的組織團體、限制法國商品進口等歷史事件內容等……。此類瓷器，都是透過歐洲貿易公司向中國訂購，而由中國以無與倫比之技術製造的精製瓷器。

　　此次展覽推動著歐洲與遠東博物館合作，樹立了新的里程碑，我特別感謝國立歷史博物館館長陳康順先生的提議和鼎力促成，此事同時也十分感謝林淑心女士及研究組參與工作同仁的全力協助。在本館方面，所有展品的遴選及圖錄文字的解說等各項準備工作，均由Regina Krahl和Jessica Harrison-Hall二位人員的參與和辛勞始得完成，藉此我想再次向兩館所有促進學術思想交流貢獻的工作同仁表示最深的謝忱，由於他們的專業知識和努力，才使展覽順利呈現在觀眾面前，我也深切期待更多的觀眾前來欣賞，藉由此項展覽，學習瞭解曾在二國間繁榮興盛卓越不凡的貿易瓷有關知識，並作為呈現結合兩國關係歷史資料，促進貴我雙方的了解，建立其良好的根基。

大英博物館館長
羅勃・安德森

Preface

It gives me great pleasure to record the close co-operation between the National Museum of History in Taipei and the British Museum in London that has brought about the exhibition catalogued in this book. This is the second occasion the two museums have joined together to display and catalogue Chinese export ceramics. In 1992 the British Museum contributed to the International Exhibition of Ancient Chinese Trade Ceramics; for this second event the Museum has assembled almost 200 porcelains in a complete exhibition. The ceramics catalogued and displayed here range from the early blue-and-white porcelains made to Western specification in the 16th century to the elaborate polychrome wares of the 18th century. All the pieces illustrated here were designed in form or ornament especially for the European market and are quite unlike those wares made for the market in China.

Besides the dinner and tea sets decorated with the coats of arms of the great aristocratic and merchant families of Europe, among the most interesting pieces are the porcelains painted with scenes copied from Western prints, particularly those which echo contemporary political concerns. These wares illustrate, for example, political figures such as John Wilkes who campaigned for the freedom of the press in England, or the political tensions between England and France which were manifested in anti-French societies, formed to restrict the importation of French goods and fashions. Such porcelains painted with scenes of contemporary interest were ordered through the trading companies of Europe and were produced with great skill by the Chinese porcelain manufacturers.

This exhibition marks another stage in the cooperation between museums in the Far East and Europe. I am grateful indeed to Director Chen Kang Shuen of the National Museum of History for proposing this exhibition and for supporting the enterprise at every stage. In the National Museum of History we have also had great help from Ms. Lin Shwu Shin and her colleagues in the research department. At the British Museum the choice of exhibits and the catalogue entries have been prepared by Regina Krahl and Jessica Harrison-Hall. I would like to thank all those who in both museums have made possible this exchange of ideas and scholarly endeavours. I hope the many visitors to the National Museum of History will have a chance to learn about the extraordinary export trade that has flourished between our nations and that we may see this project as a foundation for future research and display of the materials which link our nations' history.

Dr. Robert Anderson,
Director of the British Museum

館序

　　我國本為陶器發明的母邦，唐宋以來，便有陶瓷不斷輸出國外，而明清以後外銷瓷器愈為精美，陸海兩路輸出地區之廣、數量之大、可謂獨步全球。西方人因此得以了解我國在技藝與科學的成就，至今西方仍以中國（China）作為陶瓷（china）的代表，可說是其來有自。此次我們難得的展出來自英國所保有的中國外銷歐洲瓷器，也可以說當年外銷貿易瓷器的回流，實在饒富意義。

　　大英博物館歷史悠久，距今成立已有二百四十餘年，以其珍藏品類豐富及精采絕倫的古代文物享譽全球；尤其在專業的學術範疇，其龐大的研究陣容及嚴謹的學術態度，累積了極寶貴的研究成果，成為各國專家學者衷心期待探訪的知識寶庫。本館在一九九二年舉辦「中國古代貿易瓷國際邀請展」，應邀者計有英、比、法、德、南非、美、韓國、菲律賓等八個國家聯合展出，而大英博物館慨然提供二十五件館藏珍品瓷器參展，建立兩館合作的端緒；後來又因人員的互訪和資料的交流，雙方奠定良好的館際合作基礎，而有了進一步的往來。今年六月本館將主辦「中國古代貿易瓷國際學術研討會」，承英館配合此項會議，特再提供貿易瓷館藏精品一百六十一件，來華舉辦特展，兩館再度攜手合作，象徵今後進一步交流的長遠計劃，已經有了良好的起步，良深可慰。

　　此項特展內容的規劃，以明清時代為經，以瓷器不同的型制與彩繪為緯。而大英博物館的研究人員能將其展品分門別類，作系統的規劃與呈現，除了朝代的不同又將展品歸列為宗教、神話、生活、政治、貴族餐具、洛可可風格等多項主題，因此愈能引人入勝，其注意的焦點較之以往我國研究貿易瓷偏重於窯口、年代和運輸路線等，互異其趣。相信此一展出必能擴大貿易瓷研究的領域，也能激發研究者的興趣，實在是一項難能可貴的收穫。

　　最後特別感謝大英博物館羅勃・安德森館長對此次展覽的支持與東方部主任羅森女士的全力協助、康蕊君及霍吉淑二位女士的撰文說明，使此特展圖錄更為充實完美。付梓前夕，特綴數言以為序。

國立歷史博物館　館長

陳康順

謹誌

一九九四年五月二十日

Preface

China is a motherland of the invention and manufacture of porcelain, which began to become a major commercial product around the time of the T'ang and Sung dynasties. The Ming and Ch'ing dynasties witnessed the production of exquisitely fine porcelain wares. The export porcelain was mostly transported abroad by both sea and land to all parts of the world in great quantity.

It may be thought of as representing China's achievements both in the artistic field and in science and technology. Even today, English-speaking westerners speak of porcelain as "china".

The British Museum, already 240 years old, enjoys a worldwide reputation for the richness and excellence of its collection of antiquities. In the field of specialized learning, the British Museum's large research staff with their rigorous academic approach have built up an invaluable corpus of research work, making the museum a treasury of knowledge that experts and scholars from every country eagerly look forward to visiting. In 1992, when the National Museum of History mounted the International Invitational Exhibition of 'Ancient Chinese Trade Ceramics', eight countries namely the United Kingdom, Belgium, France, Germany, South Africa, United States, Korea and the Philippines participated in this show. The British Museum generously supplied 25 pieces of porcelain for display, thus establishing the first beginnings of cooperation between our two museums. Subsequently, through mutual visits by members of staff and exchanges of materials, an excellent basis for inter-museum cooperation has been built up by both sides which has resulted in further beneficial contacts.

In June 1994, the National Museum of History is hosting the 'International Symposium on Ancient Chinese Trade Ceramics'. The British Museum is kindly loaning us 161 superb exhibits from its trade ceramics collection for a special exhibition.

This new collaborative effort by the two museums symbolizes an excellent start to our long-range project for further exchanges in the future. As such, this is undoubtedly an event of great significance.

The scope of this exhibition extends chronologically through the various reigns of the Ming and Ch'ing dynasties, covering wares that are representative of ceramic production in each area of China. Consideration has also been given to illustrating factors such as types of vessel shape, styles of glaze decoration, and features of decorative design. In its aim of illuminating the role played by Chinese trade ceramics in world history and culture, this is a rather specialized, research based exhibition that combines art with academic knowledge. The Ming-Ch'ing transitional period witnessed a ferment of cultural and social change in the world. The evidence of these exhibits provides abundant new material for historical research, and will surely stimulate fresh interest in exploring this side of Chinese trade ceramics.

In conclusion, I would like to express a particular word of thanks to Dr. Robert Anderson, Director of the British Museum, for his support for this exhibition, and to Dr. Jessica Rawson, keeper of the British Museum's Oriental Department, for her invaluable assistance. Our appreciation also goes to Ms. Regina Krahl and Ms. Jessica Harrison-Hall of the British Museum for writing an explanatory text which usefully complements these illustrations of exhibits. As this illustrated catalogue to the special exhibition goes to press, it has been my privilege to contribute these prefatory remarks.

Chen Kang-Shuen

Chen Kang-shuen, Director
National Museum of History
May, 1994.

Introduction

by
Regina Krahl

The British Museum in London sending an exhibition of Chinese porcelain to Taipei may seem like bringing 'coals to Newcastle'. This exhibition, however, focusing on Chinese ceramics made for the West, addresses one of the few areas of Chinese crafts which are better represented in Europe than in China. In 1992 the National Museum of History organized a similar exhibition of Chinese trade ceramics, assembling pieces from eight international museums. This first exhibition gave an overview of Chinese trade ceramics of all kinds, made for the West as well as for the Near, Middle and Far East, from the Yuan (1279 - 1368) to the Qing (1644 - 1911) dynasty.

The present exhibition, consisting entirely of objects from the British Museum, is more specific in focus. Among the vast holdings of Chinese ceramics in the Museum, trade ceramics make up a large but relatively little studied group. It has been our intention to select for this exhibition all items which are of documentary interest, rare, or elaborately decorated. We have concentrated on objects which copy Western models, be it in shape, design or simply by an inscription or family crest, as being the most characteristic and contrived Chinese porcelains made for the West. The selection proved to be tantalizing and it would not have been difficult to double the number of items chosen. Nevertheless, we hope, that this catalogue brings together the best and most important export porcelains in the British Museum, many of which are here published for the first time.

The high quality and large quantity of the British Museum collection is due mainly to the intelligence and energy of one of its former keepers, Augustus Wollaston Franks, KCB (1826 - 97). Franks can not only be considered as the founder of the Museum's Chinese collection, but has come to be regarded as one of the founders of the British Museum itself (Wilson, 1984, p. 20), since his knowledge and interest were limited neither by region nor period nor medium. That more than 100 out of the 161 items included in this exhibition were acquired by Franks may partly be due to his particular interest in heraldry, but is mainly a testimony to his extremely good eye at a time when knowledge of the subject was still scant.

Foreign interest in Chinese porcelain is as old as the ware itself. This is hardly surprising since for centuries porcelain was a totally unique material. Since its beginnings in the Tang dynasty (618 - 906) it was a well-known and valuable commodity all over Asia. In Europe it was much rarer but no less highly regarded. Examples of Chinese porcelain are documented in Europe since the late 14th century, but until the 16th they appear only as single fortuitous treasures, often embellished with gold and silver mounts, and not as objects for ordinary use.

The large porcelain manufactories at Jingdezhen in Jiangxi province began to cater for foreign customers in the Yuan dynasty by adjusting their export production to foreign tastes. The most important customers at the time, Persian and other Middle Eastern merchants, are probably responsible for the large sizes, the bright cobalt-blue painting and the lavish, often geometric decoration of 14th-century porcelain; they may occasionally have commissioned special pieces - some are inscribed with Arabic words, for example - but such cases were the exception.

As soon as the Portuguese arrived in China in the early 16th century, the situation changed, since they immediately had Chinese porcelains made to their order. The first pieces to be commissioned were not adapted to specific needs or tastes but adorned either with Christian symbols relevant to the Portuguese missionaries in the Far East, or with coats of arms or names of Portuguese seafarers as a personalized 'souvenir' of the voyage to China. Since the Portuguese relationship with China was tempestuous, however, these early pieces with European features are few and far between and may not always have reached their intended customers. Some of them were sent together with regular export wares to the well-tested markets of the Middle East, where motifs such as the Monogram of Christ were probably no less exotic than the accompanying Chinese designs.

When the Dutch had established themselves as the foremost European trading nation in the Far East in the 17th century, previously unknown quantities of blue-and-white porcelain reached Europe and eventually turned porcelain from an extravagant luxury into a household commodity. Since direct trade with China, however, was almost impossible, commissioning specific porcelains at Jingdezhen was difficult. The vast amount of late Ming (1368 - 1644) and early Qing trade ceramics in the West therefore contains relatively few pieces with distinctly Western features.

It was only in the 18th century that Europeans began to trade directly at Canton, and England became one of the most active importers of porcelain. From Canton it was much easier to influence the appearance of the products from Jingdezhen; and since this was one of the Westerners' major concerns, this procedure was soon further facilitated when plain white porcelain was sent from Jingdezhen to be decorated at Canton. Commissioning porcelain was therefore easy and Western customers could indulge in any fancy they wished.

The catalogue shows a representative selection of subjects, including souvenirs of the voyage to China, manifestations of political and religious concerns, romantic scenes taken both from classical antiquity and from contemporary genre painting, any kind of table service with the owner's arms, or combinations of such themes.

An exemplary case of such commissioning - although unique in this exact form - is that of the 'Corbridge Lanx'. In 1735 a spectacular Roman silver tray ('a 'lanx'), dating from the 4th century AD, was found by the River Tyne at Corbridge, Northumberland, on the estate of the Duke of Somerset. It is a large rectangular tray depicting the Roman god Apollo on the right, with his lyre leaning against the column of a small temple, the hunter goddess Artemis on the left, with bow and arrow, greeted by Athena, with helmet and spear, as well as two other less easily identified figures, and in the foreground a jar with water pouring from it, a hound, a stag and a griffin (Johns, forthcoming).

This extraordinary find, which was originally sold by its finder, then recovered by the Duke, is now in the British Museum (fig. a; P 1993 4 - 11). It aroused much scholarly interest at the time of its discovery, when at least three other Roman silver pieces were found in the same area. It was soon much published and was obviously an object of great pride for the Duke. An expert drawing was done by W. Shaftoe, which was engraved by G. Van der Gucht. The engraving bears an inscription referring both to the piece and to its owner, giving all his titles as well as his coat of arms (fig. b; after

fig.a

fig.b

Stukeley, 1736; G 2643, courtesy of the British Library). It was published in 1736. This, however, was not the only reproduction to be made. As was not unusual for antique silver pieces at the time, a plaster cast was taken, which was gilded and framed for display; one such piece is at Audley End House, Essex (fig. c; courtesy of Lord Braybrooke. Photographic copyright English Heritage). Being made of plaster, it had of course only decorative value and could not be used, and being an actual cast, it did not contain the Duke's arms.

To combine all these features, an order was sent to China. Since an engraving existed, this was not difficult. Engravings of pictures and coats of arms were regularly sent to China on English East Indiamen to be copied on porcelain services. What is unique in this case is that a complete replica of an actual object was commissioned, and not only one. At least two examples are extant, one at Drum Castle, Aberdeenshire (fig. d; courtesy of the National Trust for Scotland), the other at Cotehele House, Cornwall, and there may well be others. These Chinese porcelain versions were used as tea trays. The exact reproduction in both shape and decoration - even down to a detail obviously misunderstood by the engraver, in the bottom left-hand corner - of such an exotic model, as well as the clever integration of the Duke of Somerset's arms in the rim border, is a prime example of the great skill of the Chinese potters and porcelain painters, as it is manifested throughout this exhibition.

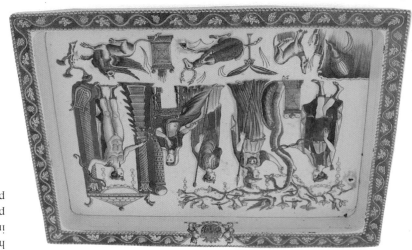

fig. d

fig. c

圖版

文字說明 / 康蕊君和霍吉淑 著

ANCIENT CHINESE TRADE CERAMICS FROM THE BRITISH MUSEUM, LONDON
Ming and Qing Porcelains Made for the West

by
Regina Krahl & Jessica Harrison-Hall

明 青花瓷

Ming, c.1520 - 1644

(cat.nos. 1 - 10)

1. 明　青花基督紋章圖盤

直徑52.5公分

此盤是特爲葡萄牙市場製作之產品。描繪一荊棘冠，以及耶穌名字之縮寫字母「IHS」，在中國山水圖中重複四次之多。這種有關基督教之主題，自十五世紀以來經常使用在西方宗教藝術品上，並且經由葡萄牙傳入中國。

1 Blue-and-white dish with Christian emblems, made for the Portuguese market

Ming dynasty, c. 1520 - 40

Diameter 52.5 cm

1979.12 - 17.1

This dish is among the earliest Chinese porcelains decorated with European motifs and was made for the Portuguese market. The connection between China and Portugal goes back to 1513/14, when the first Portuguese arrived in China. During the following decades the Jingdezhen kilns in Jiangxi province made a variety of blue-and-white porcelains with Western inscriptions - personal names, religious phrases, Western dates - and with Western motifs, like the royal coat of arms of Manual I (r.1495 - 1521), armillary spheres, or - as on the present piece - the Monogram of Christ within a crown of thorns.

This massive dish which bears the Sacred Monogram with the letters 'IHS' four times in the well, is otherwise decorated with Chinese motifs: bold peony scrolls in the centre and around the outside, clouds and landscape medallions alternating with the monograms, and *ruyi* and diaper borders.

The letters IHS are the initial letters of the name Jesus in Greek transcription, and are also understood as an abbreviation of the Latin expression 'Jesus Hominum Salvator' (Jesus, Saviour of Mankind).

The Sacred Monogram became a popular device during the 15th century and later became emblematic of the Jesuits, whose order was founded in 1534. The crown of thorns is ubiquitous in Western religious art as a symbol of Christ's Passion.

The Chinese designs as well as the shape, way of potting and the misfired yellowish glaze of this dish are all characteristic of porcelains exported to the Middle East and Southeast Asia in the early 16th century. This dish therefore probably predates the arrival of the first Jesuit missionaries in China, soon after the order was founded.

Similar dishes are in the Museo Caramulo, Caramulo, Portugal (Pinto de Matos, 1993, p. 44) ; in the Topkapi Saray Museum, Istanbul, Turkey (Krahl, 1986, vol. II, no. 750) ; in the Princessehof Museum, Leeuwarden, Netherlands (Harrisson, 1985, no. 62) ; and in the Idemitsu Museum of Arts, Tokyo (*Chinese Ceramics in the Idemitsu Collection, 1987, pl. 650*) . While these dishes were clearly intended for Portuguese customers, some of them were exported to the Middle East together with thousands of closely related export wares without such Christian emblems. This is suggested by the presence of two such dishes in the former collection of the Ottoman Sultans in Istanbul, as well as by the Leeuwarden dish, which was collected in the Saudi Arabian port of Jiddah.

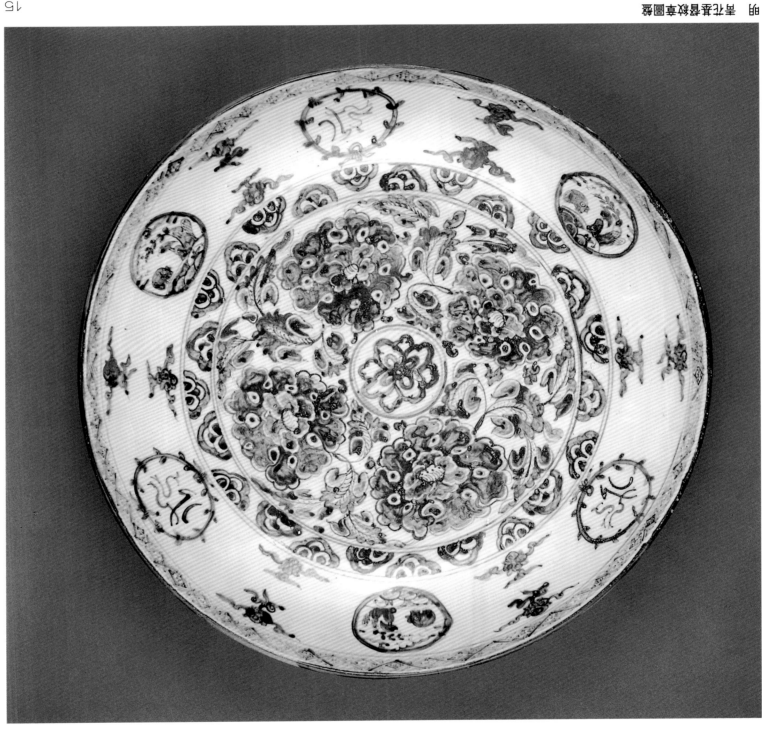

明　青花連理枝紋喜圖盤

Blue-and-white dish with Christian emblems,
made for the Portuguese market

2. 明　青花葡萄牙徽章紋盤

直徑20.2公分

此盤中央描繪的簡樸徽章，可能係屬於1570年間葡萄牙駐澳門
海軍主帥 D.Joao de Almeida 的徽章。盾牌上面繪頭盔，兩旁
有許多羽毛紋裝飾。

2　Blue-and-white dish with a Portuguese coat of arms

Ming dynasty, c. 1580 - 1600

Diameter 20.2 cm

1925.5 - 12. 1

The dish has barbed moulded sides painted in underglaze blue with fruit-
and flower-spray panels and emblems in the style of *kraak* export ware;
but the centre is unusually decorated with a stylized coat of arms
surmounted by a misunderstood helmet and framed by lavish curly
plumes.

The simplified coat of arms is difficult to identify with certainty but has
been attributed to D. Joao de Almeida, a Portuguese Chief Captain,
who settled in Macao around 1570 (de Castro, 1988, p. 24). Two
other dishes are painted with the same coat of arms and plumes but
reserved in white on a blue ground, one of similar form in the Museo
Caramulo, Caramulo, Portugal, the other of saucer shape, in the Muse'e
Guimet, Paris, France (both Paris, 1992, p.99). The armorial device
may have been taken from the title page of a Portuguese book.

3　Blue-and-white bottle with a Portuguese coat of arms

Ming dynasty, c. 1590 - 1610

Height 31.4 cm

Given by D.E. Barrett, 1960.7 - 21.1

The bottle is distinctively shaped, of square section, with domed shoulders and narrow cylindrical neck, following a European glass shape, known also from European stoneware and faience. Such bottles would have been fitted with a pewter screw top, which in this Chinese version is indicated by horizontal painted lines on the neck. They were used mainly for spirits and were designed to be stored in wooden boxes, for easy transportation, especially on ships.

Each side of this bottle is painted in underglaze blue with a Portuguese coat of arms, which has been identified as that of the families Vilas Boas and Farias, or Vaz, with a crest in form of a bird with wings displayed, and surrounded by scrolling fronds. Below the arms are four different flowers, all growing by Chinese rocks, and on the shoulder above are panels with stylized flowers reserved on a blue diaper ground. Apart from the coat of arms, the decoration is characteristic of late Ming export ware of the so-called *kraak* type.

Similar bottles are in the Fundacao Medeiros e Almeida, Lisbon, Portugal (Paris, 1992, no. 45) ; in the Staatliche Kunstsammlungen, Kassel, Germany (Kassel, 1990, no. 4) ; in the Museum De Vaart, Hilversum, Netherlands (Lunsingh Scheurleer, 1980, pl. 66) ; and another is in a private collection (Yeo and Martin, 1978, pl. 73, no. 129) .

3.　明　青花繪葡萄牙徽章酒方瓶

高31.4公分

巴霉特捐贈

器型作方其肩呈膨及圓筒樣子，其口頸有可徵驗之各種批羅，瓶身的圖飾應是運送烈洒而此設計。繪有紋飾從事的 Vilas-Boas 和 Farias或 Vaz 家族所有，其飾的瓷器飾紋飾圍中圖鳳狀：瓶花卉棲曲紋。

明　青花葡萄牙徽章紋方瓶
Blue-and-white bottle with a Portuguese coat of arms

4 Blue-and-white bowl with armorial-style shields and a Latin motto, probably made for the Portuguese market

Ming dynasty, c. 1600 - 1620
Height 17 cm, diameter 34.5 cm
Given by A.D. Passmore, 1957.12 - 16.19

This large *kraak* porcelain bowl is painted in underglaze blue with an armorial-style shield containing a hydra repeated four times on the exterior. This fabulous creature has seven heads - five reptilian and two human - scaled wings, a tail and two legs with hooves. Each shield has streamers attached on either side inscribed with the Latin motto 'SAPIENTI NIHIL NOVUM.' (to the wise man nothing is new) . As with most of these early export wares, the rest of the decorative motifs is predominantly Chinese. On the outside are Buddhist emblems and on the inside are ten panels with highly stylized flowering and fruiting plants growing by rocks, arranged around a crane in a lotus pond.

The shape of these shields and the presence of a motto suggest a Western armorial origin of this design but its source has not yet been traced. The motif has been compared (Gray, 1960) to a similar seven-headed hydra in a printed illustration in Camillo Camilli's *Impresse Illustri* (Venice, 1586) . Although this hydra is similarly depicted, it is neither contained within a shield nor is the motto found there.

The same shield design and motto appear again on the inside of a dish in the Santos Palace, Lisbon, Portugal, where it forms part of a pyramid-shaped ceiling festooned with Ming porcelain. Among those pieces which were collected by Don Manuel I, King of Portugal (r. 1495 - 1521) and his successors, it is the only piece of Chinese porcelain with a European motif and inscription (Lion-Goldschmidt, 1984 - 85, pl.18) . This would suggest that these pieces were made for the Portuguese market. An identical bowl, however, is depicted in a somewhat later Dutch oil-painting, a still-life by W.C. Heda, dated 1638 (Spriggs, 1964 - 66, pl. 68a) which proves that such pieces also came to Holland.

Although such porcelains with Western motifs and inscriptions were obviously made for Western customers, the present bowl is particularly interesting, as its type can not only be traced to 17th-century Portugal and 17th-century Holland, but also to 17th-century Persia. An earthenware bowl closely imitating this piece, made in Persia in the second half of the 17th-century, is in the Victoria and Albert Museum, London (fig. 4a; 2904.1876, courtesy of the Victoria and Albert Museum) . It has an imitation Chinese seal mark on the base which the original lacks.

The appearance of this specific design in three different countries with an interest in Chinese porcelains, suggests that in the 17th century the export trade was still fairly unstructured. This bowl belongs to a general type of late Ming blue-and-white export porcelain known in the West as *kraak* ware, which is characterized by a fairly thin body and panelled decoration. Produced at Jingdezhen and exported in bulk, it derives its name from the Portuguese ships called *carraca* (English *carrack* and Dutch *kraak*) which brought the first such pieces to Europe.

fig. 4a

4. 明 青花繪草紋及拉丁文盾紋飾碗
直徑34.5公分，高17公分
巴斯摩爾捐贈

碗上繪鱗狀四個盾牌，上圖裝飾著「Hydra」，係希臘傳神話中的怪獸，有五爬及兩個人頭，並生有蝙蝠翼上繞纏著拉丁文箴言：「智者世間，天下無新鮮事重」。此怪獸係長尾博之所服已重可參。碗的其餘刻飾作其他歐所瓷器（參考圖版4a）。

明 青花徽章紋及拉丁文箴言紋碗
Blue-and-white bowl with armorial-style shields and a Latin motto, probably made for the Portuguese market

5. 明　青花基督圖案蓋罐一對

高30.5公分

法蘭克收藏

這一對蓋罐器形別致，其把手為一赤裸人像狀，靈感可能源自
於基督受難形象。與此相似之小型象牙製人像，多半來自葡萄
牙屬地印度。

5 Pair of blue-and-white ewers and covers with a Christian motif, made for the Portuguese market

Ming dynasty, c. 1610 - 30

Height 30.5 cm

Franks collection, F.154

The ewers are unusually shaped, each having a slender body with waisted flaring neck and foot, both with raised bands. The spout is characteristic for late Ming ewers but has an additional applied scroll at the base, the handle is in the form of a rudimentary figure, similarly terminating in an applied scroll instead of legs. The ewers are painted in underglaze blue with landscape and formal borders characteristic of *kraak* export ware, and with formal rosettes of unknown origin round the centre.

The unconventional form of these ewers appears to be unique but is reminiscent of the ornate shapes found in Portuguese faience. The freely modelled figures applied to the shoulder, with their emaciated bodies and painful poses bear resemblance to small contemporary ivory figures of the crucified Christ, which were made in quantity in the Portuguese colony of Goa in India; on these ewers, however, the figures are freely adapted to serve as handles.

明　青花基督圖案蓋罐一對

**Pair of blue-and-white ewers and covers with a Christian
motif, made for the Portuguese market**

6. 明　青花基督紋罐

高12.2公分

法蘭克收藏

小罐上飾有捲髮有翼之天使，此一主題常爲葡萄牙耶穌會所引用。此罐周圍裝飾著花卉紋，枝葉纏繞，但在類似的瓶罐裡，則由花卉紋替代基督紋章。

6 Blue-and-white jar with Christian motifs, made for the Portuguese market

Ming dynasty, c. 1610 - 30

Height 12.2 cm

Franks collection, F. 1397 A

The small six-lobed jar is decorated in underglaze blue with three cherubs, their heads, with curly hair, applied in relief, their wings painted, with pendant grape vines beneath, and alternating with flower sprays.

The cherubs of the present jar, in combination with Chinese-style flower sprays, appear at first glance no more than a decorative device of Western inspiration; comparison with related jars, however, where the flower sprays are replaced by emblems of Christ's Betrayal, Crucifixion, Passion and Descent from the Cross, manifests their symbolic significance as Christian motifs even in this context, and suggests that this jar - like cat.nos. 5 and 7 - was made for Portuguese Jesuits. A jar with these additional Christian emblems is in the Fundacao Medeiros e Almeida, Lisbon, Portugal (Paris, 1992, no. 75).

明　青花基督紋罐
Blue-and-white jar with Christian motifs, made for the Portuguese market

7. 明　青花基督紋罐

高33.2公分

布羅克・余魏爾遺贈

爲澳門的葡萄牙耶穌會聖保羅大學所燒製的一批瓷器之一，爲
葡萄牙市場而製。此罐飾有聖保羅之名字縮寫「S」和「P」，以及
基督名字的縮寫「IHS」，字母四周環繞著天使。此圖案經常爲
居住中國的耶穌會傳敎士所使用，並且在書本扉頁也可見到類
似圖案。

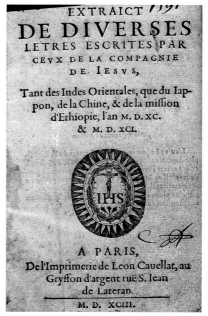

fig. 7a

7　Blue-and-white jar with Christian emblems, made for the Portuguese at Macao

Ming dynasty, c. 1620 - 44

Height 33.2 cm

Brooke Sewell Bequest, 1963 -20.4

This heavy jar with its diaper and petal-panel designs around shoulder and foot is a typical example of so-called *kraak* export ware. In the centre, however, it is painted with rare European motifs. Among highly stylized formal flower sprays are six ogival panels, two of them enclosing an oval medallion with the Monogram of Christ, 'IHS', below the Cross and above three arrows symbolizing the Trinity, enclosed by radiating rays of light and surrounded on four sides by cherubs; the four other medallions are inscribed with the initials 'S' and 'P', respectively; enclosed in an elaborate shaped frame.

The monogram IHS, which appears also on the earlier dish, cat.no. 1, became the main emblematic device of the Jesuit order and similar versions are often seen on the title pages of books by Portuguese Jesuit missionaries active in the Far East (see fig. 7 a for such a title page, published in 1593, courtesy of Sotheby's).

The initials S and P are those of the Jesuit College of St. Paul (Sao Paulo) at Macao, which at the time functioned as a university and whose only remaining part after a fire in 1835 is the stone facade and steps, which today are Macao's most famous landmark. The present jar is apparently one of a small number of such pieces ordered by the College, others being today in the Casa-Museu Dr. Anastacio Goncalves, Lisbon, Portugal (Paris, 1992, no. 74); in the G. Alpoim Calvao collection, Cascais, Portugal (de Castro, 1988, p. 28); and in a private Japanese collection (mentioned, Paris, 1992, p.159).

The flower scrolls which are similarly seen on other contemporary *kraak* ware are inspired by Western motifs.

明 青花基督紋罐

**Blue-and-white jar with Christian emblems, made for the
Portuguese at Macao**

8. 明　青花基督圖案方瓶

高38.5公分

布羅克‧佘魏爾遺贈

此件方瓶兩邊描繪中空的十字架、被遺棄的荊棘冠，以及其他
圖案，來象徵耶穌之死亡。另兩邊繪有一群在雲中奏樂的天使，
暗示耶穌之復活。器型有些誇張，源自十七世紀荷蘭玻璃及陶
器。

8 Blue-and-white bottle with Christian motifs, probably made for the Dutch market

Ming dynasty, c. 1620 - 44

Height 38.5 cm

Brooke Sewell Bequest, 1963.5 - 20.7

The square blue-and-white bottle has flat sides with slightly curved tops, a tubular neck and a stepped collar. Two sides are painted with a cross with a crown of thorns and a ladder leaning against it in a garden setting where banana plants are growing. A cockerel, a whip, and a dog are in the foreground. On the other two sides are a host of cherubs playing horns and beating drums among the clouds, and on the ground below are a Chinese house and a pagoda. Each side is bordered by flowering scrolls and the neck of the bottle is painted with Western-style flowers.

These design elements symbolically depict the death of Christ and his resurrection. The empty cross and the ladder evoke Joseph of Arimathaea's night rescue of Jesus' body, after the Crucifixion, and the plants refer to the Garden of Gethsemane where Jesus was entombed. The cockerel symbolizes Peter's triple denial of Jesus before the cockerel crowed, as predicted by Jesus at the Last Supper. The whip symbolizes the torture of Jesus before execution. The dog turning to look at the crow is holding a lighted candle in its mouth; this is a 17th-century symbol for the religious order of the Dominicans based on the Latin origin of their name, *Domini canes*, meaning 'dogs of the Lord' (Paris, 1987, p.114). The jubilant angels on the other two sides above the Chinese landscape possibly herald the resurrection of Christ and his ascent to heaven.

The bottle's shape - like that of cat.no. 3 - has a European prototype, although here it has become rather exaggerated. Dutch square-section glass and stoneware bottles were used in the 17th and 18th centuries to transport by sea alcoholic beverages and oil for lighting lamps. Another bottle of this type is at l'Hôtel d'Orbigny, La Rochelle, France (Paris, 1987, no.30). In its overall style this bottle is more closely related to wares made for the Dutch than the Portuguese market. A comparable bottle with Chinese designs only, fitted with a late 17th-century Dutch silver mount, is in the Ashmolean Museum, Oxford, Great Britain (Oxford, 1981, no.45).

明　青花基督圖案方瓶
**Blue-and-white bottle with Christian motifs, probably made
for the Dutch market**

9. 明　青花波斯人物紋蓋罐

高48公分

罐上描繪四位波斯射手，可能取材自一幅波斯細密畫。用中國山水和歐洲花卉紋鑲邊，以中國人物取代外國人。此類器物是為荷蘭市場的需求而訂製。

9 Blue-and-white jar and cover with Persian figures

Ming dynasty, c. 1620 - 44

Height 48 cm

1965.7 - 26.1

The massive blue-and-white jar shows four archers in oval cartouches, each identically represented in great detail with plumed turban with a trailing end, long mustache and beard, buttoned coat with a scarf tied around the waist, holding a bow and arrow and carrying a quiver with further arrows on his back. The four panels partly cover a landscape border with Chinese figures, banana and other plants, stupa-like structures and Western-style houses. The rest of the jar is decorated with exotic flower scrolls with tulips, carnations and other stylized blooms. The cover is decorated to match with four panels with Chinese figures between tulips, and with a landscape scene on the knob.

The archers are probably copied from a Persian source. Similar figures are depicted on Persian textiles as well as in Persian paintings and drawings of the first half of the 17th century. Pieces such as this jar were, however, not necessarily made for the Middle Eastern market, where so far no comparable example has come to light. A companion jar was in the collection of Queen Mary II（r. 1688 - 94）at Hampton Court Palace, southwest of London（Lane, 1949 - 50, pl. 9 e）. An almost identical jar where the cartouches, however, contain Chinese figures in Chinese landscapes, is in the Staatliche Kunstsammlungen, Kassel, Germany（Kassel, 1990, pl. 33).

The non-Chinese flower motifs are derived from earlier, more formal designs like those seen on the jar, cat.no. 7, but are here painted in thin outlines with stippled details as if imitating the stitches of embroidery.

明　青花波斯人物紋蓋罐
Blue-and-white jar and cover with Persian figures

10. 明 青花瓶一組

（燈）高12.5公分 （盤）直徑29.9公分 （罐）高20.7公分 （芥茉瓶）高
4.8－6.3公分

為荷蘭市場專製，出自沈船。

這一批器物是明末之際，針對荷蘭貿易市場而製作之典型貿易
瓷，包括了貓形夜燈、盤、蓋罐及芥茉瓶。有一艘載有亞洲貿
易瓷的貨船在1643年左右沉沒於南中國海。此批物乃沉船內所
發現之數千件瓷器中的一批。

10 Group of blue-and-white vessels made for the Dutch market, recovered from a shipwreck

Ming dynasty, c. 1640 - 44

Diameter（dish）29.9 cm, heights（cat）12.5,（jar）20.7 cm,
(mustard pots) 4.8 - 6.3 cm

1984.3 - 3.6 - 8, 10, 16, 19; 1985.11 - 19.38

This small group of underglaze-blue decorated pieces was among some 23,000 vessels recovered from the wreck of an unidentified Asian ship in the South China Sea（Sheaf and Kilburn, 1988, pp. 12 - 80）. The dish, painted with a bird in a landscape and eight radiating panels of alternating flower and *lingzhi* sprays is typical of late Ming export ware of the *kraak* type. The night-light in the form of a crouching cat, on a detachable base, with pierced eyes, ears, nose and mouth to reveal the light from a flaming wick within is, however, unusual. The squat, lidded jar with a metal knob and handles, is decorated in the 'Transitional' style characteristic of the last years of the Ming dynasty, with a bird among bamboo, prunus and other flowering plants. The four covered mustard pots have notches in their rims for spoons and are also painted in the 'Transitional' style with landscape motifs in fan-shaped panels, and with nature scenes.

These vessels were recovered from an unidentified Asian ship whose precise date of sinking is unknown. Its cargo consisted basically of two different types of ware made at Jingdezhen at the end of the Ming dynasty: very late versions of *kraak* porcelain, such as the dish in the present group, and examples of 'Transitional' porcelain, such as the jar and mustard pots. The discovery of two covers for oviform jar's inscribed with a cyclical date corresponding to 1643 make a fairly precise dating of the wreck possible.

This ship may have been on its way to Indonesia, probably carrying besides porcelain, also spices, silk and other commodities for sale to the Dutch, whose East India Company had offices in Batavia, modern Jakarta, Indonesia.

明　青花瓶一組
Group of blue-and-white vessels made for the Dutch market,
recovered from a shipwreck

早清 青花和彩瓷

Early Qing, 1644 - c.1722

（cat.nos. 11 - 25）

11. 清　青花拉丁文藥罐

高23.5公分

巴西爾‧伊耳尼底斯夫人遺贈

器型和紋飾均仿自歐洲，用來盛裝乾藥材之陶罐。上有拉丁文
縮寫的藥材名稱，並且裝飾天使以及植物。枝叢上棲息著一隻
鳥，其下有許多小動物。

11　Blue-and-white apothecary jar with a Latin inscription

Qing dynasty, c. 1660 - 80

Height 23.5 cm

Hon. Mrs. Basil Ionides Bequest, 1963.4 - 22.6

The rounded body is waisted in the middle and is painted in underglaze blue with two large overall plants, drawn in a formalized manner derived from European rather than Chinese models, with confronted birds perched on the branches and small confronted animals on the ground below. This design is interrupted at the waist by two cartouches with cherub vignettes above, one side inscribed 'THER.ES merag.', an abbreviation for the Latin words *Theriaca Essentia Meraca,* the name of a medicinal drug, the other with further flower motifs.

Such drug jars, generally made of faience with blue-and-white or polychrome decoration, were in common use in 17th-century pharmacies throughout Europe, but go back to ancient Islamic models. They were sometimes painted with the drug they were meant to contain in dried form, or else with some unconnected floral design, and often with cherubs.

The present piece once belonged to a larger set of identical jars with different inscriptions, of which three others are preserved, one in the Victoria and Albert Museum, London (Clunas, 1987, pl. 14); another from the Thornhill collection in the North Staffordshire Polytechnic, Stoke-on-Trent, Great Britain (Sun-Bailey, 1983 - 4, pl. 17); and the third in the Virginia Museum, Richmond, U.S.A. (Little, 1983, no. 52). It is not known how large the set originally was, nor for whom it was made. Both the Portuguese and the Dutch also exported the drugs themselves from China and it is not impossible that these drug jars might have been exported complete with contents; in general, the quantities of drugs exported were, however, much larger.

Stylistically this jar appears to have been made during the tumultous times following the end of the Ming, when European trade with south China was difficult and sporadic and porcelain made specifically to Western orders is rare.

清 靑花拉丁文藥罐
Blue-and-white
apothecary jar with a
Latin inscription

12. 清　彩瓷俄羅斯皇家徽章紋藥罐

高17.5公分（斷面）

法蘭克收藏

描繪戴有皇冠之雙頭鷹，握著笏及劍，四周圍繞著玫瑰花環。
許多此種紋飾的瓶罐，不論是盛裝乾藥材或濕藥材，都保存下
來，而絕大部分遺留在俄國。據說是爲俄皇彼得大帝（1682－
1725年在位）的莫斯科藥房而訂製的。雖然象徵俄國雙頭鷹紋
章，但描繪得不甚正確。

12　Polychrome painted apothecary jar with the imperial arms of Russia

Qing dynasty, c. 1685 - 1710

Height 17.5 cm（cut down）

Franks collection, F. 604

The jar is painted in red, green, brown and purple enamels with a double-headed eagle holding a sceptre and a sword, its centre filled by an oval shield with stylized plumes, and with a crown between the two crowned eagle's heads, all enclosed by entwined thorny branches bearing rose-hips, which form a circular frame.

The jar originally had a short straight neck and widely flaring rim and thus followed the characteristic shape of European drug jars, which are often decorated with a wreath of flowering or fruiting plants. The plant on the present jar appears to be a rambling rose - on related vessels it is painted complete with blossoms（Arapova, 1992, pl. 1）- depicted in a European style.

The double-headed eagle as represented on this jar, holding sceptre and sword, is the heraldic bird of the Austrian Empire. There is no indication, however, of an Austrian order of such jars. The majority of extant jars of this type, as well as of matching ewers for liquid medicine, appears to be preserved in Russia, both in the Hermitage, St. Petersburg, and in the State Historical Museum, Moscow（ibid, pls. 1 and 2, and p. 26, note 5）. This set is believed to have been made for Peter I's（r. 1682 - 1725）Moscow pharmacy, which in 1710 is recorded to have been stocked with jars bearing the imperial Russian eagle（ibid, p. 21）. Correctly, however, the Russian heraldic bird is holding sceptre and orb, as it appears on a later Chinese service（cat. no. 123）, and the jars in Moscow in 1710 may well have been different ones, possibly made of European faience or glass. The reason for the appearance of the Austrian bird on these pieces, however, is still unresolved.

清　彩瓷俄羅斯皇家徽章紋藥罐
Polychrome painted apothecary jar with the imperial arms of Russia

13. 清　青花盤

直徑37.5公分

巴西爾‧伊耳尼底斯夫人遺贈

盤中之人物乃描繪羅馬神話中的酒神巴可士，身披葡萄藤，手持一串葡萄和酒杯。他置身於荷蘭式室內，地面鋪滿瓷磚，此造形經常描繪於荷式青花瓷器。盤子的邊緣採凸起之花瓣造形，也是荷式陶瓷的特徵之一，淵源於銀器或鉛錫合金器皿。

13　Blue-and-white plate, made after Dutch pottery models

Qing dynasty, c. 1680 - 1700

Diameter 37.5 cm

Hon. Mrs. Basil Ionides Bequest, 1963.4 - 23.2

The large plate has a raised rim with moulded gadroons, following a Dutch faience shape which itself is derived from metalwork. It is heavily potted and decorated in underglaze blue. The central medallion shows a figure of Bacchus, the god of wine in Roman mythology, in a Dutch-style interior with a tiled chequered floor. The god is shown naked except for garlands of grape vine round his head and his hip, raising a goblet in one hand and holding a bunch of grapes in the other, and is standing between a large wine jar and a table with a bottle and another goblet. The medallion is enclosed within a broad border of scrolling vines.

Interiors with tiled floors as they are common in Dutch houses and often depicted in Dutch paintings, are also often seen on blue-and-white faience plates made at Delft in the Netherlands. Such a dish, also with a gadrooned rim but of octagonal form (not unlike cat.no. 15) is in the Musée de Cinquantenaire, Brussels (Hudig, 1929, pl. 205) .

An identical Chinese dish, also from the Ionides collection, is in the Victoria and Albert Museum, London (Hervouet and Bruneau, 1986, no. 13.9) ; another is in the Mottahedeh collection (Howard and Ayers, 1978, vol. I, pl. 34) .

清　青花盤

Blue-and-white plate, made after Dutch pottery models

41

14. 清　青花歐洲人物及法文紋蓋杯和托盤

（杯）高7.2公分　（托盤）直徑13.7公分

法蘭克收藏

此組瓷器繪有戴著皇冠的國王及王后和法文銘文：「王國恩德遍及萬方」。這件的器型、紋飾及出處等尚在研究中。類似的蓋杯，曾發現於1690年左右的越南頭頓附近南方之沉船。

14　Blue-and-white cup with cover and saucer, with European figures and a French inscription

Qing dynasty, c. 1690 - 1700

Height（cup）7.2 cm, diameter（saucer）13.7 cm

Franks collection, F.582

The underglaze - blue decoration on this tall covered cup and saucer is divided into radiating panels and the main panels contain a crowned European King and Queen seated on a throne in an interior. A misspelt French inscription around the outside rim of the cup reads 'L'EMPIRE DE LA VERTU EST ETABLIS JUSQU'AU BOUT DE L'UNERS'（sic）（the empire of virtue stretches to the end of the universe）. The radiating panels contain alternately a kneeling Chinese figure below a flock of flying birds, and a sapling. On the base of the cup is a stylized square seal mark.

These crowned figures have been variously but unsatisfactorily explained. In the 19th century they were believed to represent the historical figures of Louis IX of France（1226 - 70）and his mother Queen Blanche of Castille（Jacquemart and Le Blant, 1862, pl.xvi, fig. 1）. Later they have been identified as Louis XIV（1661 - 1715）and his Queen（Lunsingh Scheurleer, 1974, p.98 citing J. Helbig）. Until the source of this design - perhaps a medal or print - is discovered, any such identification remains, however, hypothetical.

Twenty-five covers with this design were recovered from a shipwreck off the coast of Vietnam, 100 nautical miles south of Vung Tau near Con Dao Island（Christies, Amsterdam, 8th April 1992, lot 856）, one of which is now in The Royal Museum of Scotland, Edinburgh. The cargo of this Asian trading vessel can only be approximately dated on the basis of an inkstick with a cyclical date equivalent to 1690, which provides a *terminus post quem*.

Other pieces with this design are to be found for example in the Ashmolean Museum, Oxford, Great Britain（Macintosh, 1977, pl.86）, in the Musée Guimet, Paris, France（Hervouet and Bruneau, 1986, no.9.94）, and in the Victoria and Albert Museum, London（Honey, 1927, pl.111）.

清　青花歐洲人物及法文紋蓋杯和托盤
Blue-and-white cup with cover and saucer, with European figures and a French inscription

15. 清　青花英國徽章紋八角盤

直徑48.5公分

法蘭克收藏

此八角盤，對於一些早期知名的徽章裝飾餐桌器具影響甚遠。
徽章紋出自於牛津大主教（Rt.Reverend　William Talbot
1658－1730，參看圖版15b 的書籤），器型源於銀質餐具和荷
蘭青花瓷。

fig. 15a　　　　　　　　　fig. 15b

15　Blue-and-white serving platter with an English coat of arms

Qing dynasty, c. 1690 - 1710

Diameter 48.5 cm

Franks collection, F.734 ＋

In the centre of this blue-and-white serving platter, within an octagonal frame, is a coat of arms. Its shield shows a lion striding on its back legs, the helmet above bears elaborate plumes, and the crest is a lion standing on all fours on a coronet. A ribbon for the motto below has been left blank. The cavetto is painted with Chinese antiques such as porcelain vases, scrolls and books. At the top within a double circle, the lion crest is repeated. The outer edge of the rim is moulded in relief with a ribbed border and raised ridge.

The charger was made for the Rt. Reverend William Talbot（1658 - 1730）while he was Bishop of Oxford, and bears his coat of arms. The arms, crest and mantling have been copied from one of his bookplates such as the one illustrated, also in the British Museum（fig. 15 a; P＋D Franks 28869）. Talbot was also a distinguished member of the House of Lords, renowned for his extravagance. An engraving by George Vertue（1684 - 1756）after Sir G. Kneller, also preserved in the British Museum（fig. 15 b; P＋D 1858.2 - 13.212）, shows him somewhat later, in 1720, as Bishop of Salisbury, wearing the robes of Chancellor

of the Garter. The engraving was later inscribed 'And now Lord Bishop of Durham 1722'.

This piece is part of the earliest known fully armorial table service, decorated in underglaze blue, made to order for the English market. An identical service but with a different coat of arms was made around the same time for Talbot's son-in-law, Exton Sayer（Howard, 1974, p. 164）. Both stylistically and from the quality of its materials, this charger may be dated to the Kangxi period（1662-1722）.

The shape of this octagonal serving platter with ribbed edge is found in silverware of the period and was also copied in Dutch Delft faience. A smaller Delft plate of the same shape and with the same border but painted with a Dutch interior scene is in the Musée de Cinquantenaire, Brussels, Belgium（Hudig, 1929, pl. 205）.

An identical platter is in a private Brazilian collection（Veiga, 1989, pl.13）and an oblong octagonal platter of the same service is in the Mottahedeh collection（Howard and Ayers, 1978, vol. I, pl.40）.

清　靑花英國徽章紋八角盤
Blue-and-white serving platter with an English coat of arms

16. 清　彩瓷葡萄牙徽章紋蓋碗

高37.5公分

這件爲盛湯用深碗，描繪歐式渦捲紋以及葡萄牙徽章，此徽章
紋係葡國議會贈予國王 D・路易（1700－1755），可能是路易
國王於1720年結婚時所使用的。碗蓋上有縮寫字母「L」和「A」，
可能符合 Luis Ataide，但也有人認爲徽章紋係代表義大利麥
里尼家族。

16 Polychrome painted tureen and cover with a Portuguese coat of arms

Qing dynasty, c. 1700 - 1722

Height 37.5 cm

1910.5 - 9.4

The large, heavily potted bowl has a high foot and a wide bell-shaped cover（with replaced knob）; above the foot is an unglazed band. The piece is painted in underglaze blue and red, green, some aubergine and black enamels and gilding with formal arabesque scrollwork, which on the bowl is symmetrically arranged around a coat of arms on either side, and on the cover around a gilt monogram. Inside the bowl is a similar arabesque border with fruit festoons below the rim.

The coat of arms which is surmounted by an animal under a coronet and supported by a grotesque mask, appears also on other similarly decorated pieces（e.g. Lunsingh Scheurleer, 1966, pl. 99）as well as on services with different decoration（de Castro, 1993, p. 70; Howard and Ayers, 1978, vol. II, pls. 457 and 457 a）. It has been identified as belonging to D. Luis Peregrino de Ataide（1700 - 1755）, Counsel to the Portuguese King John V, who married in 1720, when the present tureen may have been made. The initials have been interpreted accordingly, as 'L' and 'A'.

This scrollwork decoration which ultimately goes back to designs by the influential French artist and decorator Jean Berain（1640 - 1711）, was in the early 18th century used in virtually every medium, for decorating rooms, objects, fabrics, books, etc. On Chinese porcelain such decoration appears to have been popular particularly in Portugal. It also appears in the *famille rose* palette - with additional rose - pink enamel and with a blue enamel replacing the underglaze blue - on various other heavily potted pieces in faience shapes, with other Portuguese arms（e.g. de Albuquerque, 1993, p. 60; de Castro, 1988, pp. 88 - 9）. On account of heraldic inconsistencies, the present arms have, however, also been attributed to the Italian family Marini（Howard and Ayers, 1978, vol. II, pp. 450 -51）

清　彩瓷葡萄牙徽章紋蓋碗

Polychrome painted tureen and cover with a Portuguese coat of arms

17. 清　彩瓷蓋壺一對

高28公分

法蘭克收藏

器型和設計均仿自法國盧昂瓷器，其施釉非常特殊，以青花勾
勒輪廓，施以釉上藍彩及琺瑯綠彩。

17　Pair of polychrome painted urns and covers, made after French pottery models

Qing dynasty, c. 1700 - 1722

Height 28 cm

Franks collection, F.1401

These vessels have an ogee - shaped outline, with wide shoulder, raised
rib on the lower half, and a splayed foot, and domed covers with
broad knob. They are painted with floral festoons on the upper part
and formal interlaced strapwork with foliate motifs below, drawn in
underglaze-blue outlines and filled in with blue and green enamels.

The blue - and - green colour scheme using both under - and overglaze
blue is otherwise extremely rare, although an identical pair of urns was
formerly in the Winkworth collection (Sotheby's London, 12th
December 1972, lot 124). The shape is closely following a faience
model made at Rouen, France (Chompret et al., 1933, vol. IV, pl. 72
A). The decoration which is loosely based on designs developed by
Berain was also used at Rouen, but was highly popular at the time in
any medium (see also cat.no. 16).

清　彩瓷蓋壺一對
Pair of polychrome painted urns and covers, made after French pottery models

18. 清　硬彩荷蘭徽章紋湯盤

直徑24公分

查理斯‧渥克牧師遺贈

此盤中央飾有荷蘭的德‧瓦西家族徽章紋，周圍有一箴言及製作日期「1702」字樣，其上有一皇冠。盤底以青花描繪花卉及靈芝符號，均係十八世紀早期外銷瓷的特徵。但在此一時期中國徽章紋的瓷器傳世甚少。

18 *Famille verte* **soup plate with a Dutch coat of arms**

Qing dynasty, dated 1702

Diameter 24 cm

Rev. Charles Walker Bequest, F. 867 ＋ （1887.12-18.38）

This soup plate is decorated in *famille verte* enamels with a coat of arms within a roundel, divided into eight sections, containing on the left a sheaf of wheat and a horizontal crescent moon with two gold stars on a blue enamel ground, and on the right a naked mermaid on top of a castle, and a black cross decorated with five boars' heads. The design is surrounded by the French motto 'EN PEINE CROISSANT' （in difficulty growing）, the date 'ANo 1702' and a coronet on top with tasselled ribbons. The rim bears four sprays of Chinese flowers - crysanthemum, lotus, peony and camellia and the base has an underglaze - blue *lingzhi* （fungus） mark within a double ring.

The arms have been identified as belonging to the Dutch family de Vassey, impaled quarterly. The rim decoration and the mark on the base are characteristic of early 18th - century export ware but it is very rare to find dated Chinese armorial ware of this period. Another soup plate with this coat of arms is in a private collection （Godden, 1979, pl.124a.）

清　硬彩荷蘭徽章紋湯盤
Famille verte soup plate with a Dutch coat of arms

51

19. 清　硬彩法蘭德斯市徽章紋盤

直徑24.5公分

法蘭克收藏

此盤描繪「法蘭德斯」字樣和城市徽章紋。法蘭德斯市仍位於
比利時境內。英國、法國及荷蘭等各國城市、州縣徽章紋爲裝
飾系列之類似器皿頗多，在荷蘭境內也仿製這類的五彩瓷器。

19 *Famille verte* plate with the arms of a Flemish city

Qing dynasty, c. 1700 - 1722

Diameter 24.5 cm

Franks collection, F 843 +

This plate with its barbed rim with gilt edge is painted in underglaze
blue and enamels with the crowned shield of arms of the Flemish city
of Mechelen (Malines) identified by the word 'MEGGELEN'
beneath, surrounded by confronted birds and flowers. The panels in
the well contain alternately Chinese figures in landscapes, and flower
pots and vases.

The dish belongs to one of four series of vessels painted with the arms
of the main cities and provinces or the states of the Netherlands,
England and France which differ in their supporting designs (Le
Corbeiller, 1974, p.39). Only large serving dishes, plates and barber's
basins appear to have been decorated in this way. Other pieces with the
same arms include a plate in the Musées Royaux d'Art et d'Histoire,
Brussels, Belgium (Jörg, 1989, no. III) , and a barber's bowl in the
Mottahedeh collection (Howard and Ayers, 1978, vol.I, pl.113) .

Other arms in these series include Amsterdam, Artois, Brabant,
England, Flanders, France, Friesland, Gelderland, Groningen, Holland,
Louvain, Luxemburg, Overijsel, Rotterdam, Utrecht, Zeeland and
Zutphen. Imitations of these Chinese plates were made at Delft in the
Netherlands about 1720 in polychrome earthenware, an example of
which is at the Rijksmuseum, Amsterdam, Netherlands (Le Corbeiller,
1974, pl.14) .

MEGGELEN

清　硬彩法蘭德斯市徽章紋盤
Famille verte plate with the arms of a Flemish city

20. 清　青花歐洲樂師紋盤

直徑34.2公分

巴西爾・伊耳尼底斯女士遺贈

描繪三位樂師在花園演奏，原設計爲法國藝術家尼可拉・伯納（1646－1718）的版畫，此版畫曾盛行一時。

20　Blue - and - white serving plate depicting European musicians

Qing dynasty , c. 1700 - 1722

Diameter 34.2 cm

Hon. Mrs. Basil Ionides Bequest, 1963-4-22.18

The plate is painted in underglaze blue with three European musicians around a table in a garden setting. A woman dressed in a low - cut dress with high piled - up hair and a headdress with ribbons of lace is seated and strikes the strings of a dulcimer. Two men in long curly wigs, frock coats and knee breeches, accompany her on a flute and a lute. This scene is surrounded by eight petal - shaped panels containing Chinese landscape scenes.

This scene was copied from an engraving by Nicolas Bonnart (1646 - 1718) of Paris and drawn by his brother Robert, entitled 'Symphonie du Tympanum, du Luth et de la Flute d'Allemagne' (Howard and Ayers, 1978, vol. I , pl.35a). The print was also inscribed with verses comparing the inferior pleasures of Music to those of Love (Hervouet and Bruneau, 1986, p.189).

Other dishes with this scene exist, several vary in details such as the landscape scenes in the petal cartouches and some are closer to the original print than the present piece; compare examples in the Princessehof Museum, Leeuwarden, Netherlands (Leeuwarden, 1986, no.100); in the Victoria and Albert Museum, London (Godden, 1979, no.21); in the Manchester City Art Gallery, Great Britain (Hobson, 1925, pl. X X IX, fig.3); and in the Mottahedeh collection (Howard and Ayers, 1978, vol.I, pl.35).

This 'music party' print is one of a number of late 17th - century costume prints and other Chinese porcelain designs exist of ladies with similar elaborate hair-styles, fashionable in France and named the *coiffure, a la Duchesse de Fontanges* after the mistress of Louis XIV (1661 - 1715), who established its popularity. This print also inspired the decoration of Dutch Delft faience pieces such as an early 18th - century violin at the Musée de Rouen, France (Beurdeley, 1962, fig. 11).

清　青花歐洲樂師紋盤
Blue-and-white serving plate depicting European musicians

21. 清　青花聖經圖案紋盤

直徑51公分

巴西爾・伊耳尼底斯夫人遺贈

此盤描繪約翰為年輕耶穌在河中施洗。背景繪有自天而降之鴿子，象徵聖靈。邊緣有聖經中記載基督受洗之經文。此盤是以聖經故事為題材的最早中國瓷器，另外，尚有同類紋飾的紅色琺瑯彩繪盤（參考圖版21a）。

fig. 21a

21　Blue - and - white plate with a biblical scene

Qing dynasty, c. 1715 - 25

Diameter 51 cm

Hon. Mrs. Basil Ionides Bequest, 1963.4 - 22.13

Although Christian emblems appeared already on Chinese porcelain made for the Portuguese during the Ming dynasty (see cat.nos. 1,5 - 8), this large plate is one of the earliest pieces illustrating a scene from the Bible. In the foreground the young Jesus is being baptised in a river by John ('the Baptist'), a preacher who practised this form of baptism before it became a Christian custom. In the background the Spirit of God is descending in form of a dove, as described in a Bible verse of the New Testament, in the Gospel of Matthew, chapter 3, verse 16, to which reference is made in a cartouche on the rim (abbreviated to 'Mat. 3.16'):

> And Jesus, when he was baptised, went up straightway out of the water: and lo, the heavens were opened unto him, and he saw the Spirit of God descending like a dove, and lighting upon him.

The scene is surrounded by a diaper border with Chinese landscape panels and by a dense border of flowers and fruit with four angels hidden among it and a bird opposite the cartouche, painted in a style reminiscent of Dutch Delft ware. This decoration appears also on a dish in the Mottahedeh collection (Howard and Ayers, 1978, vol. 1, pl. 306), and on another in the Victoria and Albert Museum, London (Scott, 1993, pl. 8). Another dish with the same design painted in red enamel and gold is also in the British Museum (fig. 21 a; F.597).

清　青花聖經圖案紋盤

Blue-and-white plate with a biblical scene

22. 清　彩瓷歐洲情侶攜狗散步圖盤

直徑19公分

法蘭克收藏

描繪一對年輕的歐洲情侶牽著小狗在中國式庭園散步。此圖案是早期爲荷蘭市場而燒製的典型中國貿易瓷，施琺瑯彩。傳世物中，尚有琺瑯彩邊勾勒釉下鈷藍彩同紋飾的盤子。

22 Polychrome painted dish with a European couple walking their dog

Qing dynasty, c. 1715-25

Diameter 19 cm

Franks collection, F.590

The dish is painted with a romantic scene of a young European couple walking with their dog in a Chinese garden. They have their arms round each others waists and are looking at each other. The lady is wearing a kerchief over her hair, and a long patterned dress. The gentleman is dressed in a tricorne hat, three-quarter length coat, long waistcoat, knee breeches and stockings. The dish is painted entirely in brown, iron - red and gold, except for the woman's kerchief which is green. The dish has a narrow diaper border interrupted by four floral panels.

This design is very common in early Chinese export porcelain made for the Dutch market and exists also with an underglaze-blue border. An identical example is in the Musées Royaux d'Art et d'Histoire, Brussels, Belgium (Jörg, 1989, pl.76) ; a dish with blue border is in the Mottahedeh collection (Howard and Ayers, 1978, vol. I, pl. 127). The design also appears on a somewhat later Coromandel lacquer chest of drawers (Hervouet and Bruneau, 1986, no.7.33). However, the European print from which it derives has not yet been identified.

清　彩瓷歐洲情侶攜狗散步圖盤
Polychrome painted dish with a European couple walking their dog

23. 清　仿伊萬里英國徽章紋盤

直徑40公分

法蘭克收藏

盤中央之徽章紋是馬修・馬丁的徽章。他曾任東印度公司馬克
波羅號船長。此船曾因1716年到過廣東而出名。後來他升任東
印度公司總裁。此徽章紋在盤緣出現四次之多，並分佈在花卉
紋和如意之間，是一件典型的中國仿製伊萬里瓷，製於康熙朝
。

23　Chinese *imari* plate with an English coat of arms

Qing dynasty, c. 1716 - 22

Diameter 40 cm

Franks collection, F.758 +

The large plate is decorated in Chinese *imari* style, in underglaze blue,
red enamel and gilding, with a central medallion containing a coat of
arms with elaborate fronds surmounted by a helmet and with an
animal crest; this medallion is repeated four times on the rim,
alternating with *ruyi* - shaped panels enclosing small landscape scenes,
which are joined by an overall flower scroll. The base shows a *lingzhi*
mark in a double circle.

The animal which forms the crest of this coat of arms is believed to
represent a marten, a homophone of the name Martin, the family to
whom the coat of arms belongs. This dish as well as a covered jug
(Howard, 1974, p. 176) formed part of a service made for Matthew
Martin, Captain of the East Indiaman *Marlborough*, a ship known to
have been at Canton in 1716; he later became a director of the East
India Company (*ibid.*).

This dish shows how in the Kangxi period standard export porcelain
styles were adapted to fit a Western coat of arms harmoniously into a
Chinese design. Various similar plates and dishes with floral motifs
instead of the arms were exported to the Middle East and are
preserved in the Topkapi Saray Museum, Istanbul, Turkey (Krahl,
1986, vol. III, nos. 2994 - 8). The same design was used again for
another armorial service, made around the same time for Daniel
Horsemonden of New York, a relative of whom was also involved in
the China trade and is known to have been in Canton in 1721
(Howard, 1974, p. 176; Sargent, 1993, p. 208 and pl. 2).

清　仿伊萬里英國徽章紋盤
Chinese *imari* plate with an English coat of arms

24. 清　彩瓷英國徽章紋盤

直徑39.8公分

法蘭克收藏

盤中央以青花、紅、綠琺瑯彩和金彩，描繪徽章紋，徽章紋原
屬英國釀酒者之稱的國會議員，後來為倫敦市長的韓福瑞・巴
森及其夫人莎拉・克勞莉所有。巴森市長在1719年與夫人成婚，
器面上以釉下藍彩描繪精緻的龍鳳。

24 *Famille* verte dish with an English coat of arms

Qing dynasty, c. 1719-22

Diameter 39.8 cm

Franks collection, F.626

The well of this dish is decorated with two dragons chasing a flaming
pearl and two phoenix on either side of a peony spray, all delicately
incised and coloured in pale cobalt blue, and the centre is painted with
a large coat of arms in underglaze blue, bright red and green enamels
and gilding.

The coat of arms belongs to Sir Humphrey Parsons, a wealthy brewer,
Member of Parliament and later Lord Mayor of London, and his wife
Saray Crowley, whom he married in 1719.

Several armorial services painted in *famille verte* enamels and with
Chinese motifs in underglaze blue are known. The *famille verte* colour
scheme went out of fashion soon after this service was made, with the
introduction of a rose - pink enamel at the very end of the Kangxi
period. Other pieces from this service are in the Mottahedeh collection
(Howard and Ayers, 1978, vol. II, no. 410), and in the Cooke
collection (Howard, 1974, p. 217) .

清　彩瓷英國徽章紋盤
Famille verte dish with an English coat of arms

25. 清　彩瓷英國徽章紋盤

直徑35.7公分

查理斯・渥克牧師遺贈

精緻的徽章紋上有皇冠的心形紋飾以及船隻，分別由二隻頭戴皇冠的山羊來支撐，並有題辭「Through」字樣。這徽章紋原屬奧其伯・漢彌頓，他住在靠近蘇格蘭邊境的里卡頓，曾任牙買加總督，並在1708－1747年間出任國會議員。

25 *Famille verte* serving plate with an English coat of arms

Qing dynasty, c. 1715 - 22

Diameter 35.7 cm

Rev. Charles Walker Bequest, F.772 ＋ （1887.12 - 18.32）

This large plate is decorated with an elaborate coat of arms consisting of stars, crowned hearts and ships, with a ducal coronet above and supported by a pair of goats with golden horns and crowns around their necks, attached with chains. The crest is an oak tree with a saw cutting through it and the motto 'THROUGH'. On the rim are four floral sprays, and in the cavetto floral panels on a flower-scroll ground, painted mainly in iron-red and gold.

The arms belong to the Hamilton family and their quartering reflects the family's historical marriage unions with the families Douglas and Arran. The service was probably commissioned by Archibald Hamilton of Riccarton in Linlithgow on the Scottish border Governor of Jamaica, naval captain, and Member of Parliament from 1708 to 1747. （Howard, 1974, p.226）. His youngest son, Sir William Hamilton - famous for being married to Emma, Admiral Lord Nelson's mistress - is known to have used the service to which this plate belonged while Ambassador to Naples （from 1764 to 1800）. This rare service can be dated to the late Kangxi period when rose-pink enamel was not yet in use.

清　彩瓷英國徽章紋盤
Famille verte serving plate with an English coat of arms

盛清
High Qing, c.1723 -c.1800
（cat.nos. 26 - 140）

歐洲風格瓷器
Westerners in China
（cat.nos. 26 - 37 ）

26. 清　粉彩紀念荷蘭商船停泊中國海域紋盤

直徑22.8公分

法蘭克收藏

盤中描繪荷籍東印度公司商船，在荷蘭中堡市懸掛旗子之徽章紋，以荷文標示著：「威里堡號的大副在1756年駛入中國海域」。這類瓷器是爲紀念航行而製作的紀念品。其他類似紋飾之同時期瓷器，多半是以標示有船長名稱而著名。

26 *Famille rose* plate commemorating the anchorage of a Dutch trading ship in Chinese waters

Qing dynasty, dated 1756

Diameter 22.8 cm

Franks collection, F.598

The central design depicts the broadside view of a Dutch East Indiaman under full sail in a calm turquoise sea. At the stern it flies the Dutch national flag (horizontally striped blue, white and red), at the prow the standard of Middelburg, and on top of the three masts the flag of the Dutch East India Company. The vessel has large holds for cargo and provisions. It also carries an armament comparable to a contemporary 18th - century warship. The rim is edged in a delicate pink lace border and bears a cartouche inscribed in Dutch 'CHRIST: SCHOONEMAN OPPR STUERMAN OP: T: SCHIP VRYBURG: TFR: REEDE WANPHO IN CHINA INT IAAR: 1756:' which can be translated 'Christ [ian] Schooneman, Chief Mate of the ship *Vrijburg*, in the roads off Whampoa in China in the year 1756'.

The Dutch East Indiaman *Vrijburg* is recorded as having been in Canton in 1756 and this piece is one of a number of similar pieces which served as souvenirs of the ship's voyage to China. Other similarly painted plates include one at the Zeeland Museum, Middelburg, Netherlands (Jörg, 1982, no.74). Similar plates are known, painted with the starboard view of the *Vrijburg*, also dated 1756, and inscribed with the name of the ship's Captain, Jacob Rijzik. A large serving plate of this type is in the Victoria and Albert Museum, London; and another in the Musée Guimet, Paris, France (*Oriental Ceramics*, 1981, vol. 7, col.pl. 49). Only plates are known with this decoration.

Dutch ships such as the *Vrijburg* would have left their company base in Batavia in July or early August and sailed for four weeks north - eastwards via the Banka Straits. This trip was undertaken only once each year because of the prevailing tides and local weather conditions. At Macao, the entry fee to Whampoa was paid to Chinese customs officials and a local pilot was hired to guide the ships further in. At Whampoa the ships were anchored, as the Pearl River thereafter was too shallow for such large trading vessels. The supercargoes were taken in smaller boats the final 13 nautical miles to Canton's quayside to conduct their business at the European trading stations (see cat.nos. 33 and 34).

The *Vrijburg* was built in 1748, laid to rest in 1771 and her tonnage was 1150 tons (Hervouet and Bruneau, 1986, no.2.2). This type of East Indiaman would have measured over 140 feet from stern to sternpost. She was built for the Dutch East India Company's Zealand Chamber of Commerce. A model of a similar Dutch East Indiaman, the *Zeven Provincien*, made in 1723 and one of the earliest models of a merchant ship in existence, is in the National Maritime Museum, Greenwich, London (no.1723 - 1/SLR 0418).

清　粉彩紀念荷蘭商船停泊中國海域紋盤

Famille rose plate commemorating the anchorage of a
Dutch trading ship in Chinese waters

27. 清　褐釉紀念瑞典商船停泊中國海域馬克杯

高10.2公分

法蘭克收藏

馬克杯描繪山水風景，一艘大型商船掛著瑞典國旗，與其他船一同停泊在港口，背景襯有多山的鄉間靠岸旁的住家，也都在瑞典旗幟的庇蔭下。有瑞典銘文記載「格斯塔夫·艾道夫船」字樣，該船，自1784年12月8日至1785年4月21日止停泊於港口。

Utsigt af hamnen Gnalong belägen på ön Hajnan.
aftagen då Skept Gustaf Adolph därstädes gorde öfwerligande resa fr. d. 8 Decemb. 1784 til d. 21 apr. 1785.

27 Sepia - painted mug commemorating the anchorage of a Swedish trading ship in Chinese waters

Qing dynasty, dated 1784 - 5

Height 10.2 cm

Franks collection, F.613

The mug is slightly flared towards the base and the handle has a *ruyi* terminal. It is painted in sepia with a harbour view showing a large boat under a prominent Swedish flag among other boats against a backdrop of hilly countryside with some houses, also under a Swedish flag, near the shore. The rim has a gold border.

Around the base runs a Swedish inscription written in black reading

Utsigt of hamnen Gnalong belägen på ön Hajnan, aftagen däSkept Gustaf Adolph därstädes gorde öfwerligande resa fr. d. 8 Decemb. 1784, tild. 21 Apr. 1785

which can be translated

View from the harbour Gnalong situated on the island Hainan, taken while the ship *Gustaf Adolph* lay there at anchor from 8th December, 1784, to 21st April, 1785.

The Swedish East India Company, founded in 1731, reached a peak of its shipments of Chinese porcelain to Sweden in the period between 1766 and 1786, during which this piece was commissioned. According to a letter written from the ship on 9th December, 1784, the Swedish East Indiaman *Gustaf Adolph* was forced to go into harbour due to adverse winds and lack of fresh water（Kjellberg, 1975, p. 208）.

This mug appears to be unique, but a related plate in the Historiska Museum, *Göteborg,* Sweden, painted *en grisaille,* is inscribed with the name of the same ship and with the same dates, and shows a map with a coast line and a large bay inscribed 'Gnalong'（Hervouet and Bruneau, 1986, no. 1.22）. The ship appears to have anchored in the Bay of Gallong on the south coast of Hainan island, on its way to Canton, and this mug and plate appear to have been commissioned as souvenirs of this unforeseen stopover.（Thanks are due to Christer von der Burg for help with this entry.）

清　褐釉紀念瑞典商船停泊中國海域馬克杯
Sepia-painted mug commemorating the anchorage of a Swedish trading ship in Chinese waters

28. 清　黑釉描金居住中國歐洲家庭紋盤

直徑23公分

法蘭克收藏

描繪一歐洲家族，居住在圍有欄杆的中國式建築，四周擺設中
國家具及其他物品。夫人抱著小孩，頭向著丈夫談話，以理想
化之方式描繪居住在中國的歐洲人，事實上，歐洲人幾無定居
在中國，更是很少人攜家帶眷。也見描繪中國人物紋之同款式
的瓷器（參考圖版28a）。

fig. 28a

28　Plate painted in gold, silver and black with a European family in a Chinese setting

Qing dynasty, c.1725-35

Diameter 23 cm

Franks collection, F.869

The plate is lavishly painted in gold, silver and black with a European family, the man with long curly hair, dressed in a short coat and holding a cup, standing on the balustraded terrace of a Chinese - style house and looking at a child, which is held by its mother and is heading towards him. In the background, an attendant is carrying a flower vase, and both inside and outside the house are Chinese tables laden with Chinese goods, a bowl with finger citron and other fruits, a vase holding a stalk of *lingzhi*, Chinese books, and a tripod vessel. The scene is enclosed by a shaped border densely filled with flowers and insects, and the rim shows a border of tree shrews among grape vines enclosed between other formal borders.

During the Yongzheng period（1723-35）Chinese figures were often depicted in such settings. The appearance of a Western family in these opulent Chinese surroundings is, however, unusual. Similarly painted dishes with Chinese figures are also in the British Museum（fig.28 a; F.869 A）. The present scene appears to be an idealistic rather than a truthful depiction of the life of European merchants in China.

Although before the 1750s Westerners sometimes took their families to Canton, this was not the rule and after 1760 it was definitely forbidden. Several other plates with the same design exist, one for example in the Musées Royaux d'Art et d'Histoire, Brussels, Belgium（Taipei, 1992, p. 43）

72

清　黑釉描金居住中國歐洲家庭紋盤

**Plate painted in gold, silver and black with a European
family in a Chinese setting**

29. 淸　德化窰歐洲人物中國山水塑像

高27公分

法蘭克收藏

此塑像表現一群歐洲人；身著及膝褲，頭戴三角帽，置身於山
水風景中。刻意安排戲劇性的岩石堆中有一座橋及裝飾的大門。
德化窰製作，十八世紀在歐洲盛行一時，歐洲的窰廠也曾致力
仿製。

29 Dehua sculpture showing Europeans in a Chinese landscape

Qing dynasty, c. 1680 - 1720

Height 27 cm

Franks collection, F.578 B

The hollow sculpture is in the shape of a mountain covered with flowering plants, with a two-storey Chinese gateway and a sculpted snake-dragon on top. In front of the mountain is a curving path which leads over a footbridge towards steep steps. A European gentleman wearing a tricorne hat is sitting cross-legged on the upper level of the gate, contemplating the view and two others, also in tricorne hats, buttoned jackets, boots and knee breeches and armed with pistols and powder horns, are at either end of the path. Further figures and other details are now lost.

Chinese miniature landscapes have a long tradition and were made in a variety of media such as jade and other stones, wood, bamboo, ivory, bronze and clay, for contemplation on a scholar's desk. The combination with Western figures, however, was rather made for export. Europeans at a Chinese hillside must have been a rare sight and such a representation may well be idealistic, since foreigners rarely went beyond the foreign quarters in the south-western district at Canton. Another Dehua model of a very similar mountain, but with figures missing, is in the Victoria and Albert Museum, London (no. C.33 - 1957) .

清　德化窯歐洲人物中國山水塑像
Dehua sculpture showing Europeans in a Chinese landscape

30. 清　德化窯歐洲家族塑像

高16.8公分　寬15.5公分

敦尼爾遺贈

描繪正在吃點心的歐洲家族；有孩子、小狗、猴子等寵物，以及前景的花盆。此類瓷器系列曾出現於1701年英國東印度公司訂單上。

30　Dehua sculpture of a European family

Qing dynasty, c.1700 - 1750

Height 16.8 cm, width 15.5 cm

P.J. Donnelly Bequest, 1980.7 - 28.666

This sculpted group shows a European gentleman wearing a tricorne hat, buttoned frock coat and knee breeches and a lady in a tall headdress and long dress. They are seated beside a Chinese chair on which a bowl of bread is placed, holding small cups, and are flanked by a similarly dressed boy and girl with a pet dog, pet monkey and a flower pot in front of them.

Various attempts have been made to identify the figures, which may have been modelled after an engraving, but were probably intended simply as an archetypal representation of a foreign family. Such models of 'Dutch families' were already listed in cargo sale lists of the English East India Company dating from 1701 (Godden, 1979, pp.266, 270). Such figural groups are not uncommon but, being hand - finished, they vary in detail. Similar pieces are in the Rijksmuseum, Amsterdam, Netherlands (Beurdeley and Raindre, 1987, pl.334); in the Mottahedeh collection (Howard and Ayers, 1978, vol. 1, pl.55); and in the Victoria and Albert Museum, London (no. C.108 - 1963). They were sometimes cold - painted in the West (see Godden, 1979, pl.193).

清　德化窯歐洲家族塑像
Dehua sculpture of a European family

31. 清　德化窯歐洲情侶像

高25.3公分

法蘭克收藏

描繪身著短外套、緊身褲、頭戴帽子的紳士。紳士的手搭著身穿長裙，以圍巾覆頭部之女子。這一類人像通常施琺瑯彩，但此作品卻未著釉，十分少見。

31 White porcelain sculpture of a Dutch couple

Qing dynasty, c.1750 - 1800

Height 25.3 cm

Franks collection, F.578 A

The lady wears a long dress and a kerchief over her head and holds a handkerchief; the gentleman, in a short coat, tight breeches and a straight - brimmed hat, has his arm placed around her shoulder. Both are standing on a rectangular plinth with shaped openings, in the same way as figures of Chinese immortals.

This group is unusual in having been left undecorated. Unlike the groups above (cat.nos.29 and 30) which were made at the Dehua kilns where enamels were rarely used, this sculpture was made at Jingdezhen, where porcelain was rarely left plain. It may be one of the pieces sent to Canton to be decorated there, but mistakenly sent to Europe unpainted. Similar groups, painted in different ways, are for example, in the Mottahedeh collection (Howard and Ayers, 1978, vol. II, no. 648); and in the Espirito Santo collection (Beurdeley, 1962, pl. V).

清　德化窯歐洲情侶像
**White porcelain sculpture of
a Dutch couple**

32. 清　彩瓷荷蘭淑女像

高41.3公分

巴西爾·伊耳尼底斯夫人遺贈

荷葉邊蕾絲領的淡藍色女衫和斗篷，搭配粉紅裙子、淺藍圍裙，並戴著鑲有蕾絲帽子的荷蘭仕女。裙裾飛揚，像是迎風而立的姿態。

32　*Famille rose* figure of a Dutch lady

Qing dynasty, c.1735 - 45

Height 41.3 cm

Hon. Mrs. Basil Ionides Bequest, 1963-4-22.11

The Dutch woman is standing with her hands by her sides, her clothes modelled as if blown to one side by the wind, and is painted in *famille rose* enamels. She is wearing a dark blue patterned cape, lined in purplish blue, a broad ruffled collar, pink skirt, tight, laced bodice in yellow, green and brown, pale blue blouse and cloud - patterned apron. The lace - edged headdress which covers her hair has distinctive wings over each ear; her red shoes are pointed and around her wrists are twin - strand pearl bracelets.

This figure is sometimes paired with a figure of a gentleman (Sargent, 1991, no.51) and was intended for display in the houses of wealthy Europeans. The figure is probably modelled after a costume print as yet untraced. Pictures of foreigners in characteristic costumes were popular in China as well as in Europe in the 18th century.

Such figures were produced from moulds and other examples of this model are, for example, in the Victoria and Albert Museum, London (no. C.94 - 1963); in the Mottahedeh collection (Howard and Ayers, 1978, vol.I, pl.641); in the Peabody Museum, Salem, Massachusetts, U.S.A. (Sargent, 1991, no.51); and in the Espirito Santo collection, Lisbon, Portugal (Beurdeley, 1962, pl.XVIII).

清　彩瓷荷蘭淑女像
Famille rose figure of
a Dutch lady

33. 清　赭墨金彩廣州港口西方商館紋飾大碗

高15公分　直徑36公分

哈里森收藏

描繪廣州港口內東印度公司的商館，如：荷蘭商館、英國商館、瑞典商館、澳洲商館、法國商館、丹麥商館等；這些商館的建築風格，受到歐洲之影響。此類圖案也見於用來製作其他紀念品，如：畫作、版畫、扇子、瓷器等。此件紋飾仿自當時的雕刻品（參考圖版33a，年代為1779年）。此件大碗係作為調水果酒之用。

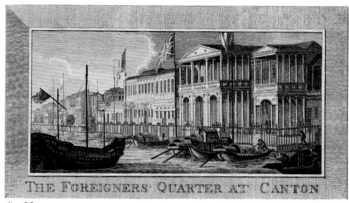

THE FOREIGNERS' QUARTER AT CANTON

fig. 33a

---

33 *Grisaille* - and - gold painted punchbowl showing the Western trading stations along the Canton waterfront

Qing dynasty, c. 1708 - 85

Height 15 cm, diameter 36 cm

Given by F.C. Harrison, F.745 ＋ (1903.11 - 18.1)

The exterior of this punchbowl is painted *en grisaille* with a continuous frieze of the trading stations, built in European style along the bund at Canton. Outside these trading stations are six national flags, flying from tall posts along the quay, which identify the buildings as those of the East India Companies of Holland, England, Sweden, Austria, France and Denmark. European merchants in tricorne hats and frock coats are painted conducting their business inside and outside of these trading stations. Much of the quay has been fenced off down to the water and small Chinese boats are moored to the harbour wall. Inside the bowl is a delicately painted floral medallion.

The factories shown here were called *hongs* by the Europeans, after the Cantonese pronounciation of the Chinese word for company or business, *hang*, and these bowls are often known as 'hong bowls'. The Western traders lived and worked in these rented trading stations built along the banks of the Pearl River in the south-west quarter of Canton, during the five-month trading season (August - January).

From about 1760 to 1800 the Canton waterfront was repeatedly depicted in oil-paintings, watercolours and engravings, so that its changing appearance is well recorded. Architectural details of the warehouses, which were re-built in 1743 in Western style, are therefore of interest for the dating of these views (Crossman, 1991, pp. 423 - 35). The appearance or lack of particular flags similarly help to pinpoint their dating. These features, however, can only provide a *terminus post quem* for the bowls since these views on porcelains as well as on ivory, silk and paper fans were not copied from life but from painted or printed pictures, sometimes of earlier date.

On the present bowl the British factory is painted with arched entrances and thicker columns than in earlier views (see cat.no. 34), as it looked around 1780 to 1785. The view can be dated before 1784 when the American flag appeared at Canton after the arrival of the ship *The Empress of China*. A similar view is seen in an early 19th-century engraving, also in the British Museum collection (fig. 33 a; P＋D 1877.10 - 13. 230) which is based on a picture dated 1789 and entitled 'The Foreigners Quarter at Canton'. In its material and potting the present bowl appears to be fairly early in date and being decorated *en grisaille* is extremely rare.

清　赭墨金彩廣州港口西方商館紋飾大碗
Grisaille - and - gold painted punchbowl showing the Western
trading stations along the Canton waterfront

34. 清　彩瓷廣州港西洋商館紋大碗

高15公分　直徑36.2公分

法蘭克收藏

描繪掛國旗的荷、英、法、澳、丹麥、瑞典等六國商館，這些
商館位於廣州之西南部，以租賃方式作為倉庫、辦公室、住屋
等。出現在這件中的廣州港景色似乎比圖版33早一些，可能是
先繪水彩，後再上色（參考圖版34a）

fig. 34a

34 *Famille rose* punchbowl showing the Western trading stations along the Canton waterfront

Qing dynasty, c. 1780 - 90

Height 15 cm, diameter 36.2 cm

Franks collection, F.746 +

Like the previous bowl （cat.no. 33）, this punchbowl is decorated with continuous scenes of the foreign trading stations along the banks of the Pearl River at Canton, but in *famille rose* enamels. Here the national flags are shown in a different order and identify buildings hired by the East India Companies of Holland, England, Sweden, France, Austria and Denmark. Chinese commercial boats are moored along the quay, and Chinese and European merchants, the latter distinguished by their tricorne hats and frock coats, stroll along the dock. Inside the bowl is a basket of flowers contained within a floral medallion.

The architectural details of the trading stations depicted on this bowl, where the British factory is shown with slender pillars as porch supports and no arches, suggest that this bowl depicts Canton at an earlier date than the previous piece （cat.no. 33） and was painted after an earlier view. A similar view appears in a scroll in the British Library, painted for the Western market between about 1760 and 1770 by an anonymous Chinese artist （fig. 34 a; K.top 116. 23. Roll.cab.12,

courtesy of the British Library）. In terms of quality, however, the present bowl does not seem to predate the last.

Hong bowls of the *famille rose* such as this piece are more common than examples painted *en grisaille*. Similarly decorated pieces include one in the Metropolitan Museum, New York （Le Corbeiller, 1974, no.49）, and another in a private collection （Godden, 1979, no. 16）. Such bowls were brought back from China as souvenirs, as part of a merchant's or seaman's private cargo; in 1785 Captain Green of *The Empress of China,* is recorded to have brought at least four enamelled bowls with factory scenes back to America.

清　彩瓷廣州港西洋商館紋大碗
Famille rose punchbowl showing the Western trading
stations along the Canton waterfront

35. 清　彩瓷茶杯及托盤

（杯）高3.6公分　（托盤）直徑10.4公分

法蘭克收藏

為荷蘭東印度公司所生產，紋飾仿自荷蘭東印度公司，在1728年間發行於遠東通行的銀幣（參考圖版35a）正面之圖案。荷蘭徽章紋分別由二隻頭戴皇冠的獅子支撐，下有荷蘭東印度公司英文縮寫「VOC」字樣，環繞四周的是拉丁文的荷蘭箴言「衆志成城」（在小事上團結，就能成就大事）。年代約為1728年。

fig. 35a

35 *Famille rose* teacup and saucer, made for the Dutch East India Company

Qing dynasty, c. 1729 - 30

Height（cup）3.6 cm, diameter（saucer）10.4 cm

Franks collection, F.797 +

The design of this teacup and saucer is composed of a crowned coat of arms supported by two crowned lions rampant, below which is the monogram 'VOC' framed by scrollwork, all painted in rose - pink, red, yellow and green enamels. Encircling this design is the date 1728 and the Latin motto 'CONCORDIA RES PARVAE CRESCUNT' (small things grow great in unity). The rim of the saucer and inner lip of the cup are painted with close parallel brush - strokes in iron-red under a narrow pink band.

The arms and motto belong to the Dutch Republic. The letters 'VOC' are the cypher of the 'Verenigde Oost Indische Compagnie', the Dutch East India Company. The design has been accurately copied from one side of a silver coin, issued by the Company in 1728 for use in the Far East. Even the ribbed milling of the coin is imitated in the rim of the saucer and the inner rim of the cup. This type of silver coin (ducatoon) was struck and issued between 1726 and 1751 (for an example dated 1741, also in the British Museum, see fig. 35 a; C + M 1947.10 - 9 .156). On its reverse is a man on horseback, which led to the coin's nickname 'The Silver Rider'.

From its foundation in 1602 until 1726 the Dutch East India Company had used regular Dutch silver dollars for its overseas trade. In 1726 it arranged - without prior governmental approval - to have coins minted with a special inscription, for trading use in the Far East. As a result of opposition by the government, however, the project had to be immediately abandoned, so that coins dated 1726 exist only as specimen drawings (Scholten, 1953). Official permission was then granted in 1728 for the minting of special ducatoons with the company cypher and these coins first arrived in Batavia on 2nd August 1729, carried by the ship *The Coxhorn*.

The tea service to which this cup and saucer belonged was arguably commissioned by the Company to commemorate the successful launch of its new coinage and may possibly have been used by its employees at the Company's different official bases throughout the Far East. Other pieces from this service include cups and saucers in the Victoria and Albert Museum, London (no. 645 & a-1907), in the Museum Boymans - van Beuningen, Rotterdam, Netherlands (Hong Kong, 1984, no.43), and in the Metropolitan Museum of Art, New York (Le Corbeiller, 1974, no.43); a plate in the Mottahedeh collection (Howard and Ayers, 1978, vol.I, pl.191); a plate, teapot, cup and saucer at the Musées Royaux d'Art et d'Histoire, Brussels, Belgium (Jörg, 1989, no.36); a teapot without lid in the Rijksmuseum, Amsterdam, Netherlands (Lunsingh Scheurleer, 1974, no.267); and a teapot in the Africana Museum, Johannesburg, South Africa (Woodward, 1974, pl.A1).

清 彩瓷茶杯及托盤
Famille rose teacup and saucer, made for the Dutch East
India Company

36. 清　粉彩茶罐 6 個

（盒）高11.8公分　（罐）高11公分

法蘭克收藏

錫盒內放置六個茶罐，上面繪有中國山水和花卉紋，在蓋子上
則寫有不同茶葉之名稱。這些茶葉是當時外銷歐洲的茗茶，茶
罐可能是用來盛裝樣本，盒子是用來保持茶葉之乾燥和芳香。

36　Pewter box with six *famille rose* tea caddies

Qing dynasty, c. 1760 - 1800

Heights（box）11.8 cm,（caddies）11 cm

Franks collection, F.1688

The straight-sided pewter box and flat cover are made in the shape of a
prunus blossom, and contain one five - lobed and five fan - shaped tea
caddies and covers, which are neatly fitted inside. The tea caddies are
painted on the sides in enamels of the *famille rose* with landscape
scenes and flower sprays, and the covers are inscribed in gold with
somewhat curiously spelled names of different teas: four black teas
named CONGO（Congou）on the central vessel, and GOBEE
（Bohea）, SAUCHON（Souchong）and PECKO（Pekoe）on the
surrounding vessels, and two green teas named HEVSAN（Hyson）
and SINGLO（Singlo）.

Although the tea trade was of major importance for European
merchants in China, no other such box, which was apparently used for
transporting a selection of tea samples, appears to be recorded. The
pewter container had a double purpose: it enabled the porcelain boxes
to be safely transported and helped to keep the tea leaves dry and
aromatic during shipment. Wooden tea chests used for shipping were
lined with an alloy of tin and lead for the same reason. In the west
silver tea caddies were also made in sets for different types of tea, and
kept in fitted containers, usually of square shape. Black, i.e. fermented,
teas were much more popular in 18th-century Europe than green teas-
just like today-and could also be kept for longer. The four black teas
inscribed on this set were the main kinds exported, Bohea being the
most sought-after until the late 18th century when the demand for
Congou became greater（Jörg, 1982, pp. 78 ff.）.

清　粉彩茶罐6個

Pewter box with six *famille rose* tea caddies

37. 清 青花中國工匠紋盤

直徑28.5公分

法蘭克收藏

盤中央描繪在松樹下工廠前正在編竹藤的三位工匠，這種圖案是仿自外銷中國水墨畫。器底有阿拉伯數字「4」字樣，是表示中國茶、生薑、果實等二十三種主題系列的繪畫作品中的第四幅。景物四周以貝殼、豐饒角、格子紋等歐式紋飾做裝飾（參考圖版126）（註：豐饒角係指盛滿花果、穀物等，以象徵豐饒的裝飾用羊角，常出現在繪畫或雕刻作品中，源於希臘神話宇宙神之羊的角。）

37 Blue - and - white plate with a scene of Chinese artisans at work

Qing dynasty, c. 1736 - 50

Diameter 28.5 cm

Franks collection, F.587

This underglaze-bule painted plate shows three Chinese artisans seated beneath a pine tree in front of a workshop splitting canes. The scene is surrounded by an elaborate border of shells, horns and lattice work. On the reverse is a Western number 4.

The central motif is unusual in that it derives from a contemporary Chinese watercolour painting made for export, depicting Chinese people at work, rather than from a Western print. In this case, the number 4 refers to the plate's position within a series of at least twenty-three different scenes recording the cultivation and processing of tea, ginger, fruits and other native plants. The rim border is Western in design and also appears on a Dutch armorial service made for the Amsterdam-based Snoek family（see cat.no. 126）and on plates painted with a pair of cockerels among rocks and plants, of which an example is in the Peabody Museum, Salem, Massachusetts, U.S.A.（Mudge, 1986, no. 202）. The original model of this border has not yet been traced.

A series of plates of different sizes, tureens and sauceboats from the same service are known; these include a plate numbered 2 with a scene of packing and sampling tea with a teapot in the foreground; the present piece numbered 4, showing men splitting canes; a plate numbered 7 with men loading containers on to a boat; a plate numbered 10 showing men carrying water along a river bank; a plate in the Fries Museum, Leeuwarden, Netherlands, numbered 11 and depicting the transport of boxes（Amsterdam, 1968-9, no. 274）; a plate in the China Trade Museum, Milton, Massachusetts, U.S.A., numbered 12, with a scene of labourers tilling the soil; a plate in the Metropolitan Museum of Art, New York, numbered 13, with scenes of men making jars（Le Corbeiller, 1974, no. 42）; a plate numbered 15 showing men hauling a barge laden with barrels; a tureen also in the Fries Museum, numbered 16 showing the loading of a barge and a customer in a shop（Rouen et al., 1971, no.222）; a plate numbered 17 painted with men weighing tea bricks; a plate numbered 18 depicting others sampling tea; another plate in the Metropolitan Museum of Art, numbered 21, decorated with workers packing baskets with small fruit（Le Corbeiller, 1974, no.42）; a sauceboat in the Fries Museum, numbered 22（listed in Amsterdam, 1968-9, no.274）; a plate in the Mottahedeh collection, numbered 23, showing the sampling and packaging of tea（Howard and Ayers, 1978, vol. 1, pl. 213）; and a plate in the Princessehof Museum, Leeuwarden, Netherlands, with ladies picking tea leaves（Harrisson, 1986, no. 114, number not listed）.

清　青花中國工匠紋盤
Blue-and-white plate with a scene of Chinese artisans at work

英國風景
Scenes of Life in England
（cat.nos. 38 - 47）

38. 清　赭墨釉金彩英國政治人物紋大碗

高18公分　直徑41公分

碗的一邊，描繪英國新聞、出版及政治界人物約翰・韋奇斯
（1727－1797）之肖像，他手持帽子，帽頂上寫著「自由」字樣。
此圖案採自英國畫家威廉・賀高斯（1697－1764）在1763年發
行的版畫（參考圖版38a）。另一面描繪三個飲酒作樂者，圖
樣採自法國藝術家查理莫古特（1728－1768）在1764年所發行
的版畫（參考圖版38b），兩邊圖案並無直接關聯性。

fig. 38a　　　　　　　　fig. 38b

38 *Grisaille* - and - gold painted punchbowl depicting an English political figure

Qing dynasty, c. 1764 - 70

Height 18 cm, diameter 41 cm

1988.4 - 21.1

On one side of the punchbowl is a portrait of a man with a distinctive squint, wearing a wig, frock coat and knee breeches. He is seated beside a desk with papers and writing utensils and is holding a cap of liberty on the end of a pole. The other side of the bowl shows a group of four gentlemen, one with pot-belly and wearing a tricorne hat forcing another to drink from a bowl while two others are looking on. A stand with sheet music and the neck of a cello are visible in front. In between these two pictures are Chinese landscape scenes with pairs of birds among flowers and rocks, exquisitely painted in *grisaille,* sepia and red.

The single figure is John Wilkes (1727 - 97), an outspoken and controversial politician, publisher and satirist, who campaigned for basic civil rights such as freedom of the press and standard procedures for police arrest.

Wilkes' irreverent behaviour brought him repeatedly into conflict with the authorities, but made him also very popular. Despite being expelled from Parliament in 1764 and later being declared an outlaw, he was re-elected as Member of Parliament in 1768, and in 1774 his popularity led to his election as Lord Mayor of London. The periodical *North Briton,* which he had founded, was famous for publishing provocative views, for attacking King George III and his prime minister, and for criticizing renowned figures such as the English artist William Hogarth (1697 - 1764) (*North Briton,* 1762 - 68). The sheets of paper seen on this bowl on the desk besides Wilkes, are in the original engraving identified as two issues of the *North Briton,* published 1762 and 1763, respectively.

This engraving which was done by Hogarth, one of Wilkes' adversaries, is a caricature which does not attempt to depict him in a flattering light. It was published on 16th May 1763 and a print is in the British Museum (fig. 38 a; P+D 1864.8-13.251). According to a contemporary comment, the print showed Wilkes with the cap of liberty 'poised over his head like a self - appointed halo, in ironic contrast to the truly diabolic squinting leer and the impression of horns created by his wig' (Palmer, 1976, p. 85).

The figures on the other side of the bowl are copied from an engraving by the French artist Charles Maucourt (1728 - 68), who worked in France and England. Various titles exist for different impressions of this design; a print in the British Museum entitled 'Night Amusements' was published in 1764 (fig. 38 b; P+D 1933.10 - 14.407). The connection between the two subjects on this bowl is uncertain. The second scene although not depicting Wilkes, may refer to the indulgent lifestyle, for which he was notorious.

During the 18th century the English public became increasingly politically aware and popular demand for historical or political curios led to the marketing of Chinese porcelain as well as English earthenware with such topical designs. An identical punchbowl is in the Mottahedeh collection (Howard and Ayers, 1978, vol. I, pl. 240); another in the Henry Francis du Pont Winterthur Museum, U.S.A. (Palmer, 1976, figs. 48 b and 49 a). While the following bowl (cat.no. 39), which also depicts Wilkes, was clearly commissioned by factions sympathetic to Wilkes' cause, the present piece seems to depict Wilkes in an unfavourable way and may have been commissioned by members of the establishment.

清　赭墨釉金彩英國政治人物紋大碗

Grisaille - and - gold painted punchbowl depicting an
English political figure

39. 清　粉彩英國政治人物像大碗

高11.3公分　直徑26.1公分

法蘭克收藏

碗上描繪二個肖像；左邊是英國出版、新聞及政治界人物約翰
・韋奇斯（1727－1797）之肖像，身穿紅色夾克，並有一箴言
寫著「有備無患」字樣。右邊的畫像是法院院長曼斯菲德
（1705～1793），身穿法袍，並寫法文「公正無私」字樣。約
翰提倡自由、反對皇權，常與當時法律有所牴觸。有一次韋奇
斯在受審時，面對鐵面無私的曼斯菲德法官。這兩個徽章紋以
及有「約翰和自由」字樣的標題，出現於1768年6月18日，當
他出任國會議員時，對支持他的選民所作的演講稿上。

39 *Famille rose* punchbowl with English political figures

Qing dynasty, c. 1768 - 75

Height 11.3 cm, diameter 26.1 cm

Franks collection, F.625

The two pseudo - armorial shields which appear both on the front and reverse of this small punchbowl contain on the left a portrait bust of a gentleman with cross - eyed look in a red jacket, flanked by flower garlands and supported by a man in black robes with a long wig and another in a blue frock coat, pink waistcoat and knee breeches. The crest is a lion above an acorn and the English motto below reads 'ALWAYS READY IN A GOOD CAUSE'. On the right is a portrait bust of a gentleman in black judicial robes, bands and full - bottom wig, flanked by chains and supported by a man in a red frock coat, green waistcoat and knee breeches, and a black devil with wings and cloven hooves. The crest is a viper above a thistle, and the French motto below is 'JUSTICE SANS PITIE' (justice without mercy). Above these designs is the caption 'Wilkes & Liberty'. The rim of the bowl has been mounted in metal.

The two portrait busts are satirical depictions of John Wilkes (1727 - 97) in red jacket, a popular English political campaigner, and Lord Chief Justice Mansfield (1705 - 93) in judicial robes. As head of the judiciary, Mansfield was unsympathetic to Wilkes and his campaigns against the establishment and once tried him for libel. Wilkes' supporters are likely to be Serjeant Glynn (1722-79), his legal adviser, and Lord Temple (1739 - 1802), his friend and patron. Conversely by Mansfield's side are probably the prime minister, Lord Bute (1713 - 92), and the devil. Wilkes' crest is the heraldic emblem of England, and Mansfield's that of Scotland. The latter may refer to the Scottish regiment that, while guarding the prison in which Wilkes awaited trial, opened fire on a crowd of his supporters outside, or simply to a general anti - Scottish feeling prevailing in England at that time.

The pseudo - armorial shields of Wilkes and Mansfield on this punchbowl appear under the title 'Arms of Liberty and Slavery' on the heading of an address by Wilkes 'To the Gentlemen, Clergy and Freeholders of the County of Middlesex' (his constituents), written in King's Bench Prison on 18th June 1768 (Franks, 1879, p. 103). This bowl which in contrast to the previous piece (cat.no. 38) was obviously commissioned by Wilkes' supporters, was probably made soon after the publication of this address, as the outbreak of war between England and America in 1775 caused loyalty to King George III and the establishment to increase and support for Wilkes to decline. Other pieces with the same decoration include a teapot (Godden, 1979, no. 149), a coffee cup (Conner, 1986, no. 119 m), and another punchbowl (Hervouet and Bruneau, 1986, no. 9.51), all in private collections; other punchbowls are in the Victoria and Albert Museum, London, and in the Henry Francis du Pont Winterthur Museum, U.S.A. (Palmer, 1976, fig. 49 b). An American silver punchbowl in the Museum of Fine Arts, Boston, U.S.A., dated 1768, bears the same inscription 'Wilkes & Liberty' (Newman, 1987, p. 292).

清　粉彩英國政治人物像大碗

Famille rose punchbowl with English political figures

40. 清　粉彩英國政治人物肖像大碗

高12公分　直徑38.3公分

巴西爾‧伊耳尼底斯夫人遺贈

裝飾有中、西花卉紋，碗內則畫有一歐洲人物肖像，十分罕見。
所畫的肖像主人爲約翰（1727－1797），在上述圖版38、39中
曾提及。類似圖案曾出現在他的演講稿以及英國陶瓷器，還有
寫著他的名字（圖版40a）。

fig. 40a

40 *Famille rose* punchbowl with a portrait medallion of an English political figure

Qing dynasty, c. 1760 - 70

Height 12 cm, diameter 38.3 cm

Hon. Mrs. Basil Ionides Bequest, 1963.4 - 22.15

The punchbowl is decorated with bold Chinese and Western - style flowers on the outside, and inside with a portrait medallion depicting a man dressed in a red coat and yellow waistcoat. He is standing behind a table with a book and quill pen, and holds open a blue curtain. Above this medallion are two cherubs with red sashes who are blowing horns and holding a flower wreath over his head. A border of bamboo and flowers separates this decoration from four flower sprays on the sides.

This combination of a portrait medallion and floral decoration is unusual. The figure depicted may be the controversial publisher and political campaigner John Wilkes (1727 - 97), who is also depicted on the previous two bowls (cat.nos. 38 and 39) and whose bust appears similarly on some of his publications (see, for example, *North Briton Tracts Etc.*, n.d. [1762 - 68], pl. 272 b). The cherubs are symbolizing fame.

A similar portrait bust is found on English tin - glazed earthenware of the late 18th century, for example on a bowl in the British Museum

(fig. 40 a; M＋LA 1910.11 - 22.1) which is inscribed 'Wilkes And Liberty No. Bu＊＊' and '45'. This refers to the publication of issue no. 45 of the caustic periodical *North Briton*, which was regarded as libellous. An identical Chinese punchbowl is in the Henry Francis du Pont Winterthur Museum, U.S.A. (Hervouet and Bruneau, 1986, no. 9.52).

清　粉彩英國政治人物肖像大碗
Famille rose punchbowl with a portrait medallion of an
English political figure

41. 清　粉彩英國皮革匠圖馬克杯

高14.8公分

法蘭克收藏

描繪皮革工匠及其助手的工作情形，並有皮鞋、長靴等皮製品，以及花卉裝飾點綴，另外，有三則銘文：「威士忌萬歲……」「富豪菲克斯及其誠實正直的家族」以及「我必須從事皮革事業」等字樣。這些紋飾可能取自當時的貿易標籤。

41　*Famille rose* tankard made for an English leather worker

Qing dynasty, c. 1760 - 80

Height 14.8 cm

Franks collection, F.779 +

This straight-sided tankard shows a leather worker, sitting on a wooden bench in a scarlet frock coat, knee breeches and a tricorne hat sewing a satchel, while another opposite him is making a shoe. Above the figures on one side is the inscription 'VIVAT RYE' (long live the rye) and in smaller letters 'I must work for leathers dear'. On the other side of the tankard the inscription is 'VIVAT [long live] Rich Phillcox whit (sic) His Honest Fammily (sic), I must work for leathers dear'. Each scene is surrounded by a frame of scrollwork and flowers interlaced with 18th-century boots and other shoes, and alternating with flowers. The tankard has a red-and-gold spearhead rim border and a red-and-gold handle with notches imitating bamboo.

The design on this mug appears to be copied from the trade label of a leather worker named Richard Phillcox. Such trade labels were used to advertise and promote goods and services. The motto 'long live the rye' refers to a kind of whisky, distilled from rye grain, for which this tankard may have been used. A similar design appears on a saucer with the initials 'R P', which may have been commissioned by the same man (Godden, 1979, no.119). Pieces of Chinese export porcelain commissioned by artisans are otherwise rare. The basic shape of this tankard is also European and is similarly found in other materials such as pewter.

清　粉彩英國皮革匠圖馬克杯
Famille rose tankard made for an English leather worker

42. 清　共濟會徽章紋酒缽和啤酒杯

（缽）高12.2公分　直徑28.3公分　（杯）高15.8公分

法蘭克收藏

這二件皆描繪共濟會之宅邸、辦公室及資深會員等圖案，並有「E」「M」等縮寫字母，可能為持有人之名字。碗上所示「1755」字樣，乃這一類器皿中發現時間最早者，散佈於全世界的共濟會，在十八世紀極盛一時。其作品特色為結合五角星及許多石匠的工具為紋飾。

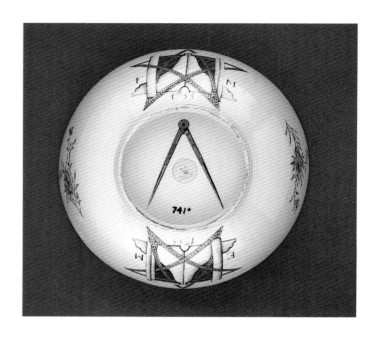

42　Polychrome painted punchbowl and tankard with Masonic emblems

Qing dynasty, c. 1755, the bowl dated 1755
Height（tankard）15.8 cm,（bowl）12.2 cm, diameter（bowl）28.3 cm
Franks collection, F.741 ＋ A, F.741 ＋

Both pieces are painted in red, black and gold with a Masonic design comprising a five-pointed star, set square, plumb-line and level, flanked by the initials 'E' and 'M'. On the bowl it is repeated three times, once on the inside and twice on the outside, inscribed with the date 1755 beneath, and on the outside it alternates with two sprays of Chinese - style flowers in *famille rose* enamels. The base of the bowl and outside of the tankard are further painted with compasses.

This design combines the principal emblems of office of the most senior members of a Masonic lodge. Freemasons are members of a non-political, non-religious, semi-secret society whose internal organization involves an elaborate system of symbolic rituals. The origin of this fraternity lies in the practices of medieval stonemasons; moving from place to place in search of building work and therefore unable to form fixed trade guilds, they established lodges wherever needed. Most of the Masonic symbols derive from stonemasons' tools.

These emblems are worn individually, like medals, on ribbons around the neck by officials of the lodge during meetings or ceremonies. The compass is the emblem of the Grand Master, the set square that of the Master of a lodge, the level is the emblem of a Senior, the plumb - line that of a Junior Warden. The five - pointed star refers to the seal of the biblical King Solomon, the construction of whose famous temple in Jerusalem provides the basis for much Masonic ritual.

The initials E and M probably refer to the owner of this set or possibly to the tavern in which a certain lodge met. Lodges themselves did not have names in the 1750s; instead, groups of Freemasons adopted the names of the taverns where they held their meetings. Liverpool creamware, Staffordshire pottery and English glass are also known with initials incorporated into Masonic designs.

The bowl appears to be the earliest dated Chinese piece with Masonic designs and the two pieces are unusual because of the simplicity of their designs. Masonic porcelain was commissioned in China from the mid-18th to the 19th century. Punchbowls and tankards seem to have been the most popular items（for a list of other important Masonic pieces, see Howard and Ayers, 1978, vol. 1, p. 328）. One of the most impressive Masonic pieces is an unusually large bowl known as the 'True Friendship Punch Bowl' in The Freemasons Hall Museum, London, which is inscribed 'this bowl made by Syng Chong, China Merchant of Canton' and was presented to the Lodge of True Friendship in 1813 by Brother Hugh Adams; it measures 56 cm in diameter and holds eight gallons（36.4 litres）of punch.

清　共濟會徽章紋酒缽和啤酒杯

Polychrome painted punchbowl and tankard with Masonic emblems

43. 清　粉彩英國愛國社徽章箴言紋茶杯

高 4 公分

法蘭克收藏

描繪英國的聖喬治；英國守護聖者，身著十八世紀服裝，騎著白馬，其長矛刺著繪有法國皇室徽章紋，一箴言寫著「為我們的國家」字樣。此標幟為反對法國之英國團體所使用。此組織之形成，是為了促銷英國商品、抑止法國服裝和產品之傾銷。這個愛國組織在1750年代盛行於英國。

---

43 *Famille rose* teacup with the motto and emblem of an English patriotic society

Qing dynasty, c. 1750 - 70

Height 4 cm

Franks collection, F.1415

The patron saint of England, St. George, is depicted on this cup wearing 18th - century costume, riding a white horse, and thrusting his lance into a shield of French *fleurs - de - lis*. Above this scene is a crest with Britannia seated, leaning against a shield with the British colours, holding an olive branch and a spear, surrounded by six flags. The supporters are a lion with a human face on the left and a double - headed eagle on the right. Below is the motto 'FOR OUR COUNTRY'. The other side of the cup is decorated with a spray of flowers and the inner rim with a spearhead border.

This pseudo - armorial design belongs to the Anti - Gallican Society, a masonic - style patriotic organization founded in London in 1745, with headquarters at Lebeck's Head, The Strand, London, and branches in the country. The Society was founded to oppose the French nation who threatened war. According to a contemporary storybook 'The society of Anti-Gallicans was so - called from the Endeavours of its Members to promote the British Manufactures, to extend the Commerce of England and discourage the introducing of French Modes, and oppose the importation of French Commodities' (*The Anti - Gallican Privateer*, 1757, p. 4). In this context St. George represents the triumph of England over France.

This pseudo - armorial design was used in a variety of ways. It appears, for example, on periodicals and songs which the Society published, and is similarly found without the supporters around the title of a map called 'A Chart of the Harbour of Corunna' of 1758 which is preserved in the British Library (no. 1103.f.16). Other Chinese porcelains with the same device include a punchbowl in the Freemasons Hall Museum, London (Hervouet and Bruneau, 1986, no. 14.19) and a teapoy in a private collection (Howard, 1974, p. 487). Besides the present cup and the following plate (cat.no. 44), at least three other different Anti-Gallican designs exist, with different borders (Howard, 1974, pp. 370, 390, 945).

清　粉彩英國愛國社徽章箴言紋茶杯
Famille rose teacup with the motto and emblem of an
English patriotic society

44. 清　粉彩英國愛國社徽章箴言紋盤

直徑21.8公分

法蘭克收藏

此件盤與圖版43之杯，皆由英國愛國組織所製。聖約翰著古羅馬服式（西元三、四世紀之式樣），並有一箴言道：「聖約翰和古英國」字樣。圖中緊握在一起的二隻手，象徵1756年爆發的七年戰爭中，英國和普魯士的結盟。

44 *Famille rose* plate with the motto and emblem of an English patriotic society

Qing dynasty, c. 1755 - 75

Diameter 21.8 cm

Franks collection, F.1414

This octagonal plate was made for the same society as the cup above (cat.no. 43), but belonged to a different service. It is similarly painted with a pseudo-armorial panel among plumes and floral sprays depicting the patron saint of England, St. George, but here in Roman costume dating to his lifetime (c. 3rd to 4th century AD). He is riding a white charger, brandishing a sword and holding a circular shield, while his lance is in mid-air. The horse is trampling underfoot a shield with French *fleurs-de-lis*. Above this panel is a crest representing Britannia, leaning against a shield with British colours, holding an olive branch and a spear, with a ribbon bearing the motto 'ST GEONGE (sic.) AND OLD ENGLAND' below. Beneath the medallion are two clasped hands.

This pseudo-armorial emblem, like that of the previous cup (cat.no. 43), belongs to the patriotic Anti-Gallican Society who endeavoured to promote English business and discourage trade with France. This plate is probably slightly later in date than the cup and may have been commisioned after 1756, when the start of the Seven Years' War caused nationalism and support for the Society to increase again. The two clasped hands may represent the alliance of England and Prussia during the Seven Years' War (Howard and Ayers, 1978, vol. I, p. 243).

Other pieces from the same service include a plate in the Mottahedeh collection (Howard and Ayers, 1978, vol. I, pl. 239); another plate in the China Trade Museum, Milton, Massachusetts, U.S.A. (Milton, 1982, no. 85); and a platter in the Hervouet collection (Sotheby's Monaco, 22nd June 1987, lot 1687); for other services ordered by the Society, see cat. no. 43.

清　粉彩英國愛國社徽章箴言紋盤
Famille rose plate with the motto and emblem of an English
patriotic society

45. 清　粉彩諷刺蘇格蘭紋大碗

直徑28.5公分

法蘭克收藏

碗的兩面是仿自羅伯‧狄頓在1783年　月11日於倫敦出版（參
考圖版4 a）的版畫，是一通俗的諷刺畫；內容為一位名叫索
尼的蘇格蘭紳士坐在廁所裡，並有一首諷刺蘇格蘭人的詩文。

fig. 45a

45 *Famille rose* punchbowl with a design satirising the Scots

Qing dynasty, c. 1783 - 5

Diameter 28.5 cm

Franks collection, F.744 +

This punchbowl is painted on one side with a grimacing Scotsman, dressed in a brightly coloured tartan jacket, kilt and tam o'shanter, seated in a latrine with his legs thrust down two holes in the board and his sword beside him. To the right, a thistle is painted on the wall, growing out of an upside - down crown with the Latin motto of Scotland above 'NEMO ME IMPUNE LACESSIT' (nobody wounds me with impunity); to the left are two pasted-up pictures, one showing a woman, the other a giant with beard and crook towering over a kneeling man, with the caption 'O Sawney why leavs thou thy Nelly to moan'(sic). The inner rim is painted in gold with an unusual border of ears of corn.

The reverse of the bowl is inscribed with details of the engraving on which this design is based, giving the name of the artist 'R. Dighton delin.', and the name and address of the publisher and date of publication, 'Published Jn. Smith No. 35 Cheapside Robt. Sayer Jn. Bennett No. 53 Fleet Street, as the Act directs 11 September 1783' and a rhyme entitled 'SAUNEYS MISTAKE':

> When first to the South sly Sauney came forth
> He was shewn to a place quite unknown in the North;
> That he is mistaken you soon will explore

Yet he scratches and S--s. as no man did before.

Reproduced on the front and reverse of this punchbowl are the upper and lower sections of a vulgar satirical English print. Such prints were made from engraved metal plates and mass - produced for sale to the public, either direct from the publishers or through shops. The publishers of this print, Robert Sayer and John Bennett, were foremost among the London publishers of popular prints at the time and according to their catalogue of 1775 charged 3d. (old pennies) for black - and - white prints, 6d. for 'neatly coloured' ones (*Sayer and Bennett's Catalogue of Prints for the Year 1775*, reprinted 1970). The present bowl is most unusual for reproducing the name of the artist, Robert Dighton (1752 - 1814), and precise publication details.

The print itself appears to be lost, so that this picture survives only on Chinese porcelain. Similar prints with the archetypal Scotsman, Sawney, were used to satirise the Highlanders from the mid -18th century and an amusing print 'Sawney in the Bog House' also in the British Museum and attributed to James Gillray, was published four years earlier, in 1779 (fig. 45 a; P+D 1868.8 - 8.4951). To send a print to China, commission a piece of porcelain, have it painted and shipped back to Europe, could take two years or more.

This design is only known from punchbowls, and identical examples exist in the Espirito Santo collection, Lisbon, Portugal (Beurdeley, 1962, no. 70), and in the Royal Museum of Scotland, Edinburgh (Hervouet and Bruneau, 1986, no. 9.45). It also exists with a different rim border (Bonhams London, 8th December 1993, lot 72).

清 粉彩諷刺蘇格蘭紋大碗

Famille rose punchbowl with a design satirising the Scots

46. 清　彩瓷英式狩獵圖碗

高15公分　直徑34.3公分

法蘭克收藏

此碗描繪歐洲紳士騎著駿馬，帶著一群獵犬，追捕狐狸、野兔。Punch大碗是英國人調製雞尾酒時所用，狩獵在當時成爲英國最流行的運動項目，而此種飲料專供狩獵者飲用。此圖案源自英國發行的兩種不同系列運動版畫。

46　*Famille rose* punchbowl with English hunting scenes

Qing dynasty, c. 1750 - 70

Height 15 cm, diameter 34.3 cm

Franks collection, F.625 A

Two naturalistic landscape scenes with hunting parties are painted on the outside of this punchbowl in *famille rose* enamels. On one side are four mounted huntsmen, two wearing round hunting horns, riding among a pack of hounds; on the other side hunters are searching for the chase among shrubs and hedgerows. In between these scenes are floral cartouches above small iron - red landscape panels, and on the inside of the bowl are a central spray of peonies and other flowers.

These designs appear to be taken from 18th-century engravings. The first scene was probably painted after 'Brushing into Cover' by Pierre Charles Canot (1710 - 77), a French artist working in England, the second after 'Beating and Trailing for a Hare' by the English artist Thomas Burford (c. 1710 - 74) (Howard and Ayers, 1978, vol. I, pl. 280 b; Hervouet and Bruneau, 1986, nos. 3.25 a,b).

Punchbowls with hunting scenes were used before and after a day's hunt. Punch, an alcoholic cocktail, made to a variety of recepies and strengths, is still served in England today where hunting continues to be a popular field sport. On porcelain, hunting scenes are most commonly found on punchbowls. A very similar piece is in the Museum of Fine Arts, Boston, U.S.A. (Hervouet and Bruneau, 1986, nos. 3.25 a, b); another with related hunting designs is in the Mottahedeh collection (Howard and Ayers, 1978, vol. I, pl. 280). Similar hunting scenes combined with an English coat of arms are also known from a dinner service (Howard and Ayers, 1978, vol. I, pl. 279).

清　彩瓷英式狩獵圖碗

Famille rose punchbowl with English hunting scenes

47. 清　粉彩英式收割圖酒缽二件

高5.5公分　17公分　直徑36公分、39.5公分

法蘭克收藏

描繪盛裝的主人，在督導工人收割玉米綑綁成束及堆積起來的情形，每個碗都寫有農莊名稱及日期：大件寫有「Warren農舍」和「1769」字樣，小碗寫著「Felden農莊」和「1779」字樣。大英博物館所藏同紋飾之第三件瓷碗，上面描寫「Thornby」和「1779」字樣。但這些碗上所繪農莊尚未考證出來。

47　Two *famille rose* punchbowls with English harvest scenes

Qing dynasty, dated 1769 and 1779, respectively

Heights 17 cm, 15.5 cm, diameters 39.5 cm, 36 cm

Franks collection, F.625 B, F.1403

These punchbowls are decorated inside and out with scenes of harvesting and are distinguished mainly by their inscriptions. The larger bowl is inscribed 'Warren Lodge' and bears the initials 'W E S' and the date '1769', the smaller one 'Felden Farm' and 'Harvest Home', with the initials 'J C' and the date 1779.

The bowls each show on one side labourers scything and bundling corn, and on the other collecting and carrying the corn sheaves, observed by a group of peasant women, one of whom is suckling a child. These two scenes are enclosed in shaped panels and alternate with the inscriptions and harvest supper scenes in smaller panels. The insides depict farm labourers piling up a strawstack, watched by a woman who leans against a wicker basket and supervised by a well - dressed gentleman in a tricorne hat. The inner rim has an elaborate shaped diaper border with butterflies and fruit - and - flower garlands.

The source of these designs is probably an 18th - century English print and these punchbowls appear to have been made for use in specific English country estates. Only punchbowls and large jugs are known with such harvest scenes. A large jug in a private collection is identical both in its

inscription and decoration to the bowl of 1779 (Hervouet and Bruneau, 1986, no. 4.17 a,b,c); other punchbowls with this decoration include an example in the British Museum inscribed 'Thornby' and 'Harvest Home' with the initials 'J C ' and the date '1779' (1963.4 - 22.14); others without inscriptions are in the Mottahedeh collection (Howard and Ayers, 1978, vol. I, pl. 283), and in the Metropolitan Museum of Art, New York (Phillips, 1956, pl. 13).

清　粉彩英式收割圖酒缽二件

Two *famille rose* punchbowls with English harvest scenes

宗教題材
Religious Subjects
（cat.nos. 48 - 53）

48. 清　德化窯白瓷聖母與聖嬰像

高26.5公分

Donnelly 遺贈

此尊聖母懷抱嬰孩耶穌像，十分類似德化窯之「觀音抱子像」。此尊歐式人物的捲髮及母親的頭飾都顯示了天主教特徵而非中國式塑像。這類作品在1699年代受到大批訂購，由西洋商船外銷至歐洲，並列於十八世紀早期皇室收藏名單中。

48 Dehua figure of the Madonna and Child

Qing dynasty, c. 1690 - 1750

Height 26.5 cm

P.J. Donnelly Bequest, 1980.7 - 28.73

The female figure is standing on the head of an animal and is holding a small boy in her arms. She is modelled after figures of the Chinese Goddess of Mercy, Guanyin, who is typically depicted on a tiger holding a child. Both mother and child, however, have European features and curly hair, the woman also wears a non - Chinese headdress and the child holds a rosary, so that this sculpture is identified as the Christian Holy Mother, the Virgin Mary carrying the infant Christ, rather than a Buddhist mother goddess.

Figures called 'Sancta Marias' (blessed Marys) are recorded, for example, in the sale list for the cargo of the *Nassau*, an English ship which returned to England from Amoy (Xiamen) in 1699 (Godden, 1979, pp. 259 - 60), but Christian Dehua figures are very rare. Dehua sculptures were shipped to Europe in great quantities but the most popular product of the Dehua kilns and possibly its best selling export commodity were figures of Guanyin. Another Dehua Madonna carrying a baby in swaddling clothes is in the Musée Guimet, Paris (mentioned by Donnelly, 1969, p. 195); a third, differently modelled, is in the Victoria and Albert Museum, London (Godden, 1979, no. 186). From dated inventories we know that figures of a woman and child, probably representing Guanyin, were also in the Dresden porcelain collection of Augustus the Strong, King of Poland and Elector of Saxony (1670 - 1733) (see cat.no. 152) and in the smaller collection of William III, King of England (r. 1689 - 1702) and Queen Mary II (r. 1689 - 1694) at Kensington House, London.

清　德化窰白瓷聖母與聖嬰像
Dehua figure of the Madonna and Child

49. 清　粉彩耶穌釘十字架圖杯和托盤

（杯）高4.5公分　（托盤）直徑12.5公分

法蘭克收藏

杯和托盤的圖案顯示聖光圍繞耶穌的頭上，和十字架上的二個小偷。前方圍觀的哀傷群眾，包括了聖母瑪麗亞及聖約翰；另一方面，羅馬士兵們的反應是擲骰子作樂。

49　*Famille rose* cup and saucer depicting the Crucifixion

Qing dynasty, c. 1740 - 60

Height （cup） 4.5 cm, diameter （saucer） 12.5 cm

Franks collection, F.923 ＋ A

Both cup and saucer are painted in enamels of the *famille rose* with the same scenes, showing Jesus on the cross between the two thieves which were crucified with him, Jesus being identified by rays of light around his head and the initials INRI on the cross, the abbreviation of the Latin 'Jesus Nazarenus Rex Iudaeorum' （Jesus of Nazareth, King of the Jews）. Behind the three crosses is a group of mourners led by the Virgin Mary and St. John. In the foreground of the saucer and on the reverse of the cup is another scene showing centurions （commanders of the ancient Roman army） enjoying themselves casting dice, a symbolic reference to the low morality of the representatives of the state responsible for Christ's crucifixion.

The same scene is frequently depicted on Chinese porcelain painted *en grisaille*, for example on a dish also in the British Museum （*Sekai Tōji Zenshu*, 1983, pl. 342） which forms part of a series of scenes from the life of Christ, from the birth to the ascension, which may all have been copied from the same illustrated Bible; representations in *famille rose* are comparatively rare.

清　粉彩耶穌釘十字架圖杯和托盤
Famille rose cup and saucer depicting the Crucifixion

50. 清　黑釉金彩德國宗教改革領袖肖像紋盤

直徑23公分

法蘭克收藏

描繪標有「Dr.M.L.」字樣及馬丁・路德（1483－1546）之肖
像，其下是耶穌向十二個門徒講道。路德是北歐基督教的新教
改革領袖，並且對聖經的重新翻譯貢獻卓著。紋飾採自荷蘭藝
術家 Frans Brun（1627－1648）之設計，並曾出現在1648年
阿姆斯特丹出版的路德翻譯新聖經版本之扉頁上（參考圖版50a）。

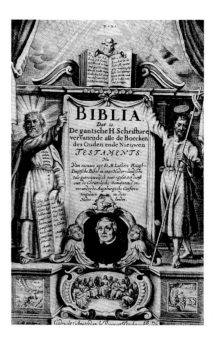

fig. 50a

50 *Grisaille* - and - gold painted plate with the portrait of a
German religious reformer

Qing dynasty, c. 1740 - 60

Diameter 23 cm

Franks collection, F.592

The plate is painted in *grisaille* and gold with a portrait bust of Dr.
Martin Luther (1483 - 1546), identified by the initials 'Dr.M.L.' below
his image, flanked by two cherubs with feathered bodies, and with a
swan above. In a separate cartouche below is Christ preaching to the
Twelve Apostles. The plate has an elaborate rim border with six
alternating scenes of boar and deer hunts.

Dr. Martin Luther was the leader of the Protestant Reformation of the
Christian Church in northern Europe and made an important and
influential new translation of the Bible. The design on the present plate
was taken from the lower half of an engraving by the Dutch artist
Frans Brun (active 1627 - 48), which was used on the title page of a
Dutch Lutheran Bible revised by Adolph Visscher and known as
Visscher's Bible, published in Amsterdam, 1648 (see fig. 50a, from an
edition in the British Library, 3035.d.4; courtesy of the British Library).
Comparison of the Chinese plate and the print, which was made from
an engraved copper plate, shows that even minute details of the
engraving were copied onto the porcelain. This Bible and its title page

were reprinted many times and the Chinese porcelain painters may in
fact have been copying a later edition than the one illustrated.

Only plates with this design are known (some with different borders)
and it has been suggested that they were made as Protestant
commemorative pieces, possibly commissioned for the bicentenary of
Martin Luther's death in 1746 (Howard and Ayers, 1978, vol. I, p. 254),
rather than being part of a dinner service. A plate with a different
border is in the Mottahadeh collection (*ibid.*, pl.248); another with a
later simplified version of this design and dated 1756 on the reverse is
in a private Brazilian collection (Veiga, 1989, pl. 111).

清　黑釉金彩德國宗教改革領袖肖像紋盤
Grisaille - and - gold painted plate with the portrait of a
German religious reformer

fig. 51a

51. 清　黑釉金彩荷蘭宗教領袖像盤

直徑35.8公分

法蘭克收藏

盤中央描繪的是里敦的喬漢・巴侯德（1510－1536），其名以
拉丁文刻於下段，他屬於激進派新教政治組織，並建立了獨立
的神權政體。此處他身著皇家王位的標幟，象徵爲領袖，其背
景是他及其信徒飽受折磨而死的情景。此圖案源自荷蘭藝術家
羅蜜恩・的・胡吉之版畫，於1701年在阿姆斯特丹出版的一本
有關教會及異教徒之書（參考圖版51a）。

51　*Grisaille* - and - gold painted plate depicting the Dutch leader of a religious group

Qing dynasty, c. 1730 - 40

Diameter 35.8 cm

Franks collection, F.918 +

The central figure is Johann Bockholdt of Leyden (1510 - 36), also
known as Jan van Leiden, whose name is inscribed in Latin,
'IOHANNES BUCHOLDI A LEYDA'. He is standing between an
attendant carrying a Bible like a tray for his crown and a groom who
is leading his horse. With his right hand he leans on the hilt of his
sword and his left touches the Bible. Behind him on the right is a cage
with a naked figure inside, suspended from a church tower. In the
background other figures are depicted being tortured. The plate has a
rococo scrollwork rim border with floral sprigs.

Johann Bockholdt, a tailor from Leyden, belonged to a group of
protestant reformers known as the Anabaptists, who preached the
rebaptism of adults who had been baptised as children. In 1534 a
militant group of Anabaptists took over the town of Münster in
northwest Germany where they attempted to create an independent
theocracy by assuming absolute power and deposing the local city
council. Bockholdt was crowned King of the Anabaptists and appeared
in royal regalia before his subjects in the marketplace of Münster. He
justified his actions such as the legalization of polygamy and the
burning of all books except for the Bible, with visions from heaven
which confirmed his authority.

Bockholdt ruled Münster for over a year, but in June 1535 the town
was successfully taken back by the authorities. Seven months later
Bockholdt and other prominent Anabaptists were publicly interrogated,
tortured and executed. As an example to potential sympathisers, the
victims were displayed in town, stretched on racks, and suspended in
iron cages from the church tower of St. Lambert's.

The design on this plate derives from a copper - plate etching by the
Dutch artist Romeyen de Hooghe (1645 - 1708), after a painting by
van Sichem. A trimmed version of this print is published in *Historie
der Kerken en Ketteren van het Jaar Onzes Heeren 1500 tot 1600* (A
History of Churches and Heretics from 1500 to 1600 A.D.) by
Godfried Arnold, Amsterdam, 1701, vol. 2, p.25 (fig. 51 a; courtesy of
the British Library, 208.g.16).

As with the previous piece (cat.no. 50), only plates are known with
this design, which may also be Protestant commemorative pieces,
possibly for the bicentenary of Bockholdt's death in 1736. Other
identical plates are in the Rijksmuseum, Amsterdam, Netherlands
(Münster, 1982, no. 189); and in the Musée Adrien Dubouché,
Limoges, France (Hervouet and Bruneau, 1986, no. 11.51). Modern
imitations of this design are also known (*ibid.*, no. 17.22).

清　黑釉金彩荷蘭宗教領袖像盤

Grisaille - and - gold painted plate depicting the Dutch leader
of a religious group

52. 清　粉彩聖經故事盤

直徑22.9公分

巴西爾·伊耳尼底斯夫人遺贈

描述舊約聖經故事中，大衛王的士兵烏利亞之妻——美麗的巴示巴，當她由婢女服侍在水池沐浴時，被以色列統治者大衛王看到。背景有一座花園，此紋飾探自1669年巴黎出版的舊約聖經故事插圖。

52 *Famille rose* plate with a scene from the Bible

Qing dynasty, c. 1730 - 40

Diameter 22.9 cm

Hon. Mrs. Basil Ionides Bequest, 1963.4 - 22.21

The plate shows a woman, naked to the waist with loose drapery around her hips and legs, seated on the edge of a pool, attended by five servants, and a man standing on a balcony above, blowing a horn. Two square shapes are visible in the distance. The rim of the plate is painted with a dense floral border.

The interpretation of this extraordinary and rare design has become possible by the discovery of an illustration in an Old Testament, published by P. Le Petit in Paris in 1669 (Hervouet and Bruneau, 1986, p. 262). This print, made from an engraved copper plate, illustrates the story of David, King of Israel, and the beautiful Bathsheba, wife of Uriah the Hittite, one of David's soldiers, which is told in the second book of Samuel, chapter 11, verses 2 - 27. Whilst walking on the roof of his palace, David saw a beautiful woman washing herself in a pool below. Having ascertained that her husband was away in the army, he seduced her, and when she became pregnant, he ensured that her husband died in battle and married her himself.

The design on the print is much more detailed than that on the Chinese plate, which was painted after a reversed copy. On the plate Bathsheba is prominently depicted, bathing in a square pool attended by servants, but the crowned King David on the roof, carrying one of his attributes, a harp, has been turned into a man blowing a horn. The squares in the background are a simplified interpretation of a formal garden in the engraving. Plates with this design are comparatively rare but an identical plate is in a private collection (Hervouet and Bruneau, 1986, no. 11.11).

清　粉彩聖經故事盤
Famille rose plate with a scene from the Bible

53. 清　赭墨金彩蘇格蘭徽章紋聖經故事紋盤

直徑41.5公分

法蘭克收藏

描繪舊約故事，德高望重的猶太人摩底該，成了宮廷陰謀的犧牲者，由於其養女的介入而獲救。此處，描繪他得意洋洋地凱旋狀。盤底以琺瑯彩繪有法國家族「索尼底克斯」以及「伯威克希」家族的徽章紋。

53 *Grisaille* - and - gold painted plate with a biblical story and a Scottish coat of arms

Qing dynasty, c. 1736 - 45

Diameter 41.5 cm

Franks collection. F.893 ＋

The large plate has a broad flat rim and is painted overall *en grisaille* with details in gilding with a biblical scene, closely copied from an engraving. It shows a man with long beard in lavish robes riding a richly appointed horse, being led through a city by a man in a turban who clears the way, and proceeded by trumpeters; around him people are shown suffering.

The story depicted is the Triumph of Mordecai, which is told in the Bible, in the book of Esther in the Old Testament. It is the story of a virtuous Jew who was about to be destroyed together with his people, the Jews, by a selfish prince in the royal household, but was saved through intervention of his niece and adopted daughter Esther, who was Queen. Here he is shown being led in triumph through the city after the looming evil has been averted, which is probably referred to by the suffering figures on the ground. The design is believed to be based on a painting by the French artist Eustache Le Sueur (1617 - 55; Howard, 1974, p. 335).

This dish is unique in its subject, and together with the following (cat.no. 54), is one of the very rare pieces painted in the style of Western faience with an overall picture. Both dishes are copying an engraving unusually precisely, as if every line of the engraver's hatching had been reproduced. Both this dish and the following are further remarkable and highly unusual in bearing a coat of arms on the reverse. The arms, painted in blue, gold, red and black, have been identified as belonging to the family French of Thornidykes and Frenchlands in Berwickshire (*ibid.*). Two other plates decorated with a copy of an engraving of flowers bear the same arms (*ibid.*, p. 334). These plates do not seem to form part of a service, but were probably made for display. This design is also known in a modern copy (Hervouet and Bruneau, 1986, no. 17.26).

清　赭墨金彩蘇格蘭徽章紋聖經故事紋盤
Grisaille - and - gold painted plate with a biblical story and
a Scottish coat of arms

古代希臘、羅馬神話系列
Greek and Roman Mythology

（cat.nos. 54 - 62）

54. 清　黑釉金彩希臘神話和蘇格蘭徽章紋盤

直徑42公分

法蘭克收藏

此盤之反面有和圖53極相似的徽章紋，並且裝飾風格十分類似，可是圖案描繪卻完全不相干；盤中描繪其母爲維納斯女神，其父爲凡人，後來成爲希臘特洛伊戰爭英雄的阿奇里斯少年，被其母浸泡於陰間之河，使其身體刀槍不入（註：見荷馬史詩伊里亞德 Iliad）。

54　*Grisaille* - and - gold painted plate with a scene from Greek mythology and a Scottish coat of arms

Qing dynasty, c. 1736 - 45

Diameter 42 cm

Franks collection, F.892 +

This large plate is a companion piece to the last (cat.no. 53) and is similarly painted with a faithful copy of an engraving, but the stories depicted are unconnected. The present plate shows a lady immersing a child in a river, with two others attending behind. To the left is a half undressed lady resting on an overturned water jar, and a winged female figure holding a laurel wreath and palm frond, both in front of a table with a wine jug, fruit bowl and other vessels; to the right is a man with ugly features, carrying a burning brazier, and a centaur (half man, half horse) appears in a phantastic landscape in the background.

The central scene depicts the infant Achilles, the later Greek hero of the Trojan War, being dipped into the Styx, the river of the underworld, by his mother Thetis, who thus made his body invulnerable except for the heel by which she held him. The lady resting on the water jar may also be a reference to Thetis, the sea goddess. Behind her is a winged Nike, who symbolizes victory. The man to the right is Hephaestus, the Greek god of fire and heavenly smith, who forged an armour for Achilles when he re-entered battle at Troy. The centaur represents Cheiron, protector of

immortal Thetis and her mortal husband, and tutor of Achilles.

The design of this plate has been attributed to the French painter Eustache Le Sueur (1617 - 55; Howard, 1974, p. 335). Paintings by Le Sueur, similar in composition and style, are reproduced in early 19th - century engravings in Landon, 1803 - 17, but the present scene is not included.

The reverse of this plate is painted with the same coat of arms as the previous piece (cat.no. 53), which has been identified as belonging to the family French of Thornidykes and Frenchlands of Berwickshire (*ibid.*). This design appears very similarly again painted in sepia on a smaller plate (Hervouet and Bruneau, 1986, no. 13.37), and on another in the Victoria and Albert Museum, London (no. C.76 - 1963), both of them lacking the coat of arms.

清　黑釉金彩希臘神話和蘇格蘭徽章紋盤

Grisaille - and - gold painted plate with a scene from Greek
mythology and a Scottish coat of arms

55. 清　彩瓷希臘神話人物盤

直徑23公分

巴西爾‧伊耳尼底斯夫人遺贈

坐臥在風景中的情侶，乃是希臘太陽神阿波羅——理想中代表
男性美之化身，以及他的情人。

55 *Famille rose* **plate with figures from Greek mythology**

Qing dynasty, c. 1730 - 40

Diameter 23 cm

Hon. Mrs. Basil Ionides Bequest, 1963.4 - 22.22

The plate is painted in enamels of the *famille rose* and shows a couple
seated under a tree, the lady dressed in a blue-and-auberging robe
and wearing a jewel - like ornament in her hair, the man naked except
for draped pink and yellow scarves, and holding a lyre. Around the
rim are sprays of chrysanthemum and rose.

The scene shows Apollo, son of the highest Greek god, Zeus, who is
clearly identified by the lyre with which he won several musical
contests among the immortals. Apollo was notorious for his amorous
pursuits, but the lady depicted on this plate is not clearly identified. It
has been suggested that she represents Daphne (Brighton, 1986, no.
122), but the intimate pose of the couple would seem to speak against
this identification since Daphne was one of Apollo's great loves which,
however, he failed to conquer.

A plate with this design as well as another with matching decoration of
a different immortal couple, are in the Zeeuws Museum, Middelburg,
Netherlands (Lunsingh Scheurleer, 1966, pl. 224). They were both
probably copied from the same series of prints.

清　彩瓷希臘神話人物盤
Famille rose plate with figures from Greek mythology

56. 清　粉彩羅馬神話人物盤

直徑22.5公分

法蘭克收藏

此盤以象徵性手法描繪火的元素，盤中央描述羅馬神話中地位
最高的主神 Jupiter 在訪問火神 Vulcanus，有許多小天使忙
著爲他的煉爐工作，其上是愛神維納斯，象徵愛之火，乘坐馬
車駕雲而至。這件作品和圖版57原屬於四件一組，四行：地、
水、火、風中的一部分，紋飾仿自法蘭西斯哥‧阿爾巴尼
（1578－1661）所繪圖案（參看圖版56a）。

fig. 56a

56 *Famille rose* plate with figures from Roman mythology

Qing dynasty, c. 1736 - 45

Diameter 22.5 cm

Franks collection, F.1404

This plate shows two bearded gods, one among rose - pink drapery,
holding a thunderbolt and accompanied by a black eagle, the other on
a draped blue cloth holding a shield, surrounded by putti; those in the
foreground are shown shooting bows and blowing a pipe, while others
in the background are working a forge. Overhead a goddess is arriving
in a chariot on a cloud, holding two torches.

The scene is a mythological representation of the element Fire and
shows Jupiter, the highest Roman god, ruler over heaven and thus
commanding thunder and lightning, visiting Vulcanus, the god of fire
and heavenly smith, at his forge. The goddess in this case is Venus, the
goddess of love, who is here symbolizing the fire of love; the putti
represent Amor, the personification of love.

Together with the following plate (cat.no. 57), this piece belongs to a
(now uncomplete) set of four, depicting the elements. The designs have
been copied from the first two paintings of a set of four, executed in
1635 by Francesco Albani (1578 - 1661) for the Cardinal of Savoy and
later King of Sardinia. The scenes are explained in Albani's
correspondence with his client (Hervouet and Bruneau, 1986, p. 318).

The paintings are reproduced in form of engravings in an early 19th -
century book on famous painters (fig. 56 a, after Landon, 1803 - 17;
courtesy of the British Library, 132.e.6 - 30).

Other plates of this design are in the Musée Guimet, Paris, France
(Beurdeley, 1962, no. 129); and in the Martin Hurst collection
(Hervouet and Bruneau, 1986, no. 13.92). A complete set of plates
depicting all four elements is in the Henry Francis du Pont Winterthur
Museum, U.S.A. (Palmer, 1976, pl. 7). These designs, being taken
from circular paintings, would seem to have been particularly
appropriate for reproduction on plates; but the present design appears
also on other items of a tea service, namely a teapoy, tea cup and
saucer in the Musées Royaux d'Art et d'Histoire, Brussels, Belgium
(Taipei, 1992, p. 40).

134

清　粉彩羅馬神話人物盤
Famille rose plate with figures from Roman mythology

清　粉彩羅馬神話人物盤

直徑22.9公分

法蘭克收藏

與圖版56一樣，以象徵性手法描繪四行之一「風」，紋飾探自
法蘭西斯哥之設計（參考圖版57 a）。以一群小天使來表現風
神Aeolus，其中一個天使仍在盆子內，另一個卻衝入雲端。坐
在孔雀接著的馬車上的是Juno女神，也就是主神 Jupiter 之妻。

fig. 57a

57 *Famille rose* plate with figures from Roman mythology

Qing dynasty, c. 1736 - 45

Diameter 22.9 cm

Franks collection, F.1405

This plate is a companion piece to the last (cat.no. 56) and was copied
from the same series of paintings by Francesco Albani depicting the
elements (see fig. 57 a, after Landon, 1803 - 17; courtesy of the British
Library, 132.e.6 - 30). It shows a bearded god seated in a landscape,
naked except for some rose - pink drapery, holding a casket which
contains a winged putto, while another putto is rushing off on a cloud,
playing a drum. Overhead a goddess is approaching in a peacock -
drawn chariot, surrounded by several winged beings, under a rainbow.

This scene is a symbolic representation of the element Air and depicts
Aeolus, the Roman god of winds, which are symbolized by putti, one
of which has been let loose while another is still kept at bay. In the
chariot above is Juno, the wife of the highest Roman god, Jupiter. Like
the previous design, this scene has been discussed by Albani in
correspondence with his client, where he explains that the element Air
has traditionally been symbolized by Juno.

清 粉彩羅馬神話人物盤
Famille rose plate with figures from Roman mythology

58. 清　黑釉金彩希臘神話紋盤

直徑23公分

法蘭克收藏

此盤描繪赫克力士，希臘神話中之英雄；天神宙斯之子，註定
要完成十二項艱鉅的任務，來展現其超能力及勇氣。這些任務
象徵邪不勝正。此處，他正屠殺獅型怪獸「尼猛」，是一隻非
常凶猛危險的野獸，無法以普通的武器殺害。

58 *Grisaille* - and - gold painted plate with a scene from Greek mythology

Qing dynasty, c. 1740 - 50

Diameter 23 cm

Franks collection, F.916 +

The plate shows a man naked except for a draped cloth, with a club raised in one hand and a chain which encircles a lion's neck in the other, with flags and other martial trophies at their feet. This design is separated from an elaborate shaped diaper border with peacocks by a fine golden flower-scroll in the well.

The scene depicts Heracles, a semi-god and hero of Greek mythology, and a popular subject of classical and later art. As a penance for slaying his own children whilst under a spell of madness and in order to gain immortality he was condemned to perform twelve super-human tasks, which symbolize the triumph of good over evil. The present plate depicts the first of these tasks, the slaying of a dangerous lion which had terrorized the inhabitants of Nemea and could not be killed with weapons of metal or stone. He achieved the task by choking the beast to death.

The engraving copied on this plate is as yet unidentified. The lacy golden flower-scroll band is reminiscent of gilding on German porcelain from Meissen, of the early 18th century. An identical plate is in a private collection (Hervouet and Bruneau, 1986, no. 13.29).

清　黑釉金彩希臘神話紋盤

Grisaille - and - gold painted plate with a scene from Greek mythology

59. 清　黑釉羅馬神話及英國徽章紋鹽盤

高4公分　寬7.7公分

法蘭克收藏

器型淵源於英國銀器（參考圖版59a）。蛋形瓶上端描繪著羅馬黎明女神奧秀拉，每日清晨駕著馬車穿越天際，並且迎接她的兄長太陽神——希羅斯。前面則描繪屬於馬修‧漢布森的英國徽章紋。

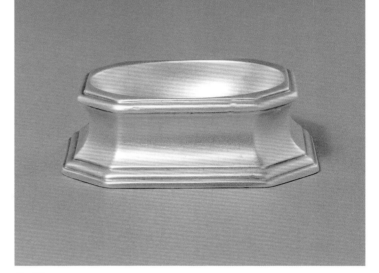

fig. 59a

59 *Grisaille* - painted salt cellar with a scene from Greek mythology and an English coat of arms

Qing dynasty, c. 1740 - 50

Height 4 cm, width 7.7 cm

Franks collection, F.1438

This small oblong octagonal vessel has a high splayed foot, flat protruding rim and a shallow oval depression on top for the salt. This is painted *en grisaille* with a goddess holding a burning torch and accompanied by a cockerel, driving a chariot through the sky pulled by winged horses. The sun is appearing behind her. The foot of the vessel bears a coat of arms, the back and sides flower sprays.

The goddess represents Eos, the Greek goddess of dawn, who causes the day to break by leading her brother Helios, the sun god, into the sky. The engraving on which this design is based is not yet identified. The coat of arms belongs to the Humbertson family and it has been suggested that the service was commissioned by Matthew Humbertson of Humbertson, Lincolnshire (Howard, 1974, p. 334) for whose son-in-law a very similar service was made, which included the salt cellar below (cat.no. 60).

In Europe salts were made in a great variety of shapes, styles and sizes, ranging from lavishly ornamented tall standing salts which were used at ceremonial banquets, to simple squat salt cellars for every - day use.

The form of the present salt which derives from English silverware is known as a 'trencher - salt' and was the most common shape between 1710 and 1740; a related silver example made by the London silversmith Paul de Lamerie in 1712, is in the Ashmolean Museum, Oxford, Great Britain (fig. 59 a; courtesy of the Ashmolean Museum). Such silver salts are also known with a coat of arms, crest or cypher engraved on one side of the foot.

A dinner plate from this service is also in the British Museum (F.1407).

清　黑釉羅馬神話及英國徽章紋鹽盤

Grisaille - painted salt cellar with a scene from Greek
mythology and an English coat of arms

60. 清　黑釉希臘神話及英國徽章紋鹽盤

高4公分　寬7.7公分

法蘭克收藏

此件與上述鹽盤（圖版59a）十分類似。圖案上端描繪希臘神話中的海神普塞頓，以及其情人希拉，快被海神善妒的妻子變成狗耳怪獸。徽章屬於馬修‧漢布森女婿威廉麥克芝少校所有，他於1745年結婚。

60　*Grisaille* - painted salt cellar with a scene from Greek mythology and an English coat of arms

Qing dynasty, c. 1740 - 50

Height 4 cm, width 7.7 cm

Franks collection, F.1437

This vessel is similar in shape to the previous (cat.no. 59). Its shallow depression on top is painted *en grisaille* with a man with a long beard, holding a trident, standing on a chariot pulled by hippocampi (fabulous creatures, half horse, half fish) and accompanied by tritons blowing horns. He is heading towards a woman surrounded by five dog - headed serpents. The foot bears at the front a coat of arms with a stag's head on a shield and the Latin motto 'DATA EATA (sic) SECUTUS' (I have followed my appointed destiny), on the reverse a crest in form of a flame, with a banner inscribed with the Latin motto 'LUCEO NON URO' (I shine but do not burn), and on the sides flower sprays.

The scene illustrates a story from Greek mythology and shows Poseidon, brother of Zeus and god of the sea, and his lover Scylla who is being turned into a dog - headed monster by Poseidon's jealous wife Amphitrite, who put magic herbs into her bath.

The arms and the crest belong to Major William Mackenzie who around 1745 married Mary Humbertson, whose father had a very similar service made (cat.no. 59; see Howard, 1974, p. 334).

清　黑釉希臘神話及英國徽章紋鹽盤

Grisaille - painted salt cellar with a scene from Greek
mythology and an English coat of arms

61. 清　青花羅馬神話杯和托盤

（杯）高7公分　（托盤）直徑14公分

巴西爾・伊耳尼底斯遺贈

描繪羅馬海神 Neptune，駕馭著一群海豚橫越海洋，並有海中精靈寧夫以及人魚相伴。紋飾採自亞伯拉罕，布勒曼（1564－1651）之圖畫，後來他的兒子菲特列（1610－1669）用在雕刻上。

61　Blue - and - white coffee cup and saucer with a scene from Roman mythology

Qing dynasty, c. 1760 - 80

Height (cup) 7 cm, diameter (saucer) 14 cm

Given by the Hon. Mrs. Basil Ionides, 1953.10-15.1

This set shows a bearded old man holding a trident, being carried across the sea by a team of dolphins. He is accompanied by water nymphs and mermen, one of whom plays a horn. The rim of the saucer is further decorated with a narrow diaper border.

The picture shows Neptune, the Roman god of the sea and its inhabitants. The scene may illustrate an episode told by Virgil in the *Aeneid*, book I, lines 124 - 143, where Neptune calms the waves with his trident after the chief goddess, Juno, had intervened in the Trojan war by unleashing a storm to combat the retreating Trojan army.

The drawing from which this design derives is the left half of a composition from a copy book by the Dutch artist Abraham Bloemaert (1564 - 1651), which is preserved in the Metropolitan Museum of Art, New York (Le Corbeiller, 1974, no. 28). The drawing was later engraved by Bloemaert's son, Frederick (c. 1610 - 1669).

Other pieces with the same decoration include a pattipan in the Princessehof Museum, Leeuwarden, Netherlands (Jörg, 1982, no. 50), and a plate in the Metropolitan Museum of Art, New York (Le Corbeiller, 1974, no. 28); a straining saucer in the Mottahedeh collection comes from a similar service with additional flower sprays (Howard and Ayers, 1978, vol. 1, no. 336).

清　青花羅馬神話杯和托盤

Blue - and - white coffee cup and saucer with a scene from Roman mythology

62. 清　彩瓷羅馬神話人物圖咖啡杯和托盤

（杯）高7.4公分　（托盤）直徑14.2公分

巴西爾・伊耳尼底斯夫人遺贈

杯和托盤顯示羅馬神話中的愛神——邱比特，被描繪成長著翅膀、頭戴三角帽之裸身小男孩，佩帶鼓和劍，對著一隻蜻蜓打鼓。圖案淵源於德國設計圖。

62 *Famille rose* coffee cup and saucer with a figure from Roman mythology

Qing dynasty, c. 1770 - 80

Height（cup）7.4 cm, diameter（saucer）14.2 cm

Hon. Mrs. Basil Ionides Bequest, 1963.4-22.8

This cup and saucer show a winged putto with an outsized tricorne hat. wearing a drum on a decorative strap and a sword attached to a sash around his waist. walking through a landscape and playing the drum to a dragonfly. The rims of both pieces are decorated with floral garlands punctuated by six ribbon bows. and the cup has a gilded handle.

Putti. which derived from images of the Roman god of love, Cupid, are frequently depicted in baroque and rococo painting. The present piece derives from a popular European porcelain model, first recorded as a three - dimensional decoration of a vase made at Meissen in Germany in the early 1750s and known as 'Putto als Tambour' (putto as a drummer). It is also known from porcelain figures made at Meissen and Fürstenberg in Germany, and at Chelsea in England. An example from Chelsea is in the Fitzwilliam Museum, Cambridge, Great Britain (fig. 62 a; Fisher loan, 82 a, courtesy of the Fitzwilliam Museum). Other figures in this series include putti playing the bagpipes or dressed as soldiers or lawyers (Zick, 1978, pp. 95 - 3 , and cat. no. 135).

fig. 62a

An identical saucer from a private collection is illustrated by Hervouet and Bruneau (1986, no. 8.24).

清　彩瓷羅馬神話人物圖咖啡杯和托盤
Famille rose coffee cup and saucer with a figure from
Roman mythology

洛可可風格
Romantic Rococo Paintings
（cat.nos. 63 - 75）

63. 清　黑釉金彩結婚圖荷蘭徽章紋盤

直徑22.7公分

法蘭克收藏

盤中央描繪一寓言式的婚禮，一對年輕的新郎和新娘，被眾神和樂師圍繞著，底下以拉丁文寫著「我對你的愛，海枯石爛永不改變」字樣，兩側的柱子上端是荷蘭夫婦的徽章紋。

63　*Grisaille* - and - gold painted plate with a symbolic wedding scene and Dutch coats of arms

Qing dynasty, c. 1736

Diameter 22.7 cm

Franks collection, F.591

The plate shows a bride and groom in a domed columned interior beside an altar with two perched loving doves, led by a figure with a burning torch, and accompanied on the right by mythological figures among clouds, one of them crowning the groom with a wreath, another offering a heart, and a winged cherub holding a finger to his mouth, and musicians on the left. In the foreground mermaids and merman are emerging from among rushes, some blowing horns. The arched entrance is superscribed with the Latin vow 'SEMPER AMOR PRO TE FIRMISSIMUS ATQUE FIDELIS' (my love for you will always be steadfast and true). The pillars on either side are supporting two coats of arms, the left - hand one bearing the misspelled Latin motto 'NULLUS VOLAT ATTIUS ALES' (no winged Attius flies). Behind the pillars is a figure holding a mirror on the left and one with a fruit basket and wheat sheaves on the right.

The picture is a symbolic wedding scene, full of emblems of love and marriage. In the clouds above the altar, holding a heart, is Juno, the mother goddess and wife of the highest Roman god, Jupiter, accompanied by a peacock. Crowning the groom is Venus, the Roman goddess of love, and the cherub represents Cupid, her male counterpart. The mirror represents truth and the fruit fertility.

The print from which this design was copied has not yet been traced. The arms belong to Johan van Gergen van der Gijp and Elisabeth Arnaudina van Beaumont Cornelis, who were married on 18th November 1736. Another plate with these arms is in the Musées Royaux d'Art et d'Histoire, Brussels, Belgium (Jörg, 1989, no. 78).

Plates with this marriage scene exist in different sizes, with different rim borders and bearing the coats of arms of different couples. All known plates with his design were made for the Dutch market and bear Dutch arms (*ibid.*, p. 204). Similar plates with different arms are in the Rijksmuseum, Amsterdam, Netherlands (Lunsingh Scheurleer, 1974, no. 284); and in the Mottahedeh collection (Howard and Ayers, 1978, vol. II, no. 391); and a large serving plate is in the Victoria and Albert Museum, London (Clunas, 1987, pl. 49).

清　黑釉金彩結婚圖荷蘭徽章紋盤

Grisaille - and - gold painted plate with a symbolic wedding scene and Dutch coats of arms

64. 清　彩瓷裸像蓋罐

高22公分

巴西爾‧伊耳尼底斯夫人遺贈

此罐帶有壺嘴以及半圓形的蓋子。繪有可愛的全裸或半裸有翼之小天使，其中一些小天使還戴著冠冕，是一極不尋常，難以解釋之設計。

64   *Famille rose* **jug and cover painted with naked and semi - naked figures**

Qing dynasty, c. 1750 - 80

Height 22 cm

Hon. Mrs. Basil Ionides Bequest, 1963.4 - 22.3

This covered jug has a rounded body, tall spouted neck and cover. Its sides are divided by overglaze-blue lines into two tiers of four sections. The lower sections each contain a naked or semi - naked figure dancing within a rococo frame with a coronet. The upper tier shows four figures in blue loin cloths, with their arms raised and their hair standing on end. The handle is decorated with an iron - red floral design.

This comical design can not yet be explained as its Western source is still unidentified. It has been suggested that it is an armorial design belonging to the German family Bucholtz of Brandenburg whose coat of arms depicts a naked woman with long hair holding a coronet in her left hand (Rietstap, 1903, vol. 1, pl. CCCXLIV). Other pieces from this unusual dinner service include an oval platter in the China Trade Museum, Milton, Massachusetts, U.S.A. (Milton, 1982, no. 84) and a sauceboat and dinner plate (Christie's London, 1st November 1993, lots 127 and 128).

清 彩瓷裸像蓋罐
Famille rose jug
and cover painted with naked
and semi - naked figures

65. 清　彩瓷天使吹泡泡圖蓋壺

高13公分　寬19公分

巴西爾‧伊耳尼底斯夫人遺贈

茶壺描繪兩個相擁在一起的邱比特，注視著第三個邱比特在吹泡泡，泡泡飄到金字塔上，四周圍繞著藝術的象徵。紋飾源自查理‧尼可拉斯‧可欣（1715－1790）為一本書所畫的插圖。

65　*Famille rose* teapot and cover decorated with cherubs blowing bubbles

Qing dynasty, c. 1740 - 60

Height 13 cm, width 19 cm

Hon. Mrs. Basil Ionides Bequest, 1963.4 - 22.5

The rounded teapot with straight spout is decorated both on the front and reverse with the same scene of two cherubs embracing and watching a third blowing soap bubbles over a pyramid, in a landscape with a large slab of stone to the right. Underneath this scene are a mask, bagpipes, a crown and a sceptre. The scene is repeated on the cover without the cherubs. The border around both neck and cover consists of scrollwork and suns with human faces.

The unusual scenes on this piece have not been satisfactorily explained. The three cherubs may represent Love, the bagpipes and mask seem to refer to the arts of Music and Drama. The scene was clearly copied from a specific European picture, and it has been suggested that it may derive from engravings by Charles Nicolas Cochin (1715 - 90), the Younger (Hervouet and Bruneau, 1986, no. 13.99).

This teapot is rare but relates closely to two saucers which are more finely painted with the same design, one in the Rijksmuseum, Amsterdam, Netherlands, the other in a private collection (Hervouet and Bruneau, 1986, nos. 13.99 and 13.100).

清　彩瓷天使吹泡泡圖蓋壺
Famille rose teapot and cover decorated with cherubs
blowing bubbles

66. 清　赭墨彩秋景英國族徽紋盤

直徑26.7公分

巴西爾・伊耳尼底斯夫人遺贈

盤中央描繪著在裝滿葡萄的果籃間嬉遊的五個小天使，象徵著
秋季。這種紋飾取自於1780年出版之法郎西斯哥・巴特羅吉之
雕刻作品集。他又摹仿希波羅尼所描繪的一組四季圖。盤子邊
緣所繪的小動物是英國大商賈兼銀行家──馬丁家族之徽章。

66 Sepia - and - *grisaille* painted plate with a symbolic depiction of Autumn, and an English family crest

Qing dynasty, c. 1780 - 1800

Diameter 26.7 cm

Hon. Mrs. Basil Ionides Bequest, 1963.4-22.19

The centre is delicately painted with a medallion in sepia showing five putti at play among baskets of grapes. The well has a formal border and the rim flower festoons and a small crest of a marten, all *en grisaille*.

This design is copied from a set of allegorical depictions of the seasons, designed by C.P. Cipriani, engraved by Francesco Bartolozzi and published in the 1780s. The present design represents Autumn and an example of the engraving which provided the model, together with a cress basket from the same service are in the Metropolitan Museum of Art, New York (Phillips, 1956, fig. 55 and pl. 75 top). Matching dishes with the corresponding picture of summer are also known and the armorial service probably included pictures of all four seasons, but examples of spring and winter appear to be lost. The engravings are surrounded by similar borders, but are lacking the crest. The animal, being a rebus of the name Martin, may belong to the English merchant banking family of that name (Howard and Ayers, 1978, vol. I, p. 377; see also cat.no. 23).

清　赭墨彩秋景英國族徽紋盤

Sepia - and - *grisaille* painted plate with a symbolic
depiction of Autumn, and an English family crest

67. 清　彩瓷歐洲佳偶圖盤

直徑23公分

巴西爾・伊耳尼底斯夫人遺贈

描繪一對佳偶坐在陽台上，紳士彈奏樂器，仕女正在餵食長尾鳥。邊緣四個玫瑰紅框裡繪有風景畫，白色琺瑯彩花卉渦捲紋圍繞四週。這類紋飾的淵源猶待考證。

67　*Famille rose* plate showing a Western couple

Qing dynasty, c. 1736 - 45

Diameter 23 cm

Hon. Mrs. Basil Ionides Bequest, 1963.4-22.24

The plate shows a couple seated on a terrace, enclosed in an ornamental rococo frame with a central medallion which serves a long - tailed bird as a swing. The gentleman is playing the oboe, while the lady is feeding the bird. The rim is exquisitely painted with four Chinese landscape vignettes in rose - pink, within a flower scroll of white enamel.

The Western original for this scene has not yet been traced. The plate belongs to a rare type of early *famille rose* pieces painted in white enamel on the white porcelain ground, with details incised into the enamel, a technique known as 'bianco sopra bianco' (white - on - white) which evokes the effect of lacework.

Other plates of this design are in the Costa collection, Lisbon, Portugal (Hervouet and Bruneau, 1986, no. 8.8), and in a private Brazilian collection (Veiga, 1989, pl. 131).

清　彩瓷歐洲佳偶圖盤

Famille rose plate showing a Western couple

68. 清　黑釉金彩歐洲佳偶及荷蘭銘文杯

高4公分

法蘭克收藏

杯的一邊繪有身著高貴服飾的歐洲佳偶，紳士注視著正舉杯傾飲的仕女。反面則寫荷蘭銘文：「爲了妳的健康，夫人」，以及「1733」年字樣，這杯可能是爲贈送夫人而製作的禮物。

68　*Grisaille* - and - gold painted cup with a Western couple and a Dutch inscription

Qing dynasty, dated 1733

Height 4 cm

Franks collection, F.596

The cup is painted on one side with a Western couple, the lady in elaborate robes and with long curly hair, holding a small tea cup, the gentleman, also with long hair and wearing a wide coat over a buttoned vest, gazing at the lady. On the reverse is a dated inscription written in a florid hand, reading 'GESONTHEYD JUFFROUWE(sic) Ao 1733', which means 'to your health, my lady; in the year 1733'. The rim is bordered inside by a golden flower scroll.

This cup with its Dutch inscription and date is very rare, but the couple is similarly depicted on other Chinese pieces, enclosed by elaborate floral borders, for example, on four saucers (Hervouet and Bruneau, 1986, nos. 7.5 - 7.8); the couples on these saucers differ very slightly from each other, some showing both the lady and gentleman holding cups. The present piece with its inscription may have been commissioned as a birthday gift for a lady, and the inscription seems to be copied from a handwritten note.

清　黑釉金彩歐洲佳偶及荷蘭銘文杯

Grisaille - and - gold painted cup with a Western couple and
a Dutch inscription

69. 清　彩瓷浪漫圖飾蓋瓶

高37.5公分

巴西爾・伊耳尼底斯夫人遺贈

此瓶繪有二種人物圖；描寫有一青年從梯子下來，將鳥巢放在情人的圍裙上，另一種是一對情侶和籠子裡的二隻雞。兩種都襯有風景背景，技巧相當出色。二種圖案均仿自威尼斯派畫家寬可波・阿半哥尼（1675－1752）的畫作。有一些英國陶瓷器紋飾也摹仿其圖案。第一種圖叫「氣」，源自四行（Four Elements）系列之一，第二種叫「夏」，也是四季系列之一。

69　*Famille rose* vase with romantic scenes

Qing dynasty, c. 1770 - 90

Height 37.5 cm

Hon. Mrs. Basil Ionides Bequest, 1963.4-22.7

This tall vase is decorated with two romantic figure scenes in large oval cartouches between flower sprays and pastoral vignettes. The main scenes show on one side a young man descending a ladder to place a bird's nest in his lover's apron with an open bird cage to one side, and on the other an amorous couple with a pair of caged hens, both couples surrounded by well - painted landscape settings and framed by garlands of flowers and butterflies painted in underglaze - blue and gold. The smaller vignettes show a man fishing in a river, and another walking his dog in the countryside.

The escape of birds from their cages is an allusion to the loss or potential loss of virginity (Holmes, 1991, p. 98). This theme is emphasized by the secluded settings and by the youths' unbuttoned shirts.

The main designs are both based on prints by the Venetian painter and engraver Jacopo Amigoni (1675 - 1752), who worked in England between 1729 and 1739. The former is entitled 'Air' and comes from a series of the Four Elements, the latter is entitled 'Summer' and is part of a Four Seasons' group. Contemporary French artists such as Nicolas Lancret (1690 - 1743), Antoine Watteau (1684 - 1721), and Francois Boucher (1703 - 70) are well known for similar romantic paintings.

Amigoni's work was not only copied onto Chinese porcelain but was also used at ceramic manufactories in Europe, and related designs are recorded from Venetian, German and Russian porcelain, from Dutch Delft faience and Spanish pottery, and from English ceramics made at Worcester, Coalport and Battersea (Toppin, 1946, pp. 266 - 76). A covered box enamelled in rose-pink with the print 'Air', made at the Staffordshire kilns in England is also in the British Museum (fig. 69 a; M＋LA 1895,6 - 3,82).

fig. 69a

162

清　彩瓷浪漫圖飾蓋瓶
Famille rose vase with romantic scenes

70. 清　彩瓷修士調戲仕女圖咖啡杯及托盤

（杯）高6.6公分　（托盤）直徑11.6公分

巴西爾・伊耳尼底斯夫人遺贈

描繪一位修道士丟棄聖經和唸珠，抓住鄉村少婦不放，充滿情
慾和諷刺。此圖似源自十分流行的版畫作品，此作品明顯的諷
刺僞善的教會聖職人員，倡導獨身，自己卻無法遵守戒規。

70 *Famille rose* **coffee cup and saucer, with a monk molesting a young woman**

Qing dynasty, c. 1750 - 70

Height（cup）6.6 cm, diameter（saucer）11.6 cm

Given by the Hon. Mrs. Basil Ionides, 1953.10-15.4

The scene on this set shows a tonsured monk in a brown monk's habit and sandals, abandoning his bible and rosary to seize a young rustic woman in a tightly laced bodice, long skirt, shawl and mob - cap, who is pushing him away. They are depicted under a tree with a church and a river bank in the background, and only a dog watching.

The subject is both erotic and satirical. It probably derives from a popular print which satirised the hypocracy of the Church whose monks swore a vow of celibacy but did not necessarily observe it. Erotic subjects were extremely popular with the European market and numerous mildly pornographic designs were copied onto or specially created for Chinese porcelain during the 18th century (see also cat.nos. 74 and 75).

Other pieces with identical decoration include a plate in the Victoria and Albert Museum, London (no. C.79 - 1963), and another in a private collection (Hervouet and Bruneau, 1986, no. 7.113).

清　彩瓷修士調戲仕女圖咖啡杯及托盤

Famille rose coffee cup and saucer, with a monk molesting
a young woman

71. 清 赭墨彩浪漫人物圖盤

直徑22.5公分

法蘭克收藏

紋飾採自約翰・史密斯雕刻作品：「算命師」，描繪一紳士坐在地上，請求一揹著嬰孩的婦女替他看手相。前景描繪二個少年，牽著紳士的馬和二隻狗。

71 *Grisaille* - and - sepia painted plate with a romantic figure scene

Qing dynasty, c. 1736 - 50

Diameter 22.5 cm

Franks collection, F.917 +

The scene depicted on this plate shows a well-dressed gentleman with lavish plumes on his hat, seated on the ground, holding the hand of a simply dressed woman with long hair, who is carrying a baby on her back. Two boys are holding his horse in the background and two well - bred dogs are reclining in the foreground. The rim border consists of shaped diaper panels joined by flower festoons, centred on three peacocks. The design is painted in black except for the figures' skin, the horse and one dog, which are all drawn in sepia.

The picture was taken from an evocative engraving by the English artist John Smith, who worked in the late 17th century, entitled 'The Fortune Teller' (Howard and Ayers, 1978, vol. II, p. 373), and depicts a man asking a gipsy woman to predict his future by reading the lines of his hand.

The intricate rim border is in the style of borders developed at the Du Paquier porcelain manufactory at Vienna, Austria in the early part of the 18th century. Other dishes with this design are in the Mottahedeh collection (Howard and Ayers, 1978, vol. II, pl. 365); and in the Victoria and Albert Museum, London (mentioned, *ibid.*, p. 373).

清　赭墨彩浪漫人物圖盤

Grisaille - and - sepia painted plate with a romantic figure scene

72. 清　彩瓷士兵紋茶盌及托盤

（杯）高5.5公分，（托盤）直徑14公分

法蘭克收藏

描繪一愁眉苦臉的士兵，坐在砲台廢墟中，他的駿馬陪伴在側，
遠處是冒煙的城垛。此圖案來源可能是當時的諷刺漫畫。盾牌
上有縮寫字母「C」，據說係詮釋為英國卡斯特家族。

72　*Famille rose* teacup and saucer depicting a soldier, and bearing a cipher and crest

Qing dynasty, c. 1770 - 90

Height（cup）5.5 cm, diameter（saucer）14 cm

Franks collection, F.881 ＋

The cup and saucer are painted with a scene suggesting the aftermath of a battle. They show a hussar with a prominant moustache, wearing a tall hat, braided doublet, fur - trimmed jacket and a sword, seated on a broken cannon or vehicle. His saddled horse is lying on the ground beside him, and smoking battlements are in the background. The rim of the saucer is surrounded by a rose - pink trellis border and contains a shield with the initial 'C' framed by floral garlands, with a lion's head as a crest.

The source for this design, probably a cartoon of a soldier from Eastern Europe, has not yet been traced. The cipher and crest are not specific enough to be identified with certainty, but it has been suggested that the service to which this tea cup and saucer belonged has been commissioned by the English Cust family（Howard, 1974, p. 332）.

Other pieces known from the same service include a two-handled cup and saucer in the Mottahedeh collection（Howard and Ayers, 1978, vol. II, no. 371）; and another in the Victoria and Albert Museum, London（Howard, 1974, p. 332）; an oblong teapot（mentioned, *ibid.*）; and a plate in a private collection（Hervouet and Bruneau, 1986, no. 9. 47）.

清　彩瓷士兵紋茶盌及托盤

Famille rose teacup and saucer depicting a soldier, and
bearing a cipher and crest

73. 清　彩瓷歐洲仕女像

高44公分

巴西爾·伊耳尼底斯夫人遺贈

描繪金髮仕女，戴著一頂紅色高帽，黃色外衣內著蕾絲上裝及一襲紅長裙，擺出舞姿。技法上避免寫實但刻意表現歐洲仕女之浪漫形象（圖版32）。

73 *Famille rose* **figure of a European lady**

Qing dynasty, c. 1736 - 50

Height 44 cm

Hon. Mrs. Basil Ionides Bequest, 1963.4 - 22.10

The lady is modelled in an agitated pose, as if dancing, with her arms wide apart and her clothes swirling. She is characterized as a Western lady by her long blonde hair, which falls in loose strands onto her shoulders, is piled up under an unusual headdress in form of a green headband with tall red crown, and is fastened at the back with an ornament with long pendant pearl strings. She is wearing a pleated red skirt with golden cloud pattern, a yellow blouse with a brooch at the collar and a pearl string round the waist, and an undergarment with triple lace collar.

This fashionably attired European lady is difficult to interpret. Like the companion figure, the Dutch lady (cat.no. 32), this figure may have been modelled after a costume print; but while the Dutch lady appears to be a realistic representation of a particular nationality, the present figure looks more like an idealized, romantic image of a Western lady, perhaps depicting a costumed dancer in a theatrical performance.

清　彩瓷歐洲仕女像
Famille rose figure of
a European lady

171

74. 清　德化窰白瓷婦女像

高39公分

派翠克‧唐娜利遺贈

戴著高聳引人注目頭飾之鬌髮女子，身著長袍，香肩微露，一
手撩裙尾。這類暴露形造型十分罕見，可能是專爲歐洲人製作。

74 Dehua figure of a woman lifting her skirt

Qing dynasty, c. 1750 - 75

Height 39 cm

P.J. Donnelly Bequest, 1980.7 - 28.297

The lady is standing on a flower - decorated pedestal and is modelled
with elaborate curly coiffure under an eye - catching headdress with
tall angular reinforcement in front which is decorated with flowers. Her
long robe has slipped from her shoulder, displaying a pearl necklace,
and she is lifting her skirt with one hand, displaying short stockings.
Her second arm is missing and appears to have been seperately
attached in a socket at the side of the sculpture, possibly in order to be
moveable.

Such exhibitionistic figures, probably made as souvenirs for Westerners,
were rarely made in Chinese porcelain. It is not known whether the
present figure was copied from a sculptural model or an engraving; the
headdress is reminiscent of those appearing in engravings of the late 17th
and early 18th century, for example, in costume prints by the artist
brothers Nicolas, Robert and Henri Bonnart (see cat.no. 20), several
of which are illustrated by Howard and Ayers (1978, vol. 1, figs. 35 a,
37 a, c and d).

清　德化窯白瓷婦女像
Dehua figure of a woman lifting her skirt

173

75. 清　彩瓷仕女圖托盤

直徑16公分

法蘭克收藏

托盤前端描繪一歐洲擠牛奶少女，頭頂著牛乳桶，撩起裙角，攀越田野的柵欄。另一面則是描繪同一少女彎下腰來，裙尾高揚，春光外洩。

75　*Famille rose* saucer with surprise design

Qing dynasty, c. 1770 - 96

Diameter 16 cm

Franks collection, F.752 ＋ A

This saucer shows on the front a milk maid balancing a churn on her head and lifting her skirt to climb over a stile, with her underskirt visible. A landscape with mountains, painted in a Chinese manner, forms the background. The surprise comes by turning the piece over, where one finds the same maid bending over and lifting her skirt right up to expose her behind, while peering back at the viewer.

Several saucers of this type are known, which would seem to have been made individually, for amusement, rather than as parts of services for practical use; but a matching tea cup is in the Musées Royaux d'Art et d'Histoire, Brussels, Belgium, together with two saucers of the same design, but more finely painted (Taipei, 1992, p. 69 top); another saucer is in the Musée. Guimet, Paris, France (Taipei, 1992, p. 81).

清　彩瓷仕女圖托盤

Famille rose saucer with surprise design

器形和技法源自歐洲器物
Interpretations of Western Silver and Ceramics
（ cat.nos. 76 - 91 ）

76. 清　彩瓷中國人物徽章紋水注

高72.5公分

精緻的器形上繪有洋人印象的中國人物。一邊是端著托盤之仕女，另一邊是抽煙斗的男子。此件作品之裝飾、器形以及規模，與普龍克（Pronk 1691－1759）的設計十分相近。普龍克是成功的荷蘭藝術家，在1734至1738年間為荷屬東印度公司設計中國瓷器紋飾。此件水注有一孔，附有金屬栓子與托盤同時使用。

76 *Famille rose* water fountain and cover with chinoiserie figure medallions

Qing dynasty, c. 1735 - 40

Height 72.5 cm

OA + 527

The massive water fountain and its domed cover are decorated with two chinoiserie figure medallions in elaborate shaped rococo frames, one showing a lady holding a saucer, dressed in a gold - patterned blue robe and red slippers, the other a gentleman in a crenellated hat, a purple robe with golden pagodas, and red slippers, who is seated cross - legged and smoking a long clay pipe. The medallions are surrounded by frames of rose - pink diaper on a ground of turquoise, with purple diaper with scallop shells at the shoulder and with flower garlands at the foot. Below one medallion the fountain is pierced with a hole for the attachment of a metal tap.

This water fountain is believed to have been designed by the successful Dutch painter Cornelis Pronk (1691 - 1759) who between 1734 and 1738 was commissioned by the Dutch East India Company to produce designs for Chinese porcelain to be made at Jingdezhen. According to the records, he supplied designs on four occasions and in return received an annual salary from the Company of 1200 guilders. This generous remuneration reflects both the fact that he worked exclusively for the Company and his status as an established artist of topographical scenes and portraits. He did not, as far as we know, produce designs for European ceramic manufactories. The directors of the Dutch East India Company were hoping that porcelains made after Dutch designs would sell better in the Netherlands than Chinese - designed pieces. However, Pronk's employment lasted only three and a half years until the venture was abandoned as being non – profitable. Only two of Pronk's watercolour designs drawn for the Company are extant, one known as 'The Parasol Ladies' and the other as 'The

Three Doctors', and both are kept at the Rijksmuseum, Amsterdam, Netherlands. The decoration of this water fountain relates closely to Pronk's design 'The Three Doctors' which shows similar figures, border motifs, diaper - work, and a similar colour scheme; examples from a tea service are in the Musées Royaux d' Art et d' Histoire, Brussels, Belgium (Hong Kong, 1989, no. 50). In shape it is identical to a water fountain with a related design, 'The Four Doctors' (Howard and Ayers, 1978, vol. I, p. 294). Water fountains designed by Pronk measured, according to the Company records of 7th March 1735, 68.9 cm in height and 45.5 cm in width (Jörg, 1980, pp.53 - 4) which is approximately the same size as the present piece.

Such fountains were ordered together with similarly decorated oval basins to be used as sets for washing hands after a meal. A slightly smaller water fountain with the same decoration is in the Princessehof Museum, Leeuwarden, Netherlands (Harrisson, 1986, no. 111) and a matching basin was formerly in the Ionides collection (Sotheby's New York, 29th January 1987, lot 461).

Several other related designs are attributed to Pronk on stylistic grounds, such as 'The Arbour', 'The Violet Plume' (cat.no. 77), 'The Handwashing', 'The Archer', 'The Flame Dancer' and 'The Phoenix' (Howard and Ayers, 1978, vol. I, p. 294). Apart from water fountains with basins, dinner services, tea services, and garnitures were produced in blue - and - white, *imari* and other polychrome palettes with designs attributed to Pronk.

清
彩瓷中國人物徽章紋水注
Famille rose
water fountain and
cover with chinoiserie
figure medallions

179

77. 清　紫黃彩歐式棕櫚圖紋茶杯及托盤

（杯）高3.8公分　（托盤）直徑11.7公分

法蘭克收藏

此件色彩特殊，純爲裝飾性；繪有一紫色棕櫚，留有白邊，與淡黃紋飾相輝映，具有歐洲風味。風格設計與荷蘭藝術家普龍克作品類似（見圖版76）。

77　Purple - and - yellow painted teacup and saucer with a European palmette design

Qing dynasty, c. 1735 - 40

Height (cup) 3.8 cm, diameter (saucer) 11.7 cm

Franks collection, F.588 A

This tea cup and saucer are unusual both in their colour scheme and in their purely ornamental design of purple palmettes with white edges on a canary - yellow diaper ground with a rim border of purple tasseled lappets.

This abstract design, known as 'The Violet Plume', has clearly a European origin, and relates stylistically to supporting designs on a Chinese export service, which may have been designed by the Dutch artist Cornelis Pronk (1691 - 1759, see cat.no. 76). The motif of a palmette or scallop shell is used as a border on the 'Arbour' service, a coffeepot of which is in the Musée Guimet, Paris, France (Taipei, 1992, p. 95). There is also a similarity in the execution of the grille - like diaper work to other designs attributed to Pronk, for example, a blue - and - white covered milk jug with the 'Four Doctors' design in the Frans Hals Museum, Haarlem, Netherlands (Jörg, 1980, no. 43). For all these pieces, however, the attribution to Pronk cannot be confirmed through the records of the Dutch East India Company (see cat.no. 76) and the design elements on the present cup and saucer were not uncommon in the decorative arts of 18th - century Europe.

Many other pieces with this design are known, all apparently from tea and coffee services, for example a teapoy, plate, covered jug, pattipan, two tea cups and saucers in the Metropolitan Museum of Art, New York (Le Corbeiller, 1974, no. 25); a coffee cup in the China Trade Museum, Milton, Massachusetts, U.S.A. (Milton, 1982, no. 63); a teapot, tea cup and saucer in the Musées Royaux d'Art et d'Histoire, Brussels, Belgium (Hong Kong, 1989, no. 53); a tea cup and saucer in the Mottahedeh collection (Howard and Ayers, 1979, vol. 1, no. 296); and a covered jug, plate, tea cup and saucer are in the Victoria and Albert Museum, London.

This particular design was also made in a different colour scheme with red palmettes against a black - and - white diaper ground with a red tasseled lappet border; a covered jug of this service is in the Musées Royaux d'Art et d'Histoire, Brussels (Taipei, 1992, p. 94)

清　紫黃彩歐式棕櫚圖紋茶杯及托盤

Purple - and - yellow painted teacup and saucer with a European palmette design

78. 清　藍紅彩歐式狗、鳥圖紋盤

直徑22.5公分

法蘭克收藏

釉上藍彩，繪有一跳躍的狗及四個渦捲紋，包含了小鳥及鐵紅色菱紋。風格及顏色十分特殊，可能是專爲歐洲設計的，大概是陶匠狄佛所製造的，在1734年以前將此設計交給了荷屬東印度公司。

78　Blue - and - red painted plate with a European design of a dog and birds

Qing dynasty, c. 1735 - 45

Diameter 22.5 cm

Franks collection, F.1406

This dinner plate is painted in overglaze - blue enamel with a Pekinese dog in the central medallion, bounding on a blue ground with his front legs in mid - air, and four oval cartouches containing a stork, a cockatoo, two doves, and a parrot, all reserved on an iron - red diaper ground.

The colour scheme of this design appears to be unique. The dog and birds are painted in European style and the simplicity of the decoration with no supporting designs around the dog and birds is most unusual. Diaper is often used in Chinese designs but does not usually continue from the rim over the well to the centre of a plate, like on the present piece.

All these features suggest that the design has a European origin, and it bears superficial resemblance to designs by the Dutch artist Cornelis Pronk (see cat.no. 76). However, as far as we understand, his work was mainly figurative and the Dutch East India Company records of Pronk's work do not support such an attribution. A more plausible suggestion seems to be that it was created by Delft potters, who are known to have submitted porcelain designs to the directors of the Dutch East India Company to be copied at Jingdezhen before Pronk's appointment in 1734 (Howard and Ayers, 1978, vol. I, p. 296).

清 藍紅彩歐式狗、鳥圖紋盤
**Blue - and - red painted plate with a European design of a
dog and birds**

79. 清　黑底歐式黑喇叭手紋杯及托盤

（杯）高4公分　（托盤）直徑11.5公分

巴西爾・伊耳尼底斯夫人遺贈

此套作品皆繪有二個黑人，身著簡單罩衫及草鞋。其中一個吹喇叭，另一個吹號角，背景為黑色。此圖案可能仿自那不勒斯市製作的義大利瓷器。

79　Black - ground cup and saucer with a European design of black trumpeters

Qing dynasty, c. 1740 - 50

Height（cup）4 cm, diameter（saucer）11.5 cm

Given by the Hon. Mrs. Basil Ionides, 1953.10 - 15.3

Both cup and saucer are painted with two black men in simple tunics and sandals, one with a green garment sounding a trumpet, the other in yellow blowing a horn, both standing on level ground which is indicated in green. The whole design is reserved on a black ground, which is intensified by an overlayer of green enamel. On the cup the scene continues on the foot; the outside of the saucer is covered in black enamel which also includes the foot. The rims of both pieces are painted with golden spearhead borders, the inside of the cup is further painted with a small black orchid.

In its colour scheme this set is reminiscent of *famille noire* porcelains with designs mainly in yellow and green on a black ground, as they were made in the Kangxi period（1662 - 1722）and extensively copied in the early years of this century. The present pieces, however, with their spearhead rim borders, clearly date from the Qianlong period (1736 - 1795). In this period this colour scheme was not used in China and seems to have been introduced from Europe together with the design itself. The way how the design incorporates the foot of the vessels is also very unusual for Chinese porcelain and may reflect a feature of the model. The decoration is reminiscent of Italian porcelain made at Naples, whose designs were often based on the figurative decoration of classical Greek vases and therefore show - like this set - individual figures in strong silhouettes rather than picturesque figure scenes. Also in accordance with Greek pottery, the painters at Naples often used a black background for their figures, not, however, in combination with green and yellow.

184

清　黑底歐式黑喇叭手紋杯及托盤
Black - ground cup and saucer with a European design of black trumpeters

80. 清　粉彩及青花歐洲植物圖盤二件

直徑26.2公分，23公分

法蘭克收藏

二件盤子都繪有類似鳶尾花及百合花，花瓣及葉子上有二隻毛毛蟲在嚙食，並有一蝴蝶翩飛其上。此圖案雖較簡略，形式上卻非常類似馬莉亞・艾莉恩（1647－1717）的畫作。艾莉恩爲德國畫家，曾徹底的研究昆蟲和植物。盤緣以歐洲巧思的精緻交錯枝葉紋飾成。

80 *Famille rose* and blue-and-white plates with a European botanical design

Qing dynasty, c. 1725 - 40

Diameters　23 cm , 26.2 cm

Franks collection, F.589 A , F.589

Both plates are painted with the same design, but in different colouring. The enamelled plate shows an iris in blue and yellow enamel and a rose - pink lily - like flower with two caterpillars feeding on their petals and leaves, and a red butterfly hovering above. The well is painted with an underglaze - blue barbed band with gilt decoration, and the rim with a splendid border of red and purple scrolls entwined with long serrated leaves in green with yellow undersides, and interspersed with golden fruit and flower motifs. On the larger plate the same design is painted in underglaze blue only, with details in gilding. The blue-and-white plate has an iron - brown rim.

This design is very similar in style to drawings by Maria Sybilla Merian (1647 - 1717), a German - born engraver and painter of watercolours, who made intensive studies of insects and plants and published several illustrated books both on plants and on the metamorphosis of insects. Her illustrations, however, are usually more elaborate than the design on this dish, which may have been copied from a secondary source. The rim border is also derived from a European prototype and has been related to designs by the Dutch artist Cornelis Pronk (Howard and Ayers, 1978, vol. 1 , p. 304; see also cat.no. 76).

An enamelled plate of this design in the Mottahedeh collection is illustrated by Howard and Ayers (1978, vol. 1, pl. 298), who mention other services painted with related designs of flowers and insects (p. 305) and illustrate a vase from a garniture with similar motifs (fig. 298 a).

清　粉彩及青花歐洲植物圖盤二件

Famille rose and blue-and-white plates with a European botanical design

直徑22.6公分

威斯考特·狄龍捐贈

此盤細緻地描繪了歐洲港口風光，以及在貨船卸貨的碼頭上閒談的紳士。邊緣裝飾華麗的中國風景紋，施有黑色琺瑯彩和粉紅彩，錯置在花卉植物及蝴蝶之間。盤中景色十分能代表在Meissen製作的德國瓷器的特徵。

fig. 81a

81 *Famille rose* plate painted in imitation of German porcelain

Qing dynasty, c. 1725 - 35

Diameter 22.6 cm

Given by Viscount Dillon, 1923.3 - 14.199

The plate is delicately painted with a central cartouche containing a European harbour view and shows European gentlemen talking on the quay where ships have been unloaded. This vignette is surrounded by rose - pink and iron - red scrollwork with iron - red butterflies above and a swan swimming in a river below. The design on the rim is particularly ornate and unusual, and contains four landscape panels, two en grisaille and two in rose - pink, surrounded by butterflies and flowering plants against a speckled green ground.

The central scene closely resembles decoration found on German porcelain made at Meissen. Save for some earlier experiments on a small scale, the Meissen manufactury was the first to make porcelain in Europe and Meissen porcelain was copied in China almost immediately, from the 1720s. Chinese porcelain, however, being available in much larger quantities, was - despite the transport - only a fraction of the cost of the German merchandise.

Some of the Chinese imitation pieces are remarkably convincing, compare for example a Chinese cup and saucer decorated with European figures in Meissen style in the Yongzheng period (1723 - 1735), and a Meissen teapot with a similar overall design but with Chinese figures, made between 1723 and 1725, both in the British Museum (fig. 81 a; OA 1933.11 - 17.1, M+LA Franks 64). (For further Chinese porcelains decorated in the style of Meissen, see the following piece, cat.no. 82, and Hervouet and Bruneau, 1986, pp. 342 - 62).

清　彩瓷仿德瓷盤
Famille rose plate painted in imitation of German porcelain

82. 清 粉彩仿德蓋盌

高8.5公分，直徑11.8公分

法蘭克收藏

此蓋盌繪有中國山水人物，仿自1720年代早期的德國Meissen
窰廠，J.G. Höroldt做的德國瓷器。

82 *Famille rose* **bowl and cover painted in imitation of German porcelain**

Qing dynasty, c. 1736 - 45

Height 8.5 cm, diameter 11.8 cm

Franks collection, F.647

The rounded bowl has a flared upturned rim, shaped to hold a saucer - shaped cover. The bowl is painted in the centre with a chinoiserie figure design showing a Chinese gentleman with long mustache, wearing an angular hat with pendants on the flat brim, a long rose - pink garment and a red overcoat, holding a fruit bowl. He is accompanied by a small boy with a basket and is standing beside a table with vases and a jar filled with a scroll, brushes and a fan. Two insects are hovering above and on either side are flower bushes, delicately painted. The design is repeated, spaced out as a continuous scene, on the outside of the bowl and appears again on the cover, lacking the figures and insects. The foot of the bowl is gilded, its inside rim is painted with delicately interlaced scrollwork in gold, which is repeated on the rim of the cover, both being visible when the cover is in place.

The chinoiserie figure scenes as well as the interlaced rim border of this bowl and cover are in the style of German porcelain made by Johann Gregor Höroldt (1676 - 1775) at Meissen in the early 1720s. A Meissen teapot with a related figure, also standing on green ground, on the cover, and with similar golden scrollwork on the shoulder, is illustrated in fig. 81 a, together with another cup and saucer with Meissen-style decoration, made in China.

A cup and saucer with the same design are in the Mottahedeh collection (Howard and Ayers, 1978, vol. II, pl. 533).

清　粉彩仿德蓋盌

Famille rose bowl and cover painted in imitation of German porcelain

清　琺瑯彩靑花仿西班牙錢幣紋蓋盒

直徑 6 公分

法蘭克收藏，亞瑟‧莫里森夫人捐贈

二個盒子皆繪有類似的西班牙查理四世國王之肖像（在位期間
1788－1808），周邊圍繞著拉丁銘文及1808年字樣。紋飾仿自
西班牙錢幣（圖83a）。琺瑯彩盒的底面則有西班牙皇家徽章
及拉丁銘文，係仿自錢幣的另一面。器底飾中國桃樹枝圖案。

fig. 83a   fig. 83b

**83　*Famille rose* and blue - and - white boxes and covers
painted after a Spanish coin**

Qing dynasty, c. 1808

Diameter 6 cm

Franks collection, F.715 +

Given by Mrs. Arthur Morrison, 1947.7 - 19.8

Both boxes are of similar lobed form, and one is decorated in colours
of the *famille rose*, the other in underglaze blue. Both show on the
cover a portrait of King Charles IV of Spain（r. 1788 - 1808), crowned
with a laurel wreath, surrounded by a curiously transcribed Latin
inscription and the date 1808. The enamelled box also copies the
reverse of the coin and shows on the underside the Spanish royal arms
surrounded by another Latin inscription; the insides of both box and
cover show a flower - head. The blue - and - white box and cover bear
peach sprigs on the insides and another peach sprig on the base, incised
through the blue pigment which covers the sides and base.

The design is copied from a Spanish silver coin of 1808 which is
inscribed on the portrait side 'CAROLUS IIII DEI GRATIA 1808'
(Charles IV, by God's grace, 1808), and on the armorial side
'CHISPAN ET IND REX'（King of Spain and the Indies) as well as
the abbreviated denomination, '8 reales', and the mintmaster's initials.
The enamelled box closely copies both front and reverse of the coin

(see figs. 83 a and b, for an example in the British Museum, 1906.11 - 5.271)
; the blue - and - white box, however, bears only a distant relationship
to it, its inscription being illegible, and may have been copied from one
of the enamelled porcelain boxes rather than from the coin itself.

清　珐瑯彩青花仿西班牙錢幣紋盫盒

Famille rose and blue-and-white boxes and covers
painted after a Spanish coin

84. 清　描金仿歐銀器台架

高15公分

法蘭克收藏

此件造型不常見之器形，乃仿自銀器（圖版84a），是用來放置剪短蠟燭燭心所用的剪器。

84　Gold - painted snuffer stand of European silver shape

Qing dynasty, c. 1736 - 50

Height 15 cm

Franks collection, F.930 +

The piece has a shaped square base, a stem of curved profile, and a shaped receptacle of rectangular section on top, whose base is pierced on either side of the stem, and fitted with a curly handle. It is painted in gold with flower designs.

This unusually shaped piece is modelled after silver snuffer stands, made for a matching scissor-like candle snuffer which would be placed upright into the receptacle, its pointed tip protruding through the holes in its base. A related silver snuffer stand complete with its snuffer (as well as a conical candle extinguisher), made in London in 1703, is illustrated for comparison (fig. 84 a; courtesy of Sotheby's).

清　描金仿歐銀器台架
Gold - painted snuffer stand of European silver shape

85. 清　粉彩歐式雙把手蓋杯

高37.5公分

法蘭克收藏

大瓷杯的把手，施銀器上常見的浮雕，像這樣的雙把手大瓷杯稱爲愛杯，是在宴會時傳遞給佳賓以供輪飲。上面裝飾著古典器物上的火盆紋。

85　*Famille rose* loving cup and cover of European shape

Qing dynasty, c. 1790 - 1800

Height 37.5 cm

Franks collection, F.624 A

The large cup rests on a tall stem and has two curved handles and a cover with curved knob. It is painted on either side with a burning brazier with rams' heads and feet and a curling snake between its three legs. The handles and knob of the cover have red - painted leaf terminals moulded in relief, and both cup and cover have moulded scalloped petal borders painted in purple and red with details in gold. A thin border of bamboo and flowers in *famille rose* enamels is painted on the cover and on the stem.

Such large double - handled cups are called 'loving cups' and were passed round at banquets for communal drinking. The form of the brazier depicted on this cup originates in classical antiquity. Another loving cup of this form, perhaps made from the same mould, but with differently shaped handles and different decoration, is in the Mottahedeh collection (Howard and Ayers, 1978, vol. 1, pl. 577).

清　粉彩歐式雙把手蓋杯

Famille rose **loving cup and cover of European shape**

86. 清　彩瓷仿歐瓷歐式臉譜罐

高37.5公分

馬克夫人捐贈

大罐上繪有多種花、水果，翩飛的蝴蝶環繞其間。罐頸以紅釉
描金中國式花卉捲紋，罐嘴下方有西方男子浮雕之臉譜，高鼻、
捲髮、留髭、長鬚。飾有這種臉譜的罐子最先是在法國盧昂
（Rouen）製作。此後，許多歐洲窰廠也紛紛仿製。中國瓷器
裏則較少見此類作品。

86 *Famille rose* jug with a European face, imitating European
ceramics

Qing dynasty, c. 1740 - 50

Height 37.5 cm

Given by Mrs. E. Mark, 1953.10 - 19.2

This large jug is painted with several clusters of flowers and fruit
among hovering butterflies, and the neck shows a flower - scroll
pattern in gold on red, all in Chinese style. Applied in relief under the
spout is the face of a Western man with pointed nose, mustache, long
beard and curly hair. The rim was later fitted with a ribbed brass
mount.

Jugs decorated with such faces were first made in earthenware at
Rouen in France, but were later copied by many European pottery and
porcelain manufactories. Chinese versions are rare, but are also known
in blue - and - white (Sotheby's London, 6th November 1993, lot 40).

清　彩瓷仿歐瓷歐式臉譜罐

Famille rose jug with a European face, imitating European ceramics

87. 清　粉彩公雞一對

高34.3公分

法蘭克收藏

這對佇立在岩石上十分寫實的公雞，是屬於禽獸及人像系列作品之一，根據西方樣本製造。這類作品全屬裝飾性，通常與類似樣本一起陳列在壁爐、壁飾、台几、櫃子及餐桌上。

87　Pair of *famille rose* figures of cockerels

Qing dynasty, c. 1750 - 70

Height 34.3 cm

Franks collection, F.313

The cockerels are modelled as a corresponding pair, each perched with one foot raised, on brown rocks. They are painted in realistic detail with layers of overlapping feathers on the wings and scales on the feet, and have yellow feathers, brown wings, black tails, scarlet combs and wattles, and claws.

These cockerels, like all the other birds below (cat.nos. 88 - 90), belong to a series of mass - produced bird, animal and human figures made after Western models for the European market, and are purely ornamental. In Europe such pieces were displayed alongside other Chinese, Japanese and European porcelain figures on chimney pieces, wall fittings and special stands, in cabinets or on tables. The Library of the Chinese Pavillion at Drottningholm, near Stockholm, Sweden, built in 1753 as a birthday gift from Adolf Fredrik, King of Sweden, for his wife Queen Lovisa Ulrica, contained according to an inventory of 1777 four pairs of cockerels of the same size as the present birds, as well as two smaller pairs (Setterwall, Fogelmarck and Gyllensvärd, 1974, pp. 295 - 6).

Other similarly modelled cockerels of different colouring are a single one in the Mottahedeh collection (Howard and Ayers, 1978, vol. II, no. 606); and a pair in the Peabody Museum of Salem, Massachusetts, U.S.A. (Sargent, 1991, no. 66), which also owns a second pair with different bases (*ibid.*, no. 65).

清　粉彩公雞一對

Pair of *famille rose* figures of cockerels

88. 清　彩瓷鷹一對

高26.5公分

法蘭克收藏

此對鷹，栩栩如生，棲息在岩石基座上，頭部相向，羽毛描繪
得十分細膩。

88 Pair of *famille rose* figures of hawks

Qing dynasty, c. 1750 - 70

Height 26.5 cm

Franks collection, F.312

The two hawks are naturalistically modelled in corresponding poses,
perched on pierced rockwork bases, their heads turned to one side to
form a corresponding pair. The rockwork bases are splashed with
purple, blue and turquoise enamels, and the birds are perched with one
leg raised and are painted in sepia, their feathers delicately pencilled in
a darker shade and with details in gold, their eye sockets green, and
the beaks golden and red inside.

Like the previous figures (cat.no. 87), this pair of birds was made for
display in a European home.

清　彩瓷鷹一對
Pair of *famille rose* **figures of hawks**

89. 清　彩瓷雉雞

高38.5公分

法蘭克收藏

此鮮明的雉雞，單腳棲息在五彩斑斕的岩石基座上。羽毛色彩
分明：粉紅色的胸部，藍綠色的背部，羽翼及尾端則分別飾以
黃、粉紅及藍色。

89 *Famille rose* **figure of a pheasant**

Qing dynasty, c. 1750 - 70

Height 38.5 cm

Franks collection, F.313 B

The brightly coloured pheasant is modelled with one foot raised and
the other perched on a multi - coloured rocky base, naturalistically
represented with different textures for the scaly feet, the claws and the
beak, and with dense pink breast feathers, clearly distinguished wing
and back feathers and a long colourful tail.

A porcelain tube would originally have been attached to the base,
possibly to contain a taper.

清　彩瓷雉雞
Famille rose figure of a pheasant

90. 清　彩瓷鶴

高43公分

法蘭克收藏

此修長的鶴，原先是一對，並呈現互相呼應的姿勢。此鶴高貴地塑成一腳縮起，棲息於岩石上之姿態。羽毛飾白琺瑯彩，與黑色斑點形成強烈對比。

90 *Famille rose* figure of a crane

Qing dynasty, c. 1750 - 70

Height 43 cm

Franks collection, F.311

The tall figure is elegantly modelled, its neck slightly curved to one side, perched on tall rockwork with one leg raised. The bird is painted in white on the white porcelain ground, with details for feathers incised through the enamel, and feathers at the top and bottom of its wings painted in contrasting turquoise and black, its crest raised in relief and enamelled in red, and the sockets of its eyes in yellow.

This bird was originally one of a correspongingly modelled pair and - like the figures above (cat.nos. 87 - 89) - made for display.

清　彩瓷鶴
Famille rose figure of a crane

91. 清　粉彩鵝形蓋盌

高33.5公分，長34公分

E.U.S.卡特小姐捐贈

此栩栩如生的鵝形大蓋盌，乃供餐桌上使用。類似的蓋盌尚有
雞、牛、豬等不同器形，用來盛裝不同種類的食物。此種蓋盌，
器形源於德國瓷器。

91　*Famille rose* tureen in form of a goose

Qing dynasty, c. 1760 - 80

Height 33.5 cm, length 34 cm

Given by Miss E.U.S. Carter, 1931.6 - 22.8

The large naturalistically represented bird is modelled as an oval tureen
and cover to be used at table. Both pieces have overall carved feathers
which are overpainted with feathers in black and red with touches of
blue and green, the head, beak and back of the neck are also painted
in red, and the crest purple; the front of the neck has been left plain
white.

Similar tureens were made in form of cocks, ox and boars' heads, carp
and other figurative shapes, for different types of food. They were used
in combination with dinner services such as shown in the following,
and some were painted with coats of arms. Such tureens originate in
German ceramics and were made at Meissen and Höchst, but also in
other manufactories. A similar goose in the Mottahedeh collection is
illustrated by Howard and Ayers (1978, vol. II, pl. 614), where its
Western prototypes are discussed (pp. 590 - 92).

清　粉彩鵝形蓋盌

Famille rose tureen in form of a goose

英國貴族餐具

Tableware for the English Nobility

（cat.nos. 92 - 114）

92. 清　青花琺瑯釉英國徽章紋湯盤

直徑23公分

聖查理斯‧渥克遺贈

盤緣施以褐釉，並裝飾著釉下鈷藍彩，係純粹中國風格。盤中央繪有徽章紋，兩隻獅子陪飾在側，並刻有法文箴言：「重溫舊夢——美好時光將再回來」。邊緣上是Viscount的冠冕。此盤是為賽門‧哈克特所訂做的器皿之一。哈克特是傑出的法官及政治家，於1721年受封為子爵，他於1724年與伊麗莎白‧維儂結婚，1727年辭世。盤中繪有哈克特家族徽章及其夫人肖像。

92 Blue - and - white soup plate with an enamelled English coat of arms

Qing dynasty, c. 1724 - 27

Diameter 23 cm

Rev. Charles Walker Bequest, F.854（1887.12 - 18.2）

The plate has a brown rim and is decorated in underglaze cobalt - blue in purely Chinese style with four flower bouquets tied with fans on the rim and further flower motifs and a diaper border round the well. To this decoration, which is complete in itself, a coat of arms has been added in the centre, in red and black enamels and gilding, supported on either side by a lion, inscribed with the French motto 'LE BON TEMPS REVIENDRA' (the good time will come back), and surmounted by a Viscount's coronet which is repeated on the rim.

The coat of arms belongs to Simon Harcourt, a prominent barrister, Member of Parliament, Attorney General and Lord Chancellor, and his third wife, Elizabeth Vernon. He was created Viscount in 1721 and married his third wife in 1724, not long before his death in 1727 (Howard, 1974, p. 170).

清 青花琺瑯釉英國徽章紋湯盤
Blue-and-white soup plate with an enamelled English coat of arms

213

93. 清　彩瓷英國徽章紋湯盤

直徑22.5公分

C.H.布朗捐贈

此湯盤以細膩的技法繪成淡灰色的中國山水，盤中並有一盾徽章，原屬於約翰·艾爾威克所有。他於1713年至1720年出任英屬東印度公司主任，於1730年過世。

93 Polychrome painted soup plate with an English coat of arms

Qing dynasty, c. 1723 - 30

Diameter 22.5 cm

Given by C.H. Beavan, F.1410 A (1911.7-18.1)

The soup plate is painted with a faint landscape scene *en grisaille*, with an armorial panel in the centre executed in iron - red, blue and turquoise enamels and gold. The cavetto shows pomegranate medallions on a ground of large and small florets, the rim shows four cartouches with landscape scenes, one incorporating a family crest, on a diaper ground.

This soup plate is one of the earliest Chinese armorial pieces made for the English market and combines typical Chinese decoration with a European coat of arms. The arms have been identified as belonging to John Elwick of Mile End and Cornwall (Howard, 1974, p. 234), who was a director of the English East India Company from 1713 to 1720 and died in 1730. His son, another J. Elwick, was also involved in trade with China and in 1734 was supercargo on the ship *Harrison* bound for Canton.

The decorative use of heraldry in England goes back to the thirteenth century when, for example, King Henry III of England ordered a silver platter engraved with the royal arms as a present for his wife. This practice soon spread amongst the nobility and great ecclesiastics, with coats of arms appearing as architectural details, painted on walls and window shutters, and woven into tapestries (Woodcock and Robinson, 1990, pp. 172 - 86). During the 18th and 19th centuries Chinese porcelain painters most commonly copied coats of arms from heraldic book-plates, sent out for this purpose by customers (see, for example, cat.no. 104).

Other pieces from this service include another soup plate in the Metropolitan Museum of Art, New York (Le Corbeiller, 1974, no. 22); and a spoon tray in the Mottahedeh collection (Howard and Ayers, 1978, vol. II, no. 407).

清　彩瓷英國徽章紋湯盤
Polychrome painted soup plate with an English coat of arms

94. 清　粉彩英國仕女圖徽章紋盤

直徑21.9公分

法蘭克收藏

此徽章紋十分罕見，飾通常屬於仕女專用的菱形盾牌，並結合
了六隻藍綠色豹頭，可能是屬於亨利・伊卓德之女及女繼承人
所有。伊卓德在其父過世（1728年）後，繼承此一盾徽章。

94　*Famille rose* plate with the arms of an English woman

Qing dynasty, c. 1728 - 35

Diameter 21.9 cm

Franks collection, F.792 +

In the centre of the plate is a coat of arms contained within a lozenge
with six turquoise leopards' heads arranged in three rows and with an
elaborate border. The cavetto combines rose - pink diaper - work with
floral cartouches and the rim blue diaper with sprays of finely painted
Chinese - style flowers.

The dinner service to which this plate belonged is virtually unique in
that it was made for a woman. The diamond-shaped shield is used in
English heraldry to display the arms of an unmarried woman, widow
or peeress in her own right. The present service is believed to have been
made for the daughter and heiress of Henry Izod of Stainton,
Gloucestershire who died in 1728 (Howard, 1974, p. 237).

清　粉彩英國仕女圖徽章紋盤
Famille rose plate with the arms of an English woman

95. 清 彩瓷英國徽章紋盤

直徑22公分

法蘭克收藏

此盤係早期瓷器，景德鎮製作。顯示出純粹中國風格之圖案，
二隻公雞棲息在牡丹盛開的叢岩上，四周以及邊緣飾以菱形紋
飾。這樣的圖案通常會特意地設計出許多留白，就像中國畫一
樣，但在此盤裏卻幾乎全為徽章紋所填滿。此徽章屬於狄望的
古溫家族。

95 *Famille rose* dish with an English coat of arms

Qing dynasty, c. 1723 - 35

Diameter 22 cm

Franks collection, F.1408

The dish shows a Chinese design of two cocks perched on pierced
rocks among peonies, within a shaped hexafoil surround of rose-pink
diaper and a green diaper rim border. Above this design is an oval
panel containing a coat of arms under a helmet with elaborate plumes,
with a griffin crest above and with a band for a motto left blank below.

The arms belong to the Goodwin family of Torrington in Devon and
of Suffolk (Howard, 1974, p. 231). This dish belongs to the early
famille rose pieces with armorial designs which were both fired and
enamel-painted at Jingdezhen in Jiangxi province. It shows a purely
Chinese design which - like Chinese paintings - would have included a
lot of blank space; this space was here considered suitable for adding a
coat of arms.

Two similar saucers with slight differences in the design are in the
Cooke collection (*ibid.*).

清　彩瓷英國徽章紋盤

Famille rose dish with an English coat of arms

96. 清　彩瓷英國徽章紋盤

直徑39.2公分，高7.8公分

聖查理斯·渥克遺贈

此盤結合了二個徽章紋，一爲德欽色雷的亨利·塔佰，另一爲史特拉福市的凱撒琳·克拉普頓。兩人於1735年結婚，此盤可能是在其後不久製作。

96 *Famille rose* **serving dish with an English coat of arms**

Qing dynasty, c. 1735 - 40

Height 7.8 cm, diameter 39.2 cm

Rev. Charles Walker Bequest, F.733（1887.12 - 18.29）

This dish is painted in overglaze enamels and gold with a central coat of arms surrounded by rose - pink enamel mantling, and a dense lotus scroll in iron - red and gold in the cavetto, with four cartouches with beribboned emblems. The rim bears a standing lion as a crest, and three sprays of flowers tied with scrolls and a gourd, or with books and pomegranates, alternating with melons and finger citron.

The arms have been identified as Talbot impaling Clopton（Howard, 1974, p. 196）. The service was made for Henry Talbot of Dorking, Surrey, a Commissioner of Revenue, who married Catherine, daughter of Sir Hugh Clopton of Stratford - upon - Avon, in 1735. This dish and the service to which it belonged, were probably made soon after their wedding. Catherine's sister and father both had their own Chinese armorial services. Replacements were made for this service in England, later in the 18th century（Howard, 1974, p. 196）.

清　彩瓷英國徽章紋盤

Famille rose serving dish with an English coat of arms

97. 清　彩瓷英國徽章紋咖啡壺

高24.5公分

聖查理斯・渥克遺贈

方塊花式盾徽是屬於英國克里佛家族。咖啡壺側邊帶嘴之器形，乃仿自英國銀器（圖版97a），在安妮皇后當政時（1702－1714）風行一時，到了1760年代逐漸衰退。此器形在十七世紀末及十八世紀初的英國陶器上也曾出現。

97　*Famille rose* coffee pot and cover with an English coat of arms

Qing dynasty, c. 1730 - 50

Height 24.5 cm

Rev. Charles Walker Bequest, F.816 ✝ (1887.12 - 18.1)

This tapering, cylindrical coffee pot has a side spout and pointed cover with a knob and is decorated with a chequered coat of arms of blue and gold with a red band across the centre containing a crescent moon. The cover is painted with floral motifs *en grisaille*.

The form of this coffee pot, with spout and handle at right angles, derives from English silverware; a related silver example with a wooden handle, engraved with a decorative cipher, and made in London in 1705 or 1706 by Isaac Dighton is in the Victoria and Albert Museum, London . This shape was particularly popular during the reign of Queen Anne (1702 - 14) and went out of fashion in the 1760s; it is also found in English stoneware of the late 17th and 18th century, made in Staffordshire and in Fulham, London.

The coat of arms has been identified as belonging to the English family of Clifford of Chundleigh (Howard, 1974, p. 299). The service may either have been commisioned by Hugh, 3rd Baron Clifford of Chundleigh (1700 - 1732) or by his son Hugh, 4th Baron Clifford of Chundleigh (1726 - 83). French replacement pieces for this service were made by Samson of Paris (for a tankard, see *ibid.*).

清　彩瓷英國徽章紋咖啡壺
Famille rose coffee pot and cover with an English coat of arms

98. 清　青花英國徽章紋湯盤

直徑22公分

C.R.皮爾斯捐贈

此盤描繪一雉雞佇立在岩石上，繁花和修竹圍繞其間，邊緣上並有一盾徽章紋。依1731年11月19日廣東提單，得知此盤的所有者、購買日期以及輸入英國之詳情；此件爲查理斯‧皮爾斯（1703－1780）製作，是屬於二百五十件一組的瓷器之一件。

98　Blue - and - white soup plate with an English coat of arms

Qing dynasty, c. 1730 - 31

Diameter 22 cm

Given by C.R. Peers, 1919.12 - 15.3

The soup plate has a brown rim, a fine glossy glaze, and is painted in a bright underglaze blue. It shows a pheasant on a rock among flowers and bamboo surrounded by dense diaper - work in the well and with a crest of a griffin on the rim. The outside of the piece is painted with flower sprays.

The service to which this soup plate belonged is interesting because its bill of lading is preserved (in the British Library). This document records the name of the customer who ordered it, date and other details of the shipment, quantity of items shipped and their price. It is dated Canton, 19th November 1731 and reads 'Invoice of two chests of China ware, Laden on board the ship *Canton Merchant* Capt. Timothy Tullie, Commander, bound to the Port of Madras and consigned to Nicholas Morris Merchant there, on account and risque of Charles Peers Esq.' The contents of the chests are described as 'China Ware blue - and - white painted with a crest' and it is recorded that there were 100 plates, 6 soup serving dishes, 60 soup plates, 4 sets of bowls, 12 sauceboats and 12 salts totaling some 250 pieces and costing 40 taels.

The service was commissioned by the Peers family and bears their family crest (Howard, 1974, p. 174). It was ordered by Charles Peers of Chiselhampton Lodge, Oxfordshire whose son, also Charles Peers, worked for the English East India Company in Madras (1720 - 35) and also traded privately. The younger Charles Peers organized the transportation of the service from Madras on to England.

Other pieces from this service include a dinner plate, also in the British Museum (1919.12 - 15.2), two soup plates in the Metropolitan Museum of Art, New York (Le Corbeiller, 1974, no. 23), a serving plate in the Royal Scottish Museum, Edinburgh (no. 1923.465), and two large serving dishes on loan from J.R. Peers at the Victoria and Albert Museum, London (Loan nos. 5 and 6).

The Peers family also commissioned another larger and more expensive Chinese armorial service in *famille rose* enamels with their full coat of arms, rather than just the crest as on this service, which was shipped directly to England on 8th January 1732.

清　青花英國徽章紋湯盤

Blue - and - white soup plate with an English coat of arms

99. 清　粉彩英國徽章紋盤

直徑22.8公分

H.C.奧克奧爾捐贈

盤中碩大的盾徽屬於李克·奧克奧爾及其妻瑪莉·尼克爾所有。
兩匹白馬在側，圍繞在精緻細膩之紋飾裏，邊緣繪有彩色花卉
滾邊，並附有「LMO」縮寫字母。瓷器紋飾根據送達於中國的
歐洲設計圖繪製，成品由二艘船分別運送；一艘在1740年，另
一艘在1743年。發票至今還保存著，上面寫著盤子的價錢。

99　*Famille rose* plate with an English coat of arms

Qing dynasty, c. 1739 - 43

Diameter 22.8 cm

Given by H.C. Okeover, F.716 ＋（1902.5-14.1）

The large coat of arms in the centre is that of Leake Okeover（1702 -
65）impaling that of his wife, Mary Nichol, in an elaborate *rocaille*
surround, surmounted by a helmet with large red and white plumes
and with an oaktree as crest, and flanked below by two white horses
emerging from water, and by flags, all enclosed in a shell - shaped
panel. On the rim are four panels, two with the initials 'LMO' and two
with griffins above crowns, all flanked by dolphins and alternating with
European-style flowers.

The design exactly copies a pattern sent to China for that purpose and
inscribed on the reverse 'The Arms of Leake Okeover Esqre. of
Okeover near Ashbourn in the Peak in the County of Derbyshire - a
pattern for China plate. Pattern to be returned'. Deliveries of two
shipments of Chinese porcelain to the Okeover family are recorded,
one in 1740 and the other in 1743, and the bill of the former is
preserved, which shows that the original price of one plate was about
one English pound. Over 150 plates and dishes are known to have been
ordered, of which 100 were preserved in the family until recently
（Christie's London, 3rd March 1975, lots 165 - 84）. The present dish
was also given to the Museum by a member of the family. Other
examples are in the Cooke collection（Howard, 1974, frontispiece and
p. 398）. The history of this service is recorded by Howard and Ayers
（1978, vol. II, pp. 413 - 15）, who are illustrating another dish in the
Mottahedeh collection（pl. 413）as well as the original drawing and a
detail of the invoice（pls. 413 a and b）.

清 粉彩英國徽章紋盤
Famille rose plate with an English coat of arms

100. 清　英國徽章紋湯盤

直徑23公分

李區菲德伯爵捐贈

盤中呈現出情慾的揉合，田園、及異國情調的象徵。此盤是
爲紀念艦隊司令官安森（1697－1792），昇爲海軍艦隊總司
令而製作。上面繪有其徽章。邊緣的花紋包含了廣東及普利
茅斯港口風景。盤中央的麵包樹及左側的棕櫚樹仿自西爾斯·
伯瑞的畫作（參考圖版100a）。他曾陪伴安森雲遊四海，是
安森的繪圖師。1743年時，安森在廣東，1747年當他成爲男
爵時，其徽章紋有所變更。由此推斷，此盤之製作年代約爲
1743至1747年間。

fig. 100a

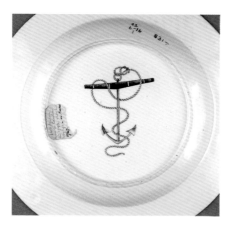

100　*Famille rose* soup plate with an English coat of arms

Qing dynasty, c. 1743 - 7

Diameter 23 cm

Given by the Earl of Lichfield, F.831（1892.6-16.6）

The plate shows in the centre a bread - fruit tree draped with a floral
garland; to the right are a colourful bird, two dogs, bagpipes, a
bonnet, a pair of crossed crooks, and in the distance a flock of sheep;
to the left a palm tree, a brazier with two flaming hearts, a pair of
loving doves, a bow and a quiver. The rim is painted with
waterscapes in long panels, one showing a pagoda, junks and
sampans between a tower and a ruin, the other ships flying the British
flag between a lighthouse and another ruin; at the top is a griffin
crest and at the bottom a coat of arms surrounded by colourful
rococo ornament and floral garlands. On the base of the plate is a
ship's anchor entwined with a cable.

The combination of pastoral, erotic and exotic emblems in the centre
is known as 'Valentine Pattern'. The symbols to the right of the bread -fruit
tree are also known as the 'Absent Master', those to the left as the
'Altar of Love' (see also cat.nos. 101 and 102). The waterscapes have
been interpreted as harbour views of the Pearl River at Canton (right) and
Plymouth Sound in Devon, England (left; Howard, 1974, p. 46).

This service was made for Commodore, later Admiral, Lord Anson

（1697 - 1792）of Shugborough in Staffordshire and bears his crest
and arms (*ibid.*, p. 323). The bread - fruit and palm trees have been
copied from drawings by Peircy Brett, Anson's draughtsman who
accompanied him on his circumnavigation of the world on *H.M.S.*
Centurion. An engraving by Brett, showing the 'Watering Place at
Tenian' was included in Lord Anson's *Voyage around the World*,
published in 1748 (pl. XXXIV, see fig. 100 a; courtesy of the British
Library).

This service can be dated quite precisely, since Anson went to Canton
in 1743, and his coat of arms was altered in 1747, acquiring a coronet
and supporters, when he was created Baron.

Other pieces from this service include a dinner plate in The National
Trust, Shugborough (Howard, 1974, p. 323).

清　英國徽章紋湯盤

Famille rose soup plate with an English coat of arms

101. 清 彩瓷英國徽章紋湯盤

直徑22.5公分

法蘭克收藏

此徽章紋盤中央有一對雉雞棲息在一塊岩石上，背景是一碩大之牡丹花朵。據查此徽章隸屬於威廉‧戴維斯，曾一度出任孟加拉之助理總督，並於1746年被授徽章。在前述盤子（參見圖100）中出現的情人圖案，分別在二個畫面點綴為盤緣。

101 *Famille rose* soup plate with an English coat of arms

Qing dynasty, c. 1746 - 50

Diameter 22.5 cm

Franks collection, F.833 +

In the centre of this soup plate are a pair of pheasants perched on rocks with giant peonies in the background. On the rim at the top is a family crest and at the bottom a coat of arms with a helmet with elaborate surrounding plumes, a ribbon left blank for the motto, and scrollwork; to the left is a panel depicting two dogs, two crooks, bagpipes and a bonnet beneath a garlanded tree, with a flock of sheep in the background; to the right another panel with a brazier with two flaming hearts, a pair of loving doves and a bow and quiver with a tree and floral festoons.

The arms and crest have been identified as those of William Davis of London and Westminster, a one - time Assistant Governor of Bengal, whose arms were granted in 1746 (Howard, 1974, p.320).

The pastoral and romantic motifs in the two rim panels are known as the 'Absent Master' and the 'Altar of Love'. These motifs were first seen on a dinner service created for the great English seaman, Commodore Anson, in 1743, a piece of which is illustrated above (cat. no. 100) and were probably designed by his draughtsman, Peircy Brett (*ibid.*, pp. 46 - 7).

A dinner plate from the present service is in a private collection (*ibid.*, 1974, p. 320).

230

清　彩瓷英國徽章紋湯盤

Famille rose soup plate with an English coat of arms

102. 清　彩瓷英國徽章紋小型深盤

直徑16.3公分

法蘭克收藏

此盤有浪漫田園之特色，可能由安森司令官的繪圖師——皮爾斯·伯瑞所創（見圖100），是爲了1747年1月喬治·寇莫戴利子爵與海斯特·愛德華成婚而訂製。徽章紋上之拉丁文箴言爲「勇氣爲最穩妥的頭盔」（勇者無懼，勇氣蓋世）。

102 Small deep *famille rose* plate with an English coat of arms

Qing dynasty, c. 1747 - 50

Diameter 16.3 cm

Franks collection, F.765 +

This small deep plate shows in the centre a pastoral landscape with a tree swathed in a floral garland, and two dogs, two crooks, bagpipes, a bonnet, and a flock of sheep in the background. The rim bears a coat of arms with a coronet, supported by a black griffin and a wolf, with the Latin motto below 'CASSIS TUTISSIMA VIRTUS' (virtue is the safest helmet), and a golden rococo scrollwork border on the rim.

The arms have been identified as those of the Cholmondeley family, with Edwards in pretence (Howard, 1974, p. 331). The service to which this deep plate belonged was made for the politician George Cholmondeley, Viscount Malpas (1724 - 64) and his wife Hester Edwards, whom he married in January 1747.

The combination of romantic-pastoral motifs in the centre of the plate is known as the 'Absent Master' and derives from a design created by Peircy Brett, draughtsman of the great English seaman, Commodore Anson (see cat.no. 100).

清　彩瓷英國徽章紋小型深盤
Small deep *famille rose* plate with an English coat of arms

103. 清　彩瓷英國徽章紋八角盤

直徑21.7公分

法蘭克收藏

八角盤上繪有中國人物圖，一仕女端坐在地，婢女持扇相隨，
侍從傾壺倒茶。盤緣描繪水墨山水圖，以及五彩徽章和頂飾，
此徽紋屬於帕威爾及克利夫蘭家族所有。

103 *Famille rose* **plate with an English coat of arms**

Qing dynasty, c. 1745 - 55

Diameter 21.7 cm

Franks collection, F.823 +

The octagonal plate is painted with a Chinese figure scene in the
centre, showing a lady seated on a carpet, holding a small square cup,
a female attendant with a large fan behind her, and a male attendant
kneeling by her side, filling her cup from a ewer. On the rim are a
family crest at the top and a coat of arms with a lion at the bottom,
with another in pretence, showing a hare, and two landscape panels,
painted *en grisaille*, on either side.

The arms bearing the lion belong to the Powell, those with the hare
to the Cleland family, which according to Howard had connections
with the English East India Company in the second half of the 18th
century (Howard, 1974, p. 314). An identical dish is in the Clive
Rouse collection (*ibid.*). Armorial services with Chinese figure scenes
are comparatively rare.

清　彩瓷英國徽章紋八角盤

Famille rose plate with an English coat of arms

104. 清　彩瓷英國徽章紋蓋罐

高12公分

法蘭克收藏

此徽章紋設計有箴言：「至死效忠，乃屬於巴威爾家族」，
是仿自彩色畫籤（參見圖104a）。據信，此蓋罐是爲任職於
東印度公司的米歇爾·巴威爾而製，他於1792年過世。

fig. 104a

104　*Famille rose* jug and cover with an English coat of arms

Qing dynasty, c. 1750 - 70

Height 12 cm

Franks collection, F.780 ＋

This small jug is decorated below the spout with a coat of arms and a crest with a helmet with elaborate plumes and the French motto 'LOYAL AU MOAT'(sic) meaning 'loyal to the death' below, within a gold - and - black rope border which is repeated on the cover. The rims of both jug and cover are further decorated with a spearhead border.

The arms have been identified as belonging to the Barnwell family and the service to which this cream jug belonged was probably ordered by Michael Barnwell, an employee of the English East India Company who died in 1792 (Howard, 1974, p. 416). The design was probably copied from a bookplate such as the one illustrated, also in the British Museum (fig. 104 a; P＋D Franks 1580).

清　彩瓷英國徽章紋蓋罐
Famille rose jug and cover with an English coat of arms

105. 清　英國徽章紋瓶一組（五件）

（瓶）高28.5公分　（杯）高23.8公分

聖查理斯・渥克遺贈

每件瓷器皆繪有徽章及頂飾，可能隸屬於英國伯奈爾家族。
此組瓶在十八世紀的歐洲十分盛行，用做室內裝飾品，陳列
在壁爐或房間的其他處。

105　*Famille rose* five - piece garniture with an English coat of arms

Qing dynasty, c. 1750 - 70

Height（jars）28.5 cm,（beakers）23.8 cm

Rev. Charles Walker Bequest, F.820 ＋（1887.12-18.4）

This garniture is comprised of three covered oviform jars and a pair of flaring vases in a form reminiscent of archaic bronze *gu*, each painted in *famille rose* enamels and gilding with a coat of arms and a crest.

The arms possibly belong to the English family of Burnell, although according to Howard the crest is not recorded as a Burnell crest （Howard, 1974, p. 572）.

Chinese porcelain was popular in Europe not only for practical use as dinner, tea and coffee services but also for interior decoration. A garniture is a set of matching vessels of uneven number, usually varying from five to nine pieces, made for display on the mantelpiece, on brackets and cornices of walls, and in cupboards and cabinets of European houses. Such garnitures became popular in Europe during the Kangxi period（1662 - 1722）.

清　英國徽章紋瓶一組（五件）

Famille rose five - piece garniture with an English coat of arms

106. 清　彩瓷英國皇家徽章紋附蓋茶壺

高16.8公分

聖查理斯·渥克遺贈

此處描繪的徽章爲1714年至1801年英國繼任君王所使用，但
非專屬任何一位皇室成員。徽章之下有渦形花紋，含有共濟
會的標記（參見圖42）。此茶壺可能是爲共濟會的某特定小
組而製，他們可能在一個名爲「國王的徽章」酒館聚會。

106 *Famille rose* **teapot and cover with the royal arms of England**

Qing dynasty, c. 1770 - 80

Height 16.8 cm

Rev. Charles Walker Bequest, F.806 ＋（1887.12-18.13）

The globular teapot has a branch-like spout, domed lid with pointed knob, and a replacement handle of metal and wicker-work. The teapot is decorated with a coat of arms enclosed within a belt, which bears the French mottos 'DIEU ET MON DROIT' (God and my honour) and 'HONI SOIT QUI MAL Y PENSE' (the shame be his who thinks ill of it), supported by a lion and a unicorn. These arms rest on a cartouche of Masonic emblems including a square, level, plumb-line, gavel, apron, sword, and lewis. The neck of the teapot and the cover have a spearhead border and the cover is further painted with delicate flowers.

This coat of arms and motto were employed by successive English monarchs from 1714 until 1801, when George III renounced his title of King of France and the arms were altered to remove the French *fleurs-de-lis* (Howard, 1974, p. 499). However, it is unlikely that the service to which this teapot belonged was made for a member of the English Royal Family. Although George III's son, Henry Frederick, was Grand Master (i.e. highest member of the Freemasons), his period of office was from 1782 to 1790 and would seem to postdate this piece. The royal arms may refer instead to the name of a tavern in which a particular group of Freemasons met, such as the King's Arms (see cat.no. 42).

The shape of this teapot with its branch-like spout is copied from European ceramics.

Other pieces with this design include another teapot with a replacement spout in the Mottahedeh collection (Howard and Ayers, 1978, vol. I, no. 319) a punchbowl in the Bullivant collection (Howard, 1974, p. 499), a teapoy in the Henry Francis du Pont Winterthur Museum, U.S.A. (mentioned by Howard, 1974, p. 499), and a tea cup in the Freemasons Hall Museum, London.

清 彩瓷英國皇家徽章紋附蓋茶壺
Famille rose teapot and cover with the royal arms of England

107. 清　彩瓷英國徽章紋貝形鹽碟

長10.7公分

聖查理斯・渥克遺贈

形如貝殼，爲餐桌上使用，可能仿自十八世紀歐洲銀器，繪有英國彫錢及阿米爾斯家族之徽章紋。

107 *Famille rose* **salt cellar with an English coat of arms**

Qing dynasty, c. 1760 - 80

Length 10.7 cm

Rev. Charles Walker Bequest, F.767 ＋（1887.12-18.23）

The salt cellar is moulded in the shape of a scallop shell. It is painted, in *famille rose* enamels and much gold, with a coat of arms in an oval panel with a crest above, surrounded by floral sprays and by a gold - and - black spearhead border.

The coat of arms has been identified as belonging to the Beauchamp family of Fifield in Essex, with those of Amyas quarterly in pretence (Howard, 1974, p. 495).

The shape of this salt cellar derives from English silverware. A similar pair of silver scallop shells, dated to 1767／8 and made by William Plummer, is in the Victoria and Albert Museum, London (no. M. 15a-1963).

清　彩瓷英國徽章紋貝形鹽碟
Famille rose salt cellar with an English coat of arms

108. 清　黑釉描金英國徽章紋蓋杯一對

高26.5公分

聖查理斯・渥克遺贈

此對蓋杯飾班克家族徽章，仿自一張畫籤。約瑟班克爵士
（1743－1820）爲一著名的自然主義者，於1764年繼承其父，
並於1779年結婚。這一對杯可能是在這段期間製作。器形乃
仿自歐洲銀器。

fig. 108a

108　Pair of covered *grisaille* - and - gold painted cups with an English coat of arms

Qing dynasty, c. 1765 - 80

Height 26.5 cm

Rev. Charles Walker Bequest, F.802 ＋（1887.12 - 18.7）

The deep cups each are supported on a bell-shaped foot, their handles made of twisted strands of clay with applied leaf terminals and their covers with applied berry knobs. They are decorated in *grisaille* and gold with a coat of arms on either side, divided into quarters, each section with a *fleur - de - lis*, and with floral garlands and a chain border around the rim, the foot and the cover.

The coat of arms belongs to Sir Joseph Banks (1743 - 1820), a celebrated naturalist and son of a wealthy merchant who became president of the prestigious Royal Society in 1778 and a Baronet in 1781 (Howard, 1974, p. 360). Banks was also interested in Chinese botany and wildlife; some of the Chinese watercolours of plants which he commissioned are in the Natural History Museum, London. The armorial design on both cups was copied from an engraved bookplate such as the one illustrated, also in the British Museum, which is inscribed 'Joseph Banks Esq.r' (fig. 108 a; P＋D Franks 1371). These cups were probably commissioned after Banks came into his parental fortune in 1764 and before he married in 1779.

The shape of such two-handled cups, which are sometimes called 'grace cups' or 'loving cups' (see cat.no. 85), derives from English silverware, and a similar pair of 17th - century English silver cups is in the British Museum (M＋LA 1973,1 - 3,1 and 2). Their original function was for drinking a final toast after grace was said at the end of a meal, for which they were passed around the table. These porcelain examples, however, may have been decorative rather than utilitarian.

清　黑釉描金英國徽章紋蓋杯一對

Pair of covered *grisaille* - and - gold painted cups with an English coat of arms

109. 清　彩瓷英國徽章紋乳蛋糕蓋杯及盤

（杯）高9公分　（盤）直徑16公分

法蘭克收藏

乳蛋糕乃雞蛋和牛奶之混合加糖焙烤之一道甜點，通常為餐飲中最後一道附菜。乳蛋糕杯不同於一般的茶杯或咖啡杯，杯上有纏繞的葉紋形把手，杯蓋上有草莓形鈕蓋，皆仿自歐洲瓷器。徽章紋屬於英國勞倫斯及艾伯莉家族。

109　*Famille rose* covered custard cup and plate with an English coat of arms

Qing dynasty, c. 1780 - 90

Height (cup) 9 cm, diameter (plate) 16 cm

Franks collection, F.634

The set consists of a small plate, squat cup with twisted handle with leaf terminals and cover with a berry - shaped knob. It is painted predominantly in gold and sea-green enamels with a coat of arms, surrounded by thin ornamental borders. The rims of both plate and cover are further decorated with a border of joined gold trefoils and a plain sea-green enamel band.

The coat of arms has been identified as Lawrence impaling Ilbery (Howard, 1974, p.645).

This type of covered cup was used to serve custard, a dessert made from milk, eggs and sugar, or similar sweets. The shape is much rarer than tea or coffee cups and is also known in English glass and silver.

清　彩瓷英國徽章紋乳蛋糕蓋杯及盤

Famille rose covered custard cup and plate with an English
coat of arms

110. 清　五彩英國徽章紋馬克杯三件

高15.2公分，13.4公分，12.3公分

法蘭克收藏

馬克杯仿自歐洲器型，把手上繪有纏繞的葉紋，三件尺寸各
有不同，並可以按徽章紋來辨別。徽章紋一邊由動物支撐，
另一邊則由半女人、半鳥狀之神話動物支撐，並且寫有一段
拉丁文箴言。此徽章屬於漢佛的奧伯瑞·維爾男爵，他在
1781年獲授男爵頭銜，於1787年成爲聖·艾爾本公爵時，徽
章紋有所變更。由此推斷這些馬克杯確爲此段時間內所做。

110　Three polychrome painted mugs with an English coat of arms

Qing dynasty, c. 1781 - 7

Heights 15.2 cm, 13.4 cm, 12.3 cm

Franks collection, F.1435

The mugs are copying a European shape, their handles made of twisted strands of clay with applied leaf terminals. They are made in graded sizes and identically decorated with a coat of arms divided into sixteen squares, between animal supporters, one in the form of a harpy, and with a crowned lion crest. The Latin motto below reads 'VERO NIL VERIUS' (nothing is truer than truth). On either side of the arms is a cypher, probably consisting of the initials H, R and V, within a blue enamelled mantle. The diaper and spearhead rim borders as well as the leaf terminals are painted in underglaze cobalt blue with details in gold.

The arms are those of Beauclerk quartering de Vere, and these mugs are believed to have been made for Aubrey, Baron Vere of Hanford, who inherited this title in 1781 and became the 5th Duke of St. Albans in 1787, when his arms would have changed (Howard, 1974, p. 712). This makes it possible to date these pieces fairly precisely.

清　五彩英國徽章紋馬克杯三件

Three polychrome painted mugs with an English coat of arms

111. 清　粉彩英國徽章紋盤

直徑25.2公分

法蘭克收藏

盤正面描繪海昱堂，蘭卡斯特州的約翰‧迦得威克（1720－
1800）中校的徽章紋。背面則有「1791年1月24日，廣東，
中國」等字樣。這類瓷器傳世的尚有若干件，背面皆有上述
不常見的銘文。

111 *Famille rose* **plate with an English coat of arms**

Qing dynasty, dated 1791

Diameter 25.2 cm

Franks collection, F.862 ✛

The front of this plate shows a coat of arms in the centre, a husk
border in the well and a spearhead border on the rim, and the reverse
is inscribed 'Canton in China 24th Jany. 1791'.

The coat of arms belongs to Lieutenant Colonel John Chadwick
(1720 - 1800) of Healey Hall in Lancashire. Several pieces of this
dinner service as well as a closely related service, made for another
member of the same family, with a slightly different coat of arms,
have been preserved, all with the same inscription on the reverse
(Howard, 1974, p. 741). Such inscriptions were not common on
Chinese export porcelain and the significance of the date here
recorded is not known.

清　粉彩英國徽章紋盤

Famille rose plate with an English coat of arms

112. 清　彩瓷英國徽章紋盤

直徑22.8公分

聖查理斯‧渥克遺贈

盤子以寓言方式呈現「希望」，描繪一沈思的仕女，握著帆，憩息在一繪有徽章的盾牌上，盤緣雕鏤。徽章紋屬於克爾‧馬丁家族。盤子是爲威廉‧克爾的一項儀式所訂製的。克爾於1790年和表妹珍‧馬丁結婚。

112 *Famille rose* plate with an English coat of arms

Qing dynasty, c. 1790 - 1800

Diameter 22.8 cm

Rev. Charles Walker Bequest, F.873 ＋（1887.12 - 18.56）

The plate has a broad pierced rim and is painted with an allegorical representation of Hope, in form of a pensive lady, gazing in the distance, holding a large anchor and resting her elbow on a coat of arms with another in pretence, all surrounded by a husk - chain with four pendants and surrounded by four anchors.

The reverse bears a largely rubbed inscription, written in black in a Western hand, of which only the words '... Ker ... Martin ... family' can be made out. Another plate of this service is known with a contemporary label reading 'This plate bears the arms of the Ker-Martin family for whom it was made' (Sotheby's London, 30th October 1972, lot 170).

The dinner, tea and coffee service to which these plates belonged is believed to have been made for the marriage about 1790 of William Ker of Gateshaw, Roxburghshire, and Jane Martin, his cousin (Howard, 1974, p. 694). Many different pieces of the service are preserved, including plates with the rim painted with allegorical representations of the Four Continents, oval dishes with the rim moulded and differently pierced (Howard and Ayers, vol. II, pls. 440

and 440 a), and openwork baskets. Although porcelain with pierced walls was made in China since the late Ming dynasty (1368 - 1644), the pierced patterns on these pieces are more closely related to European porcelain models.

It is unusual to find a Chinese armorial service of this late date with a coat of arms incorporated into a representational design rather than on its own.

清　彩瓷英國徽章紋盤

Famille rose plate with an English coat of arms

113. 清　青花描金英國徽章紋盤

直徑15.8公分

法蘭克收藏

此盤與類似紋飾的青花山水盤在歐洲最受歡迎，英國窰廠曾
在十九世紀大量仿製。徽章紋屬於英國皇室。

**113　Blue - and - white plate with gilding, with an English coat
of arms**

Qing dynasty, c. 1800 - 1810

Diameter 15.8 cm

Franks collection, F.896 +

This plate shows a Chinese landscape scene of pavilions surrounded
by trees by a lake, with a man crossing a small bridge in the
foreground. It has a wide diaper border and an armorial crest and
coat of arms on the rim.

The arms have been identified as belonging to the English family with
the surname King. The service may have been commissioned by Lt.
General Sir Henry King K.C.B. who died in 1839 (Howard, 1974, p.
738).

This and similar blue - and - white landscape designs were among the
most popular Chinese designs in the West and were much copied by
English ceramic manufactories throughout the 19th century. The
Chinese prototypes often included willows, which gave rise to the
name 'willow pattern' for this general type of design.

清　靑花描金英國徽章紋盤

Blue - and - white plate with gilding, with an English coat of arms

114. 清　紅彩愛爾蘭徽章紋盤

直徑16公分

法蘭克收藏

盤子描繪著濃密的花卉紋，此風格在十八世紀盛行於美國。
盤上施湯姆斯・耐斯比之徽章紋頂飾。耐斯比陸軍上校爲凱
文郡里莫爾人，死於1820年。盤上尚有法文箴言：「我將擁
護它」。

114　Red - painted dish with an Irish coat of arms

Qing dynasty, c. 1800 - 1820

Diameter 16 cm

Franks collection, F.1423.

The small dish has a concave rim and is painted in iron - red with
four sprays of flowers tied with emblems and a broad border of
shaped diaper panels centred on butterflies. An armorial crest in gold
and black has been added in the centre, in form of an arm holding a
truncheon, enclosed by a broad gold belt inscribed with the French
motto 'JE LE MAINTIENDRAI' (I will maintain it).

This service was probably made for Thomas Nesbitt of Lismore,
County Cavan, Ireland, a Colonel in the army and Member of
Parliament, who died in 1820 (Howard, 1974, p. 691). Replacements
for this service were made by the Spode manufactory in England (*ibid.*).

The flower - spray and border design is generally referred to as
Fitzhugh pattern after a service ordered c. 1780 by Thomas Fitzhugh,
a later Director of the British East India Company (see *ibid.*, p. 52
top left for a dish from the original service). The pattern became
particularly popular in America in the early 19th century and
examples exist in different colours (see Howard and Ayers, 1978, vol.
II, pls. 508, 516, 528).

清　紅彩愛爾蘭徽章紋盤
Red - painted dish with an Irish coat of arms

歐洲（英國以外）貴族餐具

Tableware for the non-English Nobility

（cat.nos. 115 - 140）

115. 清　粉彩蘇格蘭徽章紋盤

直徑38.3公分

巴西爾‧伊耳尼底斯夫人遺贈

此盤是為詹姆斯‧格蘭爵士（1679－1747）所訂製的，上有
其家訓「堅定不移」，以及蘇格蘭地名「克雷‧艾倫希」。
徽章採自於送至中國的徽章紋藏書票。

115 *Famille rose* serving dish with a Scottish coat of arms

Qing dynasty, c. 1725 - 35

Diameter 38.3 cm

Hon. Mrs. Basil Ionides Bequest, 1963.4-22.16

This magnificent colourful serving dish bears a coat of arms with a
scarlet shield with three gold crowns and on the left-hand side a
badge with a lion, supporters in the form of two semi - naked men
with clubs wearing leafy crowns and skirts, a helmet above, a crest of
a burning hill superscribed 'CRAIG ELACHIE', and the motto
'STAND FAST' below. The cavetto is decorated with diaper *en
grisaille* enclosing twin beribboned emblems, and well - painted flower
sprays are surrounding the centre as well as the rim where the crest is
repeated.

The armorial device in the centre belongs to the Scottish Grant family.
The service to which this large dish belonged was commissioned by
Sir James Grant (1679 - 1747; Howard, 1974, p. 242). 'CRAIG
ELACHIE' is a place in Scotland overlooking the Spey River at
Aviemore where the Grant family traditionally assembled in times of
crisis and this is symbolized by the family crest (*ibid.*).

清　粉彩蘇格蘭徽章紋盤
Famille rose serving dish with a Scottish coat of arms

116. 清　彩瓷蘇格蘭徽章紋多角盤

直徑23.4公分

法蘭克收藏

徽章紋上有三個半獅半鷹怪獸之首以及一皇冠，其上有拉丁
箴言：「聰明如蛇，溫馴如鴿」。其下是一裸體人像，以鐵
鏈繫在徽章上，徽章紋屬於羅伯森家族。

116 *Famille rose* plate with a Scottish coat of arms

Qing dynasty, c. 1784 - 90

Diameter 23.4 cm

Franks collection, F.1417

The coat of arms bears three griffins' heads and has a helmet with
plumes above, a crest in form of an arm holding up a coronet and the
Latin motto 'VIRTUTIS GLORIA MERCES' (glory is the reward of
valour). It is flanked by a serpent and a brown dove, with the motto
'WISE AS THE SERPEWT (sic) HARMLISS (sic) AS THE DOVE'.
Below is a naked figure chained to the coat of arms. The rim border
consists of bamboo stems and roses, entwined with a garland.

The arms belong to the Scottish Robertson family of Strowan (see
Howard, 1974, p. 391). The service to which this dish belonged may
have been made for Colonel Alexander Robertson who received the
family property back in 1784, after it had been annexed by the Crown
in 1745 (Howard and Ayers, vol. II, p. 419). The chained figure
below the arms represents a naked prisoner and has been explained
by Howard and Ayers (*ibid.*) as a reference to the arrest of the
murderers of King James I of Scotland by the Chief of the Clan,
Robert, in 1451. A coffee pot from a different service, made for the
same family earlier in the century, is in the Mottahedeh collection
(*ibid.*, pl. 418).

清　彩瓷蘇格蘭徽章紋多角盤
Famille rose plate with a Scottish coat of arms

117. 清　彩瓷蘇格蘭紋咖啡杯

高7公分

法蘭克收藏

徽章紋之頂飾是一裸像緊握著匕首，旁側則由一羣身著蘇格蘭格子呢裙及外套的蘇格蘭人支撐著。箴言寫著「我將保衛」及蘇格蘭湖「Loch Sloy」之名。此盤可能是爲法蘭西斯・麥克法蘭所製。他遊遍歐洲，足跡遍及各處，也曾到過西印度羣島（參見其藏書字，圖117a）。

fig. 117a

117　*Famille rose* coffee cup with a Scottish coat of arms

Qing dynasty, c. 1780 - 90

Height 7 cm

Franks collection, F.639

This coffee cup with blue enamel band and gold - and - blue spearhead border at the rim is decorated with a coat of arms with four red roses separated by a diagonal red cross, with a crest in form of a naked figure holding a dagger in his right hand. The supporters on either side are two Highlanders (men from the Scottish Highlands) wearing green tartan kilts, jackets and the traditional fur - covered pouches called sporrans, and having their swords drawn. Above the arms is the motto 'THIS I'LL DEFEND', and below the place name 'LOCH SLOY'.

The arms have been identified as belonging to the Scottish family of Macfarlane. 'LOCH SLOY' is the name of a lake in Strathclyde, Scotland. This service was probably made for Francis Macfarlane, head of the Macfarlane family in Britain, who had travelled widely in Europe and the West Indies (Howard, 1974, p. 743). The design was copied from a book plate such as the one illustrated, which is also in the British Museum (fig. 117 a; P+D Franks 19198).

清　彩瓷蘇格蘭紋咖啡杯
Famille rose coffee cup with a Scottish coat of arms

118. 清　彩瓷蘇格蘭徽章紋盤

直徑24.5公分

法蘭克收藏

盤中央盾徽含有一漂浮在水面上的方舟，有一隻鴿子嘴上叼著一根橄欖樹枝，並且有一拉丁文箴言：「歡欣鼓舞」。此徽章紋屬於蘇格蘭裘利家族，而那句拉丁文箴言是根據其家族名字之諧音雙關語而來的，盤緣飾以有綠色枝梗的小藍花，源自十八世紀法國的瓷器。

118 *Famille rose* **plate with a Scottish coat of arms**

Qing dynasty, c. 1780 - 90

Diameter 24.5 cm

Franks collection, F.761 ╈

The central shield contains an ark floating on water with a dove on top holding an olive branch in its beak, and surrounded by three flowers; it is enclosed by floral garlands. The rim bears a crest in form of a bird with the Latin motto 'LAETARE' (to rejoice) on a band above and small strewn blue flowers with green stems and leaves.

The arms have been identified as belonging to the Scottish family Jolly (Howard, 1974, p. 645). The motto is a pun on the family name. The ark and dove in the shield refer to the Biblical story of God's safe deliverance of a selection of men, animals and birds from flooding which destroyed the rest of the world. The border of strewn flowers derives from 18th-century French porcelain.

清　彩瓷蘇格蘭徽章紋盤
Famille rose plate with a Scottish coat of arms

119. 清　粉彩茶杯及托盤

（杯）高4公分　（托盤）直徑11.6公分

法蘭克收藏

可能是爲蘇格蘭市場而製造。盤中央的裝飾十分特別；描繪
一艘船，船上靠近甲板的低層有一排突出的槍。最上面支撐
淡紅色皇冠的是羅馬神話中的海神Neptune，手裏拿著一個
三叉戟，並有一隻猴子拿著劍。金色縮寫字母據說是詹姆斯·
愛德華·斯圖亞特（1688－1766）──「老僭王」，他聲稱
自己是英國及蘇格蘭王朝的繼任者，生前流亡於法國。

119 *Famille rose* cup and saucer, perhaps made for the Scottish market

Qing dynasty, c. 1750 - 60

Height (cup) 4 cm, diameter (saucer) 11.6 cm

Franks collection, F. 894 +

The tea cup and saucer show the stern of a battleship with a row of guns which protrude from under pink flaps on the lower deck. Supporting a pink crown above, which rests on a heart pierced with two golden arrows, are Neptune, the Roman god of the sea, with a trident and wearing a crown, and a monkey with a sword. In the centre is an elaborately entwined gold monogram, and the rim border is a scrolling grape vine.

The monogram is very difficult to decipher but the letters it contains have been interpreted as H, M, K, J and F and are taken to stand for the words 'His Majesty King James in France' (Howard, 1974, p. 274). This may refer to James Stuart (1688 - 1766), 'the Old Pretender', a claimant to the throne of England and Scotland who was living in exile in France and whose supporters rebelled in 1745. This service may have been ordered by a supporter of James Stuart, and it is believed that the design has deliberately been left obscure since open support for him would have been dangerous.

清　粉彩茶杯及托盤

Famille rose cup and saucer, perhaps made for the
Scottish market

120. 清　彩瓷丹麥皇室名諱托盤

直徑13公分

法蘭克收藏

此托盤是用來端茶壺的，上面繪有二個盾徽，其一是丹麥女皇裘利安娜・瑪麗亞的肖像，另外一個是其名諱縮寫字母捲曲成紋，兩側有支撐物，其上戴有皇冠。瑪麗亞是丹麥國王菲特烈五世(在位期間為1746－1766)之妻，於1752年成婚。

120　*Famille rose* teapot stand with a royal Danish monogram

Qing dynasty, c. 1752 - 70

Diameter 13 cm

Franks collection, F.759 ✛

This shaped hexafoil tray is painted with two shields in the centre, one containing a portrait of a lady in a low - cut dress, with a rose at her bosom and another in her hair, the other entwined initials. These shields are flanked by horns - of - plenty, surmounted by a crown and have as supporters Neptune, the Roman god of the sea, with a trident and a fish on the left, and another deity on the right, both standing on a green ground among flowers. The angular sides are painted with a border of diaper and leaf motifs with a peacock on top *en grisaille*, interrupted by a large schooner flying a red flag with white cross.

The portrait depicts Queen Juliana Maria, wife of King Frederick V of Denmark (r. 1746 - 66), whom he married in 1752; the initials are probably 'J M'. The ship carries the Danish flag. Another dish of this service is in the Metropolitan Museum of Art, New York (Hervouet and Bruneau, 1986, no. 14.25); for another service made for Juliana Maria, see the following plate (cat.no. 121); compare also a dish with related design, dated to 1763, illustrated below (cat. no. 138).

Trays of this form were used as supports for teapots.

清　彩瓷丹麥皇室名諱托盤

Famille rose teapot stand with a royal Danish monogram

121. 清　黑釉描金丹麥皇室徽章紋八角盤

直徑24公分

法蘭克收藏

八角盤緣描金，並飾大裘利安娜·瑪麗亞之名字及丹麥皇族
之徽章紋，盤中央描繪丹麥王菲特烈五世(1746－1766在位)
的人像，瑪麗亞爲其第二任妻子，丹麥王死後由她統治丹麥
直到1784年。

121　*Grisaille* - and - gold painted plate with the royal arms of Denmark

Qing dynasty, c. 1766 - 84

Diameter 24 cm

Franks collection, F.612

The octagonal plate is painted with a central medallion depicting an equestrian statue enclosed within a laurel wreath, and the rim is covered in gold, decorated with bands of laurel and florets, inscribed 'IULIANA MARIA', and bears a small crowned coat of arms at the bottom, reserved in the gold.

This unusual, richly gilded plate is believed to show a statue of the Danish King Frederick V (r. 1746 - 66), and is inscribed with the name of his wife, who is depicted on the teapot stand above (cat.no. 120). Juliana Maria was Frederick's second wife, who ruled Denmark after his death until 1784, and this plate was probably commissioned during that time.

清　黑釉描金丹麥皇室徽章紋八角盤
Grisaille - and - gold painted plate with the royal arms of Denmark

122. 清　藍釉瑞典皇室徽章紋盤

長29公分

艾文斯女士捐贈

此橢圓形盤子的中央描繪徽章紋：有三頂皇冠、瑞典官方標
幟，由眾相圍繞著皇冠以及寫有瑞典古堡的名字，此盤爲
1766年瑞典東印度公司主管舉行的一場儀式中使用的。

122　Blue - and - white serving dish with the royal arms of Sweden

Qing dynasty, c. 1774 - 6

Length 29 cm

Given by Lady Evans, 1921.7 - 12.1

The oval serving dish shows in the centre an underglaze-blue roundel
with three golden crowns, surrounded by a golden laurel wreath and
by overall small blue crowns, with a golden rim border and the
inscription 'GRIPSHOLM' on the rim.

The central medallion shows the royal arms of Sweden, and the
inscription gives the name of a Swedish royal castle near Stockholm
on lake Mälav. The sevice is known to have been ordered by the
Swedish East India Company and carried by the ship *Terra Nova*,
which anchored in Gothenburg in 1776. The service is first mentioned
in inventories of 1781, when it consisted of over 700 pieces, and is
reported to have cost 600 taels (Wirgin, 1979, p. 218). Of the several
royal Swedish services made in China, this was by far the largest.
Large parts of the service are still preserved at Gripsholm Castle
today (*ibid.*, pl. 5).

清　藍釉瑞典皇室徽章紋盤
Blue - and - white serving dish with the royal arms of Sweden

123. 清　五彩俄羅斯皇室徽章紋盤

直徑23公分

巴西爾·伊耳尼底斯夫人遺贈

此盤上戴著皇冠的雙頭鷹，象徵俄國徽章之鳥，握著象徵王
權的寶杖及寶珠，以及聖喬治之盾牌。此盤據信爲俄羅斯女皇
伊莉沙白時代所製作。圖案仿自一枚俄國銀幣（參見123a）。

fig. 123a

123　Polychrome painted plate with the imperial arms of Russia

Qing dynasty, c. 1745 - 60

Diameter 23 cm

Hon. Mrs. Basil Ionides Bequest, 1963.4 - 22.17

The plate is painted in red, black and gold with details in blue enamel with a crowned double - headed eagle wearing a chain and holding a sceptre and an orb, with a crown between the two heads and a red shield on its body, depicting a mounted St. George fighting the dragon. The well and rim of the dish are decorated with gilt scrollwork and a shaped diaper border with pendant florets.

This dish forms part of a service believed to have been made for the Russian Empress Elizabeth (r. 1741 - 62). The double eagle on the dish is a correct representation of the Russian imperial arms and was probably copied from a Russian silver rouble. Such roubles were minted throughout Elizabeth's reign; an example in the British Museum, dated 1742, is illustrated for comparison (fig. 123 a; C + M Banks 994). The gilt borders are related to patterns introduced by the German porcelain manufactory at Meissen.

Only plates are known from this service; several of them are preserved in the Hermitage, St. Petersburg, Russia (Arapova, 1992, pl. 5); a pair is in the Metropolitan Museum of Art, New York (Le Corbeiller, 1974, pl. 47), others are in private collections. For an earlier Chinese piece bearing the Russian imperial arms, compare cat. no. 12; and a plate from a later service is in the Mottahedeh collection (Howard and Ayers, 1978, vol. II, pl. 461).

276

清　五彩俄羅斯皇室徽章紋盤
Polychrome painted plate with the imperial arms of Russia

124. 清　彩瓷普魯士皇室徽章紋盤二件

（橢圓盤）長47公分，（盤）直徑23.2公分

法蘭克收藏

聖查理斯·渥克遺贈

兩件盤子皆繪有菲特烈大帝的普魯士皇家徽章紋。
兩側由葉片覆蓋著以支撐裏頭有毛斗篷，以及一隻普魯士老鷹在頂上。橢圓形大盤在歐洲加繪紅色簾幕以掩飾瑕疵。此盤據信在1755年左右，當船運往德國途中觸礁時遭受損害，因此這組盤子就沒有獻給國王，而在稍加修飾後轉賣給市場。

124 *Famille rose* **serving dish and plate with the royal arms of Prussia**

Qing dynasty, c. 1750 - 55

Length（oval dish）47 cm, diameter（plate）23.2 cm

Franks collection, F.606 ＋

Rev. Charles Walker Bequest, F.738 ＋（1887.12 - 18.35）

The two pieces come from the same service and are painted with a highly complicated coat of arms, which consists of forty shields, surmounted by a helmet and plumes and a royal crown, adorned with a large chain with a pendant cross. It is flanked by two supporters in form of 'wild men' with long beards and clad only in leaves, holding tall standards with black and red eagles, respectively, and standing on a pedestal with the German motto 'GOTT MIT UNS' (god with us). The whole is enveloped in an ermine - lined purple mantle which forms a crowned canopy with an eagle emblem on top with long trailing tassels. Another eagle appears on the rim of the dish, interrupting a golden rim border.

The elaborate arms are the Prussian Royal arms of Frederick II, the Great (r. 1740 - 86), their forty shields representing historical connections of the royal house. The large chain is that of the Order of the Black Eagle, adorned with a Maltese Cross.

These two pieces belong to a large service of which many items in various shapes are preserved. It is believed to have been ordered by the Prussian Asiatic Company as a gift for Frederick II, King of Prussia. He had founded the Company, which was based in the German North Sea port of Emden, in 1750, but it lasted only until 1757. In 1755 one of the four ships sailing for the Company, the *Prinz von Preussen*, ran aground shortly before her arrival home. It is believed that this ship carried this service, and since the porcelain was damaged in the accident, it could not be presented to the King, but the rescued pieces were repaired and sold on the market instead.

The oval serving dish in the British Museum has an old breakage and repair. To hide the damage, a theatrical curtain in matching red pigment with gilt details has been painted on cold (and has partly flaked off). It is tempting to speculate that this overpainting may have been done in Germany at the time of its recovery from the sea, in order to make the dish saleable.

About 200 pieces of this service were recorded before the War; 153 pieces were collected in the Hohenzollernmuseum alone, in the late 19th century (Berlin, 1973, pp. 149 - 50). A sweet - meat set is in Schloss Charlottenburg, Berlin (*ibid.*, no. C 11); a salt is in the Kunstgewerbemuseum, Berlin (mentioned *ibid.*, p. 149); a tureen and an ice - pail or jardiniere are in Huis Doorn, Doorn, Netherlands (Lunsingh Scheurleer, 1966, pl. 150); and another tureen, further dinner and soup plates and a punch bowl are recorded (Sotheby's Monaco, 22nd June 1987, lot 1693).

清　彩瓷普魯士皇室徽章紋盤二件

Famille rose serving dish and plate with the royal arms of Prussia

125. 清　彩瓷阿姆斯特丹市徽章紋盤

直徑22.7公分

法蘭克收藏

盤中央圓形徽章綴滿了牡丹以及許多花卉，周遭圍繞著五瓣牡丹、菊花、玫瑰以及其他花卉的圖案，背景飾以金色菱形紋。最上面的圖案是阿姆斯特丹市徽，其上有冠冕，兩側由獅子支撐。盤子背面繪有鮮紅色琺瑯彩，具有雍正時期以來之瓷器特色。

125 *Famille rose* soup plate with the arms of a Dutch city

Qing dynasty, c. 1725 - 35

Diameter 22.7 cm

Franks collection, F.712 +

This soup plate is decorated with a central peony-spray medallion surrounded by five shaped panels enclosing sprays of peony, chrysanthemum, rose and other flowers, one of them with a coat of arms flanked by two lions and surmounted by a coronet, all reserved on a ground of golden Y - diaper. The reverse of the dish is covered with ruby - pink enamel.

The coat of arms is that of the city of Amsterdam, Netherlands; the lions are comically depicted, with almost human faces. The dish is unusual in its well - painted flower designs and particularly in having a ruby - pink enamelled reverse . Both features are characteristic of porcelains of the Yongzheng period (1723 - 35), and the enamelled reverse in particular is very seldom found on armorial wares.

Another dish of this design is in the Rijksmuseum, Amsterdam, Netherlands (Lunsingh Scheurleer, 1966, pl. 259).

清　彩瓷阿姆斯特丹市徽章紋盤

Famille rose soup plate with the arms of a Dutch city

126. 清 彩瓷荷蘭徽章紋盤

直徑23公分

法蘭克收藏

此徽章紋屬於阿姆斯特丹的史諾克家族，與家族姓氏相同的一條魚做爲象徵之物。洛可可風格的貝殼形盤緣、豐饒角以及格子紋的裝飾都十分特殊，可能是源自於荷蘭設計圖。另一件施中國茶、薑、水果栽培圖等紋飾的青花瓷，也同樣視爲特殊的紋飾之一。

126 *Famille rose* plate with a Dutch coat of arms

Qing dynasty, c. 1736 - 50

Diameter 23 cm

Franks collection, F.858 +

The dinner plate has a central coat of arms with two golden fish between three golden stars with elaborate mantling and a crest of a begging dog beneath an arc of golden stars. The rim border is composed of large - scale horns, shells, scrolls and lattice - work panels, all executed in *famille rose* enamels.

The arms belong to the Amsterdam-based Snoek family and their emblem is a fish which in Dutch bears the same name. The rococo rim border is unusual and probably derives from a Dutch design. It is found on two other services, one with designs illustrating the cultivation and manufacturing processes of tea, ginger and fruits (see cat.no. 37) and the other painted with a central scene of cockerels (see, for example, a plate in the China Trade Museum, Milton, Massachusetts, U.S.A.; Milton, 1982, no. 17).

Other pieces from this dinner service include a plate in the Metropolitan Museum of Art, New York (Phillips, 1956, pl. 5); and another in the Mottahedeh collection (Howard and Ayers, 1978, vol. II, pl. 393), which also contains a 19th-century Japanese plate with the same arms but otherwise differently decorated, possibly in Holland (*ibid.*, pl. 394)

清　彩瓷荷蘭徽章紋盤

Famille rose plate with a Dutch coat of arms

127. 清　青花琺瑯彩荷蘭徽章紋盤

直徑28公分

聖查理斯・渥克遺贈

盤凹處施以鈷藍彩菱形滾邊，一處留白，可能是爲徽章紋預留的位子。徽章紋是一紅色松鼠吃著橡果，靠著金色的背景，其上有金色冠冕。圖案重複二次，一次在盤中央，另一個在盤緣，但是鈷藍的留白處卻始終沒有使用。此徽章紋據考證爲希區德門（1692－1764）所有，他曾服務於荷蘭東印度公司，可能在1745年將此盤帶回Groningen。

127 Blue - and - white plate with an enamelled Dutch coat of arms

Qing dynasty, c. 1740 - 45

Diameter 28 cm

Rev. Charles Walker Bequest, F.878 ＋（1887.12-18.45）

The armorial design which appears in the centre of this plate and again on the rim is a red squirrel holding a green acorn, on a golden background, surrounded by golden scrollwork and with a coronet above. The well and rim are exquisitely painted in underglaze cobalt blue with diaper borders in minute strokes. In one place the cobalt pigment was accidentally wiped off, perhaps when the dish was picked up for glazing; and at the rim a roundel was deliberately left blank for the coat of arms. On the reverse are three well-painted butterflies and flower sprays in underglaze blue.

This coat of arms has been attributed to the Dutchman A.J. Sichterman (1692 - 1764) who came from Groningen, worked for the Dutch East India Company and was director in Bengal from 1731 to 1740. It has been suggested that the service to which this plate belonged was brought back to Holland by Sichterman on his return to Groningen as part of his repatriation cargo allowance in 1745 (Jörg, 1982, pp. 143 - 4 and footnote 197).

Other pieces from this service include a bowl in the Musée Guimet, Paris, France (Beurdeley, 1962, no. 191), and a vase and cover in the Mottahedeh collection (Howard and Ayers, 1978, vol.II, no. 399). These arms also exist on a *famille rose* covered vase and beaker in the Groningen Museum, Netherlands (Lunsingh Scheurleer, 1974, nos. 101 and 102).

284

清　青花琺瑯彩荷蘭徽章紋盤

Blue - and - white plate with an enamelled Dutch coat of arms

128. 清 彩瓷荷蘭皇室徽章紋盤

直徑16.2公分

法蘭克收藏

此盤簡單描繪皇冠下二個徽章，兩側由一個半裸男子及一頭獅子支撐。徽章紋屬於荷蘭王子威廉五世（1748－1806）及其妻普魯士公主威荷米娜所有。1791年荷蘭駐廣東窰廠主任回國時，獻給威荷米娜公主。

128 *Famille rose* **plate with the royal arms of Holland**

Qing dynasty, c. 1790 - 91

Diameter 16.2 cm

Franks collection, F.902 +

The small plate is simply decorated with two armorial shields under a royal crown, one with a quartered coat of arms supported by a crowned lion, the other with a crowned eagle holding sceptre and sword, supported by a leaf - clad man with a club. Both shields and supporters rest on a purple cloud - like ground. The rim is decorated with a golden scroll border.

The arms belong to Prince William V of Holland (1748 - 1806) and his wife, Princess Wilhelmina of Prussia (1751 - 1820). The service to which this plate belonged was ordered by Ulrich Gualtherus Hemmingson, a director of the Dutch factory at Canton, and presented to Princess Wilhelmina, upon his return to Holland in 1791 (Jörg, 1982, p. 131).

The design appears on a portrait of Princess Wilhelmina, engraved by Vinkeles (1741 - 1816) after P.C. Haag (1737 - 1812), illustrated by Lunsingh Scheurleer (1966, pl. 155). Various tureens, sauceboats, salts and a mustard pot and spoon of this service are preserved, some in the collection of H.M. the Queen of the Netherlands (Jörg, 1982, pl. 52), others in the Paleis Noordeinde, Den Haag, Netherlands (Lunsingh Scheurleer, 1966, pls. 154 and 156).

清　彩瓷荷蘭皇室徽章紋盤

Famille rose plate with the royal arms of Holland

129. 清　五彩布倫本徽章紋大盤

直徑22.5公分

法蘭克收藏

金碧輝煌，以金、銀描繪的盤子，上有二個徽章，兩隻獵犬立於徽章紋旁，盤凹處飾以菱形滾邊，盤緣飾以葉形紋飾。盤緣有四處插入圖案，其中三處的徽章紋和盤心相同，另一處則是不同之徽章。主要的徽章屬於比斯崔特家族。另一件盤緣下面之徽章是隸屬於查理斯布恩，他在1716～1720年間曾任孟賈的總督，此徽章紋配飾在此盤是不小心而犯的錯誤。

129　Polychrome painted dish with a coat of arms of Brabant

Qing dynasty, c. 1723 - 35

Diameter 22.5 cm

Franks collection, F.1410

This richly gilded and silvered plate shows two coats of arms in an elaborate gilt *rocaille* surround, flanked by two hounds, surmounted by a helmet with silver and blue plumes, and with a coronet above and a lion crest. The welt is painted with a golden diaper border with blue florets and floral panels, and the rim with a border of shell and arabesque motifs, hung with rose - pink banners, and interrupted in four places by armorial shields; those on either side and a lozenge - shaped shield at the top are repeating the arms from the centre. At the bottom is a different coat of arms with a helmet, surrounded by red plumes and with two birds above.

The main coats of arms belong to the families of de la Bistrate of Anvers in Brabant, modern Belgium, and Proli of Milan and Brabant. The coat of arms at the bottom of the rim, however, is totally unconnected and belongs to Charles Boone, Governor of Bombay from 1716 - 20, for whom other services had been made in China. It was apparently added to this service by mistake (Howard, 1974, pp. 40 - 41). Correctly painted plates of this design without the additional arms are also known, for example in the Mottahedeh collection (Howard and Ayers, 1978, vol. II, pl. 459).

The unusual colour scheme as well as the decoration of cavetto and rim appear to follow European models.

清　五彩布倫本徽章紋大盤
Polychrome painted dish with a coat of arms of Brabant

130. 清　彩瓷法國徽章紋茶壺

高12公分　長19公分

法蘭克收藏

此件，施艾伯特・修尼斯公爵（1 76－1744）之徽章紋，徽章四周圍繞著描述聖靈之字樣。公爵於1724年獲得此一徽章。採用多種彩釉，並附加些微玫瑰紅，製於清雍正年間，器形源自歐洲銀器。

130 *Famille rose* teapot with a French coat of arms

Qing dynasty, c. 1724 - 25
Height 12 cm, width 19 cm
Franks collection, F.808 +

The teapot has a round squat body and a splayed foot, a spout with a dragon's head and leaf terminal, and a handle with scrolling end, probably representing the dragon's tail; the cover is surmounted by a lion knob. On one side is an armorial design with two oval shields in a decorative ring, surrounded by a chain of *fleurs - de - lis* with a medal, and with a coronet above, on a background of a blue ermine - lined cloak. On the other side are Chinese motifs such as pine, prunus, bamboo, a *ruyi* sceptre, a musical instrument and a fan. Between these designs and on the cover are different plants, baskets of fruit and various emblems, and a red - and - gold diaper border encircles the rim. The design is painted almost exclusively in colours of the *famille verte* with minimal additions of rose-pink.

The French coat of arms on this teapot has been identified as d'Ailly impaling Beaumanoir, and belongs to Louis Auguste Albert d'Ailly, Duc de Chaulnes (1676 - 1744). The armorial design is surrounded by the collar of the 'Ordre du Saint Esprit' which the Duke received in 1724 (Hobson, 1908, p. 183). The service to which this teapot belonged may have been made for this event or soon after, since this colour scheme went out of fashion early in the Yongzheng period (1723 - 35) and was replaced by a proper *famille rose* palette with rose - pink dominating over iron-red.

The shape of this teapot derives from European silverware. The cover is fastened to the spout and the handle with a silver chain, added in Europe.

清　彩瓷法國徽章紋茶壺

Famille rose teapot with a French coat of arms

131. 清　青花法國徽章紋盤二件

直徑24公分

法蘭克收藏

此二件八角盤十分相似，皆繪有荷葉圖樣配置在荷花紋旁，
圍繞著盤中央的徽章紋。其中一件，繪有一徽章，兩側立有
半獅半鷹之怪獸，上有一冠冕。另一件繪有同樣的徽章紋，
旁邊伴有另一徽章，此二件八角盤可能皆爲法國巴黎的達吾
伯爵家族所製作。可能是達吾伯爵本人之婚禮前後訂購的，
或是親戚爲其所訂購。

131 Two blue - and - white plates with French coats of arms

Qing dynasty, c. 1745 - 55

Diameter 24 cm

Franks collection, F.841 +

The two octagonal plates are very similarly painted with lotus - spray panels arranged in the shape of a lotus flower around an armorial device in the centre. One of the plates shows a single coat of arms flanked by two griffins under a coronet; the other shows the same coat of arms paired with another.

Both plates were probably made for the family of the French Comte Davous of Paris, and were ordered either by the same man before and after his marriage, or by a father and son, or two brothers (Howard and Ayers, 1978, vol. II, p. 444). Although the two plates were probably not painted by the same hand, they are so similar in material and style, that a difference in date cannot be detected, and they may well have been ordered at the same time. A similar pair is in the Mottahedeh collection (*ibid.*, pl. 450).

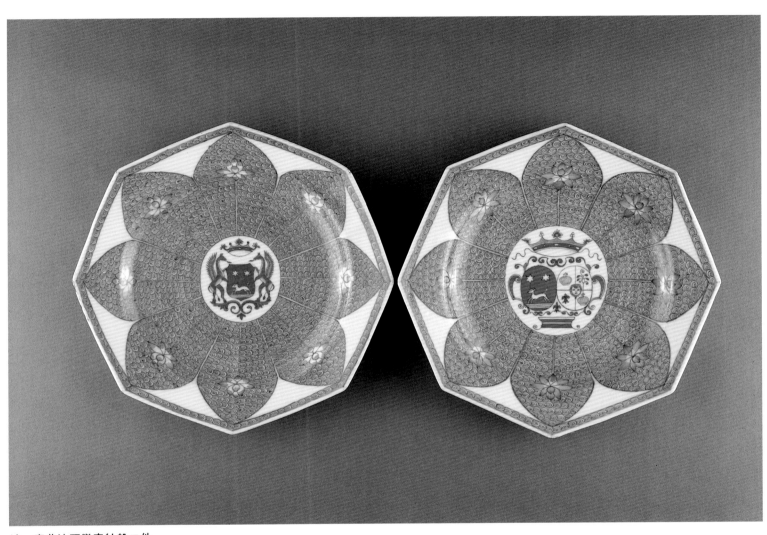

清　青花法國徽章紋盤二件

Two blue - and - white plates with French coats of arms

132. 清　粉彩法國徽章紋咖啡杯、茶杯及托盤

（咖啡杯）高 8 公分　（茶杯）高 5 公分　（托盤）直徑13.5公分

法蘭克收藏

紋章旁圍繞著繁盛的羽飾，其下寫有法國字「LE GRAND」（偉大），邊緣以貝殼紋及相關紋飾做爲裝飾。

132 *Famille rose* beaker, cup and saucer with a French coat of arms

Qing dynasty, c. 1740 - 50

Height (beaker) 8 cm, (cup) 5 cm, diameter (saucer) 13.5 cm

Franks collection, F.846 ＋, F.846 ＋ A

The beaker is shaped as a deep cup, without a handle, but the smaller cup has an elegant curved handle with small flanges on top. All three pieces of this set are painted in a distinct colour scheme, consisting mainly of light blue, rose-pink and white enamel, with a quartered coat of arms under a helmet with lavish　blue-and- white　plumes, with a bird as crest and a ribbon inscribed 'LE GRAND' below. The rim border consists of decorative shells, feathers and similar motifs.

The French family Le Grand had branches particularly in Normandy. The rim border is reminiscent of European - inspired shell borders such as those on a blue - and - white and an enamelled service, examples of which are illustrated above (cat.nos. 37 and 126).

清　粉彩法國徽章紋咖啡杯、茶杯及托盤

Famille rose beaker, cup and saucer with

a French coat of arms

133. 清　彩瓷葡萄牙徽章紋船形盛醬器

長18.5公分

聖查理斯・渥克遺贈

此一沈重的扭轉式把手船形瓷器，正面綠地繪滿葉紋，兩側
開光繪有中國式風景，口緣下方是葡萄牙奧伯托主教(1789-
1814)之徽章紋。

133 *Famille rose* **sauceboat with a Portuguese coat of arms**

Qing dynasty, c. 1800 - 1814

Length 18.5 cm

Rev. Charles Walker Bequest, F.852 ＋ (1887.12 - 18.20)

The heavily potted sauceboat has a curved handle, made of two twisted strands of clay with applied flower - shaped terminals, and is painted with a lobed panel under the spout enclosing a coat of arms, and two smaller panels with chinoiserie scenes on either side, with decorative borders in rose - pink around the rim and below, all on a green enamel ground with formal golden leaf sprays.

This sauceboat formed part of a dinner service commissioned by D. Frei Antonio de Sao Jose de Castro, Bishop of Oporto, Portugal, from 1789 to 1814. Other pieces of this richly decorated and unusually coloured service are in the Henry Francis du Pont Winterthur Museum, U.S.A. (Palmer, 1976, pl. 11); another sauceboat is in the Museu Nacional de Arte Antiga, Lisbon, Portugal (Pinto de Matos, 1993, p. 55 left).

The commission of this service reflects the continued interest in Chinese porcelain by Portuguese customers, long after the Portuguese had ceased to be the foremost European trading power in the Far East.

清　彩瓷葡萄牙徽章紋船形盛醬器

Famille rose sauceboat with a Portuguese coat of arms

134. 清　粉彩歐洲徽章紋茶杯、咖啡杯及托盤

（咖啡杯）高6.1公分　（茶杯）高3.2公分　（托盤）直徑11.6公分

法蘭克收藏

這件歐式徽章紋圖案，呈現十朵紅玫瑰靠在銀色盾牌上，頂
飾一隻狗，嘴裏叼著一朵玫瑰。此徽章隸屬於誰，尚未可考。
在十八世紀，杯子和托盤一組，通常是以一個托盤配茶杯及
咖啡杯的成套方式銷售。

134 *Famille rose* **tea cup, coffee cup and saucer with a
European coat of arms**

Qing dynasty, c. 1723 - 35

Height (coffee cup) 6.1 cm, (tea cup) 3.2 cm, diameter (saucer)
11.6 cm

Franks collection, F.609

The tea cup, coffee cup and saucer are decorated with a coat of arms
with a silver shield with ten red roses arranged in rows, and a crest of
a dog with a red rose in its mouth, and with panels of fruit and floral
sprays, surrounded by pink and pale blue diaper-work. The cups have
spearhead rim borders inside and the tea cup a small orchid at the
bottom. The set is exquisitely painted, the fruit and flower sprays in
the style characteristic of porcelain from the Yongzheng period (1723-35).
Silver, which has in the course of time tarnished to a silvery black,
was rarely used on later export porcelain.

The coat of arms is still unidentified (Howard, 1974, p.231). Sets of
cups and saucers were generally sold in this way in the 18th century,
with one saucer serving both cups.

清　粉彩歐洲徽章紋茶杯、咖啡杯及托盤
Famille rose tea cup, coffee cup and saucer with a
European coat of arms

135. 清　粉彩字母縮寫紋茶罐

高11公分

法蘭克收藏

此方形茶罐之兩面皆有姓名縮寫，由「C」、「J」兩字母的
紋飾纏繞，由一月桂冠及皇冠所包圍。茶罐肩部繪有花卉渦
形紋及菱形紋飾。這樣的蓋罐在歐洲是用來裝茶葉。

135 *Famille rose* tea caddy with a monogram

Qing dynasty, c. 1730 - 40

Height 11 cm

Franks collection, F.1424

The vessel is rectangular in section, with flat front and reverse and
barbed sides, and has a matching angular cover. Both front and
reverse are painted with entwined initials, perhaps 'C' and 'J', on an
oval blue medallion, enclosed by a laurel wreath and surmounted by
a coronet, and at the sides the initials are repeated on a paler blue
shield, all on a ground of golden Y - diaper. The upper corners and
the top of the cover are painted with flower scrolls, the top of the
shoulder and sides of the cover with diaper designs.

Tea caddies were in Europe used for keeping tea leaves and were
made both of silver and porcelain. The Western prototypes came
originally in sets, placed in a fitted container, and were therefore
rectangular in section, for easy storage.

清　粉彩字母縮寫紋茶罐
Famille rose tea caddy with a monogram

136. 清　粉彩歐洲徽章紋杯及托盤

（杯）高4.5公分　（托盤）直徑12.5公分

法蘭克收藏

此件把手杯及托盤上描繪一組象徵浪漫的戶外風景。例如仕
女的帽子及圍巾、號角、葡萄藤、花環，以及繫在權杖上的
徽章。徽章紋尚未查證屬於那一個家族。設計源自法國瓷器。

136 *Famille rose* **cup and saucer with European coats of arms**

Qing dynasty, c. 1750 - 70

Height（cup）4.5 cm, diameter（saucer）12.5 cm

Franks collection, F.610

This handled cup and saucer are painted with a group of emblems
evoking a romantic outdoor scene, which include a lady's hat and
scarf and a horn under a grape vine, as well as two coats of arms,
one painted on a scroll, the other on an oval medallion, both tied to
a staff and joined by a flower garland. This design is surrounded by
small strewn flower sprays, and the rims have a red toothed border.

The motifs combined on this set are known as 'Trophies' and are
found on French porcelain. The arms have not yet been identified.

清　粉彩歐洲徽章紋杯及托盤
Famille rose cup and saucer with European coats of arms

303

137. 清　彩瓷歐洲徽章紋茶罐

高14公分

聖查理斯·渥克遺贈

此件豐肩多角茶罐，飾以蓓蕾形鈕蓋，描繪二個尚未可考之
徽章紋和皇冠，該款式在歐洲市場非常普遍。

137 *Famille rose* tea caddy with European coats of arms

Qing dynasty, c. 1750 - 70

Height 14 cm

Rev. Charles Walker Bequest, F.819 ＋ （1887.12-18.19）

This tea caddy, of rectangular section, has a somewhat protruding
domed shoulder and a cylindrical neck; a cylindrical cover fits inside
the neck and has a bud - shaped knob. Both front and reverse are
painted with two coats of arms, one depicting a hunt, surrounded by
plumes, with a bow on top and surmounted by a coronet. The sides
show small flower sprays and the shoulder and cover shaped diaper
surrounds. The bud on top is gilded.

The arms on this piece are unidentified. The shape of this tea caddy is
known from both silver and European porcelain, particularly from
Germany, where the cover, however, generally fits over the neck.

清　彩瓷歐洲徽章紋茶罐
Famille rose tea caddy with European coats of arms

138. 清　彩瓷歐洲夫婦名字縮寫紋盤

直徑22.9公分

聖查理斯‧渥克收藏

盤子施黑釉，深褐釉及金彩，二個盾徽裏纏繞著姓名縮寫字
母，上有一皇冠，兩側由手執碩大棍棒的半裸人像支撐，盤
面心形紋有「1763」字樣。歐式風格之盤緣挿有小型琺瑯彩
圓徽。同款式繪有不同姓名縮寫字母者，十分聞名，專爲荷
蘭及丹麥市場製作。

138 Polychrome painted plate with the monograms of a European couple

Qing dynasty, dated 1763

Diameter 22.9 cm

Rev. Charles Walker Bequest, F.891 ＋ （1887.12 - 18.52）

The dish is painted *en grisaille* with sepia and gold with two shields
enclosing entwined initials, supported on large stone pedestals,
surmounted by a coronet and flanked by two supporters in form of
semi - naked, leaf - clad 'wild men' holding large clubs. The date 1763
is inscribed within a heart at the bottom. The rim border consists of
elaborate shaped diaper panels entwined with flowers and leaves,
centred on three peacocks and with a small enamelled medallion at
the bottom, with a dove beneath rays of light, symbolizing the
presence of God.

Several related dishes with different monograms are known, which
were probably made for marriages, all apparently for the Dutch or
Danish markets; dated examples are, however, rare (compare
Howard and Ayers, 1978, vol. II, pp. 398 - 9; and Hervouet and
Bruneau, 1986, no. 14.26). The design is related to that of the teapot
stand made for Queen Juliana Maria of Denmark (cat.no. 120).

清　彩瓷歐洲夫婦名字縮寫紋盤
Polychrome painted plate with the monograms of a
European couple

139. 清　彩瓷姓名縮寫紋杯和托盤

（杯）高4.5公分　（托盤）直徑12公分

法蘭克收藏

杯及托盤上繪有一盾徽，包含著「JCW」的姓名字母縮寫，
上有一皇冠，兩側由天使支撐，並有「1776」字樣。

139 *Famille rose* **cup and saucer with a monogram**

Qing dynasty, dated 1776

Height（cup）4.5 cm, diameter（saucer）12 cm

Franks collection, F.850 ✛

The oval medallion in the centre of the design contains entwined
initials, perhaps 'J C W', enclosed in a rococo surround, with two
loving doves perched on top, two cherubs holding trumpets floating
above with a coronet in the middle, and the date 1776 below. The rest
is decorated with flower sprays and a toothed rim border.

This set was clearly made for a marriage, and related pieces with
initials under a crown flanked by angels, but differently painted, were
already made earlier (compare Hervouet, 1986, nos. 14.43 and 14.44).

清　彩瓷姓名縮寫紋杯和托盤
Famille rose cup and saucer with a monogram

140. 清　彩瓷姓名縮寫紋盤

直徑23.5公分

法蘭克收藏

盤子上繪有一騎著海馬吹奏喇叭的全裸男子，旁邊是纏繞的
縮寫字母紋，上有一皇冠和閃耀的太陽光。盤中央有尚不可考
的徽章紋圖案，如此不對稱構圖，是十分罕見。

140 *Famille rose* plate with a monogram

Qing dynasty, c. 1770 - 90

Diameter 23.5 cm

Franks collection, F.763 +

The plate is painted with a deity riding a sea horse and blowing a
horn, emerging from waves beside the entwined initials 'G H'
surmounted by a coronet. Rays of the sun are appearing on the upper
left - hand side, just inside the rim, and are shining on this scene. The
rim is painted with festoons of roses.

This dish is very unusual for its asymmetrical composition, with the
sun on one side. The central design is unidentified, but the
combination of an armorial-style design and initials may have been
designed for a marriage.

清　彩瓷姓名縮寫紋盤

Famille rose plate with a monogram

歐洲塡彩中國貿易瓷

Chinese Porcelain Decorated in the West

（cat.nos. 141 - 161）

141. 彩瓷法國製小罐

法國（1870－1900）

高8.2公分

伍德渥遺贈

小罐上之徽章紋及拉丁文箴言「美德無敵」皆屬諾福克郡公爵何渥德家族所有。1854年在巴黎艾德·山姆森窰廠製造，爲仿中國徽章紋而製作之瓷器。罐底以紅色琺瑯彩仿中國朱印，惜仿製得並不正確。

141 *Famille rose* **jug, made in France**

C. 1870 - 1900

Height 8.2 cm

Woodward Bequest, 1981.6 - 4.8

This small cream jug has a rounded body and well - defined spout. The porcelain body is covered with a green - tinged glaze and painted in underglaze - blue and *famille rose* enamels with flowers and a coat of arms, supported by a lion and a unicorn with a branch in its mouth, surmounted by a pink - and - gold crown, with the Latin motto 'SOLA VIRTUS INVICTA' (virtue alone is invincible). The rim, handle and base are edged with a gold - decorated underglaze - blue band and a golden spearhead border. A small red - enamel seal mark on the base imitates Chinese characters.

The jug is one of a large number of porcelains made in European workshops at the end of the 19th and beginning of the 20th century in imitation of Chinese pieces. It was made at Edmé Samson et Cie, the most famous porcelain manufactory copying Chinese wares, established in 1854 in Paris. It was probably ordered as a replacement for a broken piece from a Chinese armorial service, and bears the motto and arms of the English Howard family, Dukes of Norfolk. A Tankard with the same arms, also made in France, is in a private collection (Brighton, 1986, no. 142).

The French imitation pieces differ from the Chinese originals in a variety of ways, particularly in their body material and enamel colours, but also in the painting manner. The seal mark on the base of the jug is an imitation of a Chinese mark which the original would have lacked. Part of it could be interpreted as a sinicised 'S', in analogy to Samson imitations of Middle Eastern pieces which are marked with an Arabic 'S', and his imitations of European porcelain which are sometimes marked with entwined 'S's or impressed 'S' marks.

彩瓷法國製小罐
Famille rose jug, made in France

142.　清　荷蘭填彩中國瓷瓶

高21.5公分　1700－1720，隨後即填彩

法蘭克收藏

瓷瓶施釉裏紅，描繪三個傳說中的獅怪獸。技法具有康熙年間景德鎮窯的風味，在荷蘭以琺瑯彩填繪，描繪三位武士持劍，似乎要砍殺怪獸，圖中的樹具有日本風格。

142　Chinese porcelain bottle, overpainted in Holland

Qing dynasty, c. 1700 - 1720; overpainted soon after
Height 21.5 cm
Franks collection, F.643

The pear - shaped bottle has a thin long neck and is decorated in underglaze copper - red with three fabulous lion - like beasts with underglaze cobalt - blue eyes.

This design was embellished in overglaze enamels of the Japanese Kakiemon palette with three bearded men in aubergine dress, standing with swords poised as if about to kill the aminals among small flowers between three different trees. The design is framed at the bottom by a border of pendant floral motifs and at the rim by a border of pendant red - and - gold lappets; the lip was overpainted in brown. The unglazed base is inscribed with a simulated Chinese four - character mark in red.

Bottles of this type, decorated in underglaze red and blue, are characteristic products of the Jingdezhen kilns in Jiangxi province, of the Kangxi period (1662 - 1722). The overglaze enamel decoration was added in Holland, probably soon after. Both Chinese and Japanese porcelain was copied in Europe, where the colour scheme of the Kakiemon kilns, composed of turquoise, red, blue, green and some yellow, was particularly popular (see London, 1990, no. 183 and compare nos. 100 and 101).

Chinese porcelains overpainted in Holland are generally known as being 'clobbered', but this overpainting, mainly used to add colour to blue - and - white porcelain, is usually of a much coarser type than on the present piece.

清　荷蘭填彩中國瓷瓶
Chinese porcelain bottle,
overpainted in Holland

317

fig. 143a   fig. 143b

143. 清　荷蘭填彩中國瓷盤五件

直徑22.1公分

1720－1730

法蘭克收藏

此五件盤描繪一羣荷蘭股東，有的手持股票，有的手抓錢幣，並有荷蘭銘文說明關於1720年代歐洲經濟大恐慌之事。盤中人物包含各行各業，紋飾與1720年在阿姆斯特丹印製的一副荷蘭撲克牌類似。

143　Five Chinese porcelain plates, painted in Holland

Qing dynasty, c. 1720 - 30; painted c. 1720 - 30

Diameter 22.1 cm

Franks collection, F. 937 +

These five Chinese porcelain plates are each carved with overall floral scrolls under a blue - tinged glaze, and have barbed rims.

They were over - painted in Holland with flowering creepers around the rim, and with Dutch figures and Dutch inscriptions in the centre.

The plate illustrated top left portrays a gentleman in a blue frock coat, holding a document in one hand, standing among rats with the inscription 'mijn bank is [rot]. Ik sot' (my bank is [rotten]. I am stupid).

On the top right is a farmer with a bunch of carrots tied around his waist, and inscribed with 'op hooren is mee vech verlooren' (on hearsay much is also lost).

The plate at the bottom left depicts a gentleman in a red frock coat with a coin in one hand and a document in the other, standing among bags of coins, with the inscription 'het is alle gewonn geld' (it is all earned money).

In the centre of the bottom row the plate shows a weeping man seated on a stool, with the inscription 'de treurend knegt' (the mourning servant or knave).

The bottom right - hand plate is painted with a man holding a dagger and wearing a belted pink tabard which bears three coats of arms, those of Amsterdam (three crosses arranged vertically), Leyden (crossed keys) and Haarlem (a dagger between four stars topped with a cross); the plate is inscribed 'Op mijn tris. Ben ik bis (sic)' (through my threesome. I go to the deuce).

These plates belong to a series depicting Dutch shareholders, some holding share certificates or clutching coins, in despair over a

financial crisis. The second decade of the 18th century saw a period of immense speculation in the trading of financial shares in Europe. Many people in the Netherlands were ruined as a result of the collapse of the financial markets known as the 'Bursting of the South Sea bubble' after the collapse of the South Sea Company. This subject features in numerous contemporary satirical cartoons and prints which appeared in books, pamphlets, newspapers and on playing cards.

The source of the designs on the present plates are caricatures of Dutch shareholders from a pack of 54 'fashionable' playing cards entitled 'April - Kaart of Kaart Spel van Momus Naar de Nieuwste Mode' (April card or Momus's Game at Cards after the newest fashion), published in Amsterdam in 1720. Two of the engravings for the cards, also in the British Museum, are illustrated for comparison: the Six of Spades which corresponds with the top left - hand plate, and the Three of Diamonds, after which the bottom right - hand plate was painted (figs. 143 a and b: P + D 1858.2 - 13.86). These cards are published as a single uncut print in a collection of Dutch satirical prints called 'Het Groote Tafereel der Dwaasheid' (scenes of great folly; George, 1935, vol. II, no. 1642).

These plates were made at Jingdezhen in Jiangxi province, and were over - painted in Holland. Relatively little is known of individual Western enamellers or the workshops where such decoration was added. Plates painted with such designs are very rare and other examples with similar figures of shareholders and Dutch inscriptions include seven plates in the Fries Museum, and one in the Princessehof Museum, Leeuwarden, Netherlands (Hervouet and Bruneau, 1986, nos. 16.55 - 16.62). Another more finely painted series was in the Hervouet collection (*ibid.*, nos. 16.63 - 16.71).

清　荷蘭填彩中國瓷盤五件
Five Chinese porcelain plates, painted in Holland

144. 清　荷蘭填彩中國瓷盤

製造年代1700－1710年　填彩於1710－1720年

直徑21.5公分

法蘭克收藏

此盤描繪荷蘭東印度公司商船，船尾繪有荷蘭「西蘭省」以及「1700」字樣。圖案可能源於航運畫或印刷品。

144 Chinese porcelain dish, painted in Holland

Qing dynasty, c. 1700 - 1710; painted c. 1710 - 20

Diameter 21.5 cm

Franks collection, F. 597 A

The dish shows a three - masted ship, with flags flying at the tops of her masts, from the bowsprit and stern. Her stern is painted with an armorial design of a lion emerging from waves and with the date '1700'. A long boat is depicted to the right, carrying passengers and crew and flying a flag, and in the distance are two faintly painted ships. The rim border is painted with a regular geometric pattern in red, turquoise and black enamels.

The main ship is a Dutch East Indiaman and the arms painted on her stern belong to the Dutch province of Zealand. She flies the National Dutch flag as ensign (horizontally striped red, white and blue) and from the bowsprit the Middelburg flag (a castle on a red ground; Middelburg was Zealand's main town). At the top of each of the three masts are the 'house flags' of the Dutch East India Company (horizontally striped yellow, white and red).

The plain white porcelain dish was made at Jingdezhen, Jiangxi province, and decorated in Holland, as is evidenced by the enamels employed and by the style of painting. Several features identify this ship as a vessel of the end of the 17th or early 18th century, for example, the rounded fighting tops (platforms half way up the masts) or the sprit topmast which had disappeared by the mid-18th century. The source of the design, however, is more likely to be a marine painting or print than the actual ship itself. It is very unusual for a vessel to have a dated stern, but this is not uncommon for votive models of ships, for example, as they hung in Europe in the churches of fishing communities, to remind the congregation of the dangers and rewards of the sea. The date on this plate can therefore not be taken as the date of its decoration.

Dishes with identical decoration are in the Rijksmuseum, Amsterdam, Netherlands (Lunsingh Scheurleer, 1974, pl. 355); in the Victoria and Albert Museum, London (no. c. 317 - 1963); and in a private collection (Hervouet and Bruneau, 1986, no. 16.4).

清　荷蘭填彩中國瓷盤
Chinese porcelain dish, painted in Holland

145. 清　荷蘭塡彩中國咖啡杯

1740－1746，1747年繪

高6公分

法蘭克收藏

此徽章紋屬於威廉四世所有，他是荷蘭聯合省之統治者（統治年代1747－1751年）。銘文指出此件乃1747年5月3日威廉四世大選時所繪，做爲紀念。景德鎭燒製素杯，在荷蘭塡彩完成。

145 Chinese porcelain coffee cup, painted in Holland

Qing dynasty, c. 1740 - 46, the painted decoration dated 1747

Height 6 cm

Franks collection, F. 798＋

The coffee cup bears a royal coat of arms surrounded by a collar of the Order of the Garter with the French motto 'HONI. SOYT. QUI. MAL.Y.PENSE.(sic)' meaning 'the shame be his who thinks ill of it', and is surmounted by a coronet and supported by two crowned lions. Underneath the arms is a Dutch inscription 'd'Orange stam door gods macht verh: [verheven] d. 3. Mi: 1747' (the Orange raised through God's power on the 3rd May 1747). Around the handle are entwined branches of blossoming orange and around the lip is another border of blossoming orange. The decoration is painted with thin dull enamels of red, green and blue, with gilding.

The arms have been identified as Nassau quartering Dietz, Vianden and Catznellbogen, with smaller shields superimposed, and belong to the Stadtholder William IV, Prince of Orange (1711 - 51), ruler of all seven Dutch Provinces (r. 1747 - 51) and together with the inscription suggest that this piece was painted as a souvenir of William's appointment by the members of the States General on 3rd May 1747. The coffee cup was made at Jingdezhen in Jiangxi province but was left plain white and decorated in Holland. The dull, washed-out colours are reminiscent of Dutch Delft ceramics. Other Chinese porcelains painted in Holland as souvenirs of William IV's appointment are known, for example, a coffee cup with the same date, his portrait and initials, in a private collection (private communication of Dr. Bernard Watney). The following tea cup and saucer (cat. no. 146) are decorated with William IV's arms and those of his wife.

清　荷蘭填彩中國咖啡杯
Chinese porcelain coffee cup, painted in Holland

146. 清　歐洲塡彩中國瓷杯及托盤

1740－1750，1740－1751彩繪

（杯）高3.6公分　（托盤）直徑11.6公分

法蘭克收藏

盛開之橘花叢的小枝上施重疊式徽章紋，其頂端有一皇冠。
徽章屬於奧蘭治省的威廉四世及其妻英格蘭安娜公主所有。
奧省爲荷蘭首省。

146　Chinese porcelain tea cup and saucer, painted in Europe

Qing dynasty, c. 1740 - 50; painted c. 1740 - 51

Height (cup) 3.6 cm, diameter (saucer) 11.6 cm

Franks collection, F. 798+

The tea cup and saucer are painted with an armorial design in blue
and red enamels of two overlapping coats of arms placed on top of a
sprig of blossoming orange and topped with a red crown studded
with pearls. Around the left shield is a collar of the Order of the
Garter with the old French motto 'HONY SOIT QUI MAL Y
PENSE (sic)' (the shame be his who thinks ill of it). Inside the cup is
another sprig of blossoming orange.

The two shields contain the arms of Nassau and the royal arms of
England (Howard, 1974, p. 797) and are those of William IV, Prince
of Orange (1711 - 51), who became ruler of the Dutch Provinces in
1747 (see also cat.no. 145), and to his wife Anne of Hanover, Princess
Royal of England and daughter of George II of England, whom he
married in 1734.

This set was made in Jingdezhen, Jiangxi province, and decorated in
Europe, possibly in Holland (Honey, 1977 [1932], p. 104, fig. 11 and
p. 105). Chinese porcelain painted in Europe with armorial decoration
is much less common than pieces painted with figurative or landscape
scenes, but an identical tea cup and saucer are in the Victoria and
Albert Museum, London (no. 3719 - 1901).

清　歐洲填彩中國瓷杯及托盤
Chinese porcelain tea cup and saucer, painted in Europe

147. 清　荷蘭塡彩中國蓋壺

1710－1730，隨後不久即上彩

高14公分

法蘭克收藏

器形仿自歐洲銀器，在福建德化窰製作，專爲外銷歐洲而製，在荷蘭上彩，爲典型中國風格圖案，其中描繪坐在陽台桌旁的一對夫婦，四周圍繞著花草樹木，邊緣裝飾著花紋及蝴蝶紋。色彩以紅、綠琺瑯彩爲主。

147 Chinese porcelain ewer and cover, painted in Holland

Qing dynasty, c. 1710 - 30; painted soon after

Height 14 cm

Franks collection, F. 535+

The pear-shaped ewer has a high spout and a loop handle with a small leaf terminal, attached at right angle to the spout, and a domed cover with pointed knob.

The ewer is decorated in bright enamel colours with three panels of chinoiserie figure scenes, one showing a bearded Chinese gentleman in a blue robe, another a lady in a long green dress with short yellow overcoat, each in a balustrated garden, and the third a couple seated at a table laid for tea, also in a garden among flowers. The rim is framed by a floral border with butterflies in small panels, and the cover shows on one side a Chinese gentleman seated in a garden setting, and on the other side large pierced rockwork with flowers.

The ewer was made at Dehua, Fujian province, where side - handled ewers, originally copied from European silverware, were rarely made (for a Jingdezhen example, see cat.no. 97). The ewer was painted in Holland and the colour scheme, with red and green enamels predominating, was probably intended to imitate the *famille verte* palette.

清　荷蘭填彩中國蓋壺
Chinese porcelain ewer and cover, painted in Holland

148. 清　荷蘭塡彩中國瓷馬克杯

1700－1722，1720－1730上彩

高9.5公分

法蘭克收藏

此件施把手、平行弦紋於頸部。原爲德化窰素瓷，在荷蘭上彩。繪有兩個小男孩與一隻雉雞在庭園玩耍，在風格及顏色上皆有日本瓷器之風味。

fig. 148a

148 Chinese porcelain mug, painted in Holland

Qing dynasty, c. 1700 - 1722: painted c. 1720 - 30

Height 9.5 cm

Franks collection, F. 934＋

The mug has a globular body, cylindrical neck, and handle and is moulded with geometric patterns around the shoulder and foot, and with horizontal ribbing around the neck.

It is painted in polychrome enamels with two boys playing in a garden and a colourful pheasant in a prunus tree, and around the neck with flower sprays and a parrot.

The mug was made at the Dehua kilns in Fujian province, where this shape was very popular in the late 17th and early 18th century (seven other undecorated examples are in the British Museum). This shape is also seen in English salt - glazed stoneware, from which it may derive an example with a silver rim dated 1682, made in Fulham, London, by John Dwight is in the British Museum (fig. 148 a; M＋LA AF 16/87, 2-10, 106). John Dwight was the first potter to produce stoneware in England on a successful commercial basis. This shape is also found in earlier German stoneware.

The painted decoration was added in Holland in the style and palette of Japanese Kakiemon porcelain.

328

清　荷蘭塡彩中國瓷馬克杯
Chinese porcelain mug, painted in Holland

149. 清　荷蘭填彩中國瓷杯

1700－1720，隨後不久即上彩

高 7 公分

法蘭克收藏

德化窯燒製，上有浮雕八仙，後來在荷蘭以紅、綠琺瑯彩上色，原來的中國人物描繪成歐洲人。

149　Chinese porcelain cup, painted in Holland

Qing dynasty, c. 1700 - 1720; painted soon after

Height 7 cm

Franks collection, F. 891

The octagonal cup is moulded in relief with eight small figures representing the Eight Daoist Immortals, and with two ranks of lotus petals below. The base is impressed with a Chinese seal mark giving the name of the potter, reading *Zhongtun shi* (Mr. Zhongtun).

The figures are overpainted and have been turned into chinoiserie figures, standing in different attitudes, wearing different hats and green, aubergine and blue garments; they are surrounded by stylized flower motifs reserved on an overall red ground, and the lotus petals below are painted with small sprigs on a green ground, or in a pale red. A red scroll border was added to the inside rim and the foot.

The cup was made at Dehua, Fujian province, and is a characteristic product of the late Kangxi period (1662 - 1722). The painting was added in Holland. Since the Chinese immortals had not come out very clearly in the moulding, they could easily be adapted to vaguely Chinese - looking figures of Western taste.

清　荷蘭填彩中國瓷杯
Chinese porcelain cup, painted in Holland

150. 清　荷蘭填彩中國瓷蓋壺

1680－1720，1725－40上彩

高17公分

法蘭克收藏

一邊繪有樹上的鳥巢，四周圍繞著小鳥，另一邊則在最上面
繪一盆盛開的花草，其下是孔雀籠。德化窰製造，在歐洲以
琺瑯彩精巧地上釉而完成。

150 Chinese porcelain ewer and cover, painted probably in Holland

Qing dynasty, c. 1680 - 1720; painted c. 1725 - 40

Height 17 cm

Franks collection, F. 943＋

The pear-shaped ewer is thinly potted and highly translucent; it has a long curved spout and handle and a flat cover with small knob.

It is painted on one side with a bird's nest in a tree and birds perched on the tree and below it, and on the other side with a large flower pot with an exuberantly flowering plant on top of a peacock cage, all painted in colours of the *famille rose*, with landscapes indicated in the background in pale rose - pink and other colours.

The ewer was made at Dehua, Fujian province and, with its flat cover, is unusual in shape. The very finely painted enamel decoration has formerly been attributed to a German workshop but is now considered to have been added in Holland. (thanks are due to Dr Bernard Watney for this information). Other Dehua ewers of this shape with identical decoration are known (Sotheby's London, 8th July 1969, lot 84 A).

清　荷蘭塡彩中國瓷蓋壺
Chinese porcelain ewer and cover, painted probably in Holland

151. 清　意大利填彩中國瓷杯

1690－1710，1730－1740上彩

高7.5公分

德化窰生產，施紅色釉，以十分細膩的筆法，描繪聖經故事中有關耶穌的事蹟。杯上有畫工卡羅・溫德琳・安倫泰的簽名，他於意大利翡冷翠工作。

151　Chinese porcelain cup, painted in Italy

Qing dynasty, c. 1690 - 1710; painted c. 1730 - 40

Height 7.5 cm

1924.7 - 17.1

The cup is of deep beaker form with flared rim.

It is painted in red enamel in extremely fine brushwork with a continuous, highly detailed scene depicting a story from the Bible. It shows Jesus in a landscape surrounded by large crowds of people. Some of whom are carrying baskets. The foot of the cup is gilded. The cup is signed on the base in minute writing 'Carlo Wendelin Anreiter di Ziernfeldt, Fierenze'.

The story depicted is known as the miracle of the loaves and fishes and tells how Jesus, who had retired into the desert, was followed by a large crowd; this was unexpected and they had not enough food. He, however, fed them all by breaking the few loaves of bread and distributing the few fish they had brought among the thousands of followers who all got enough while much was left over. Johann Carl Wendelin Anreiter of Zirnfeld was a porcelain painter working in Vienna, Austria, as well as in Florence, Italy, particularly in the 1730s.

清　意大利塡彩中國瓷杯
Chinese porcelain cup, painted in Italy

152. 清　德國塡彩中國瓷杯

1700—1720，1720—30上彩

高 7 公分

法蘭克收藏

此白瓷杯飾有梅枝，德化窯製品。在德國以黑釉描繪波蘭王奧古斯都（1670—1733）之加冕徽章紋。奧古斯都王收藏有大量的中國、日本及歐洲之瓷器。

152　Chinese porcelain cup, painted in Germany

Qing dynasty, c. 1700 - 1720; painted c. 1720 - 30

Height 7 cm

Franks collection, F.947 +

The Chinese white porcelain cup is decorated with applied sprigs of prunus.

The applied decoration is emphasized in black enamel and gilding, and three crowned coats of arms surrounded by leaves are painted in between. Inside the cup is a crowned monogram, at the rim and the foot are finely painted and gilded lace borders, and on the base is a flower-head.

The arms belong to Augustus the Strong, Elector of Saxony, King of Poland (1670 - 1733), whose extensive collection of European, Japanese and Chinese porcelains was recorded in an inventory in 1721 and is still largely housed at Dresden, Germany. Augustus began to collect porcelain from 1715 and reputedly was so fond of acquiring it that he gave a regiment of dragoons in exchange for twelve large Chinese jars (London, 1990, p. 65).

The cup is of a well-known type made at the Dehua kilns in Fujian province, which was copied by many European manufactories. Dehua wares were more often overpainted in Europe than wares from Jingdezhen which rarely came to Europe undecorated. The black enamel decoration was added in Germany, possibly by Ignaz Preissler of Kronstadt in Bohemia, who was active c. 1720 - 39.

清　德國塡彩中國瓷杯
Chinese porcelain cup, painted in Germany

153. 清　德國填彩中國瓷杯

1700—1722，1720—1730上彩

高7.5公分

法蘭克收藏

景德鎮製，紋飾來自希臘神話；描繪半神半人的大力士赫克力斯消滅蛇形怪獸。此件可能是在德國波頓左魯伯填彩完成。

153　Chinese porcelain cup, painted in Germany

Qing dynasty, c. 1700 - 1722; painted c. 1720 - 30

Height 7.5 cm

Franks collection, F 946 ＋

The tall cup bears on the base a small uneven underglaze - blue ring. The cup was painted in Germany in black enamel with a continuous frieze, depicting a mythological scene which shows various stages in the destruction of a snake-like monster. On one side a snake - like winged monster is depicted in a landscape setting attacking a group of goats, and on the other side it is being destroyed by a semi - naked figure with a club who is surrounded by men with flaming torches. Two other snake - like beasts are seen escaping into trees. A fly is painted inside the cup off - centre, in a very naturalistic way. The foot - ring bears traces of red pigment and gilding.

The decoration depicts a story from Greek mythology, and shows the destruction of the multi - headed Lernaean hydra by the semi - god Heracles who is typically represented half - naked and with a raised club (see cat. no. 58). This task was the second of the twelve labours he was condemned to perform before gaining immortality, as a penance for slaying his own children. He overcame the monster, which grew two new heads every time one head was cut off, with the help of others using torches.

The cup was made at Jingdezhen, Jiangxi province, and was painted in Germany probably by Ignaz Bottengruber of Breslau, who was active c. 1723 - 30

338

清　德國填彩中國瓷杯
Chinese porcelain cup, painted in Germany

154. 清　德國填彩中國瓷杯及托盤

1690－1710，1720－1730上彩

（杯）高7.2公分，（托盤）直徑13.1公分

法蘭克收藏

景德鎮素瓷，在德國由波希米亞的瓷器畫工普瑞斯勒填彩完成。作品繪有中國人物，四周纏繞捲紋，是當時的流行樣式。

154　Chinese porcelain cup and saucer, painted in Germany

Qing dynasty, c. 1690 - 1710; painted c. 1720 - 30

Height (cup) 7.2 cm, diameter (saucer) 13.1 cm

Franks collection, F. 1442

The cup is of deep beaker shape with flared rim and the saucer has curved sides. Both pieces are plain white and each is marked with a beribboned lozenge in a double ring in underglaze blue.

They are painted in red and gold with an elaborate chinoiserie scene which shows on the saucer a large figure with conical hat holding an umbrella, with a smaller one behind him, both standing on a decorative pedestal, flanked by two other figures with fancy hats, seated and kneeling on brackets formed by the surrounding scrollwork, which contains perched birds and formal fruit motifs. The cup is matchingly painted with a similar pair of figures standing in conversation, two others standing singly, and a figure kneeling, with a fan, among similar scrollwork.

Cup and saucer were made at Jingdezhen, Jiangxi province, but were apparently sent to Europe without decoration. They were painted in Germany by the well - known porcelain painter Ignaz Preissler of Kronstadt, Bohemia, who was active c. 1720 - 39. Such chinoiserie scenes with idealized Chinese figures in romantic settings were highly fashionable in Europe at the time and appeared in interior decoration, in paintings and on objects of all sorts.

Characteristic elements of this chinoiserie style are figures in voluminous robes with pointed or other fanciful hats, holding umbrellas, long stiff fans or small folding fans, either among elegant scrollwork with pseudo-architectural ornament (like on the present piece and on the following, cat. no. 155), or surrounded by an exotic and often fantastic fauna and flora (like on the bottle below, cat. no. 156). Stylistically the present scenes are closely related, for example, to the chinoiserie wall and ceiling paintings at the Pagodenburg, a chinoiserie pavilion built between 1716 and 1719 in the grounds of Schloss Nymphenburg, a palace in Munich, Germany (Impey, 1977, pls. 185 and 195).

清　德國塡彩中國瓷杯及托盤
Chinese porcelain cup and saucer, painted in Germany

155. 清　德國填彩中國瓷杯及托盤

1710－30，隨後不久即上彩

（杯）高4.5公分，（托盤）直徑13.4公分

法蘭克收藏

如同圖版154作品，也是波希米亞的普瑞斯勒所繪。人物纏枝花卉紋圍繞著在中央的異國風景，施釉下藍彩爲邊，以雕瓷爲飾而完成。

155 Chinese porcelain tea cup and saucer, overpainted in Germany

Qing dynasty, c. 1710 - 30; overpainted c. 1720 - 30

Height (cup) 4.5 cm, diameter(saucer) 13.4 cm

Franks collection, F.1443

This cup and saucer are decorated with carved stylized flower designs between underglaze - blue cash - diaper borders. The inside of the cup also shows a carved flower - head, the outside of the saucer two underglaze - blue leafy branches.

Both cup and saucer were overpainted in bright red and gold. The saucer shows in the centre an exotic landscape with palm trees, and pavilions with curved roofs in front of a monumental pierced rock, and a phoenix in the sky; this is surrounded by a dense band of scrollwork with two chinoiserie figures on either side, one with an umbrella, the other with a fan, both holding on to the scrolling stems around them, which incorporate birds, flowers and bunches of fruit. The cup is painted on the outside with a similar band with two pairs of figures, one pair similar to those of the saucer but with conical hats, the other with pig tails , holding an umbrella and a fruit bowl, respectively, all seated in the surrounding scrollwork among birds and flowers.

This cup and saucer were made, carved and painted in underglaze blue at Jingdezhen, Jiangxi province, and overpainted in Germany, possibly because plain white porcelains from China were not easily obtainable. The painter of this set, however, Ignaz Preissler of Kronstadt in Bohemia, who also painted the cup and saucer above and the bottle below (cat. nos. 154 and 156), may have chosen blue - and - white porcelains deliberately. According to contemporary correspondence he painted much Chinese porcelain, "particularly that with blue borders" which was bought for him in Prague by his patron, Count Kolowrat (Honey, 1977 [1932], p. 107).

Exotic landscape gardens such as depicted in the centre of this saucer were in the 18th century laid out at many European palaces and mansions, with fancy pavilions, rockwork grottos and exotic plants; an engraving of the garden at Petit Trianon, built slightly later in the 18th century at Versailles outside Paris, France, depicts a very similar setting (Impey, 1977, pl. 152 top left).

清　德國塡彩中國瓷杯及托盤
Chinese porcelain tea cup and saucer, overpainted in Germany

156. 清　德國填彩中國瓷瓶

1710－22，隨後不久即上彩

法蘭克收藏

景德鎮製作，雕以花卉紋，可能是由波希米亞的普瑞斯勒上
彩，繪有許多中國人物，周遭是一些異國奇花異草。

156　Chinese porcelain bottle, overpainted in Germany

Qing dynasty, c. 1710 - 22; overpainted c. 1720 - 30

Height 24.5 cm (reduced)

Franks collection, F.948+

The cylindrical bottle is decorated with overall carved lotus scrolls on the body and rose and camellia sprays on the neck, which originally was slightly flared; the base bears underglaze - blue double rings.

The sides are overpainted in black and gold with an elaborate exotic figure scene, showing on one side a Chinese gentleman with a tall fan, and a lady accompanied by a servant with a fruit bowl, and between them a figure kneeling on the ground as if performing a kotow and a large phoenix swooping down at him; on the reverse, separated by large trees, is another exotic-looking couple with a child heading towards the scene, the man carrying a sword, the lady a fan, and above them another phoenix. A mountainous landscape with a pyramid, pavilions and other buildings is visible in the background and decorative shrubs are filling the foreground.

The bottle was made at Jingdezhen, Jiangxi province, and is a typical piece of Kangxi porcelain (1662 - 1722). The painting is closely related to that of the previous cups and saucers (cat. nos. 154 - 5) and was probably done by the same painter, Ignaz Preissler of Kronstadt in Bohemia.

Depictions of phoenixes - known in Europe as *hoho* birds (an adaptation of their Japanese name) - were an integral part of chinoiserie designs.

清　德國填彩中國瓷瓶
Chinese porcelain bottle, overpainted in Germany

157. 清　德國或荷蘭填彩中國瓷杯和托盤

1710－30，隨後不久即上彩

（杯）高5.8公分，（托盤）直徑12.7公分

法蘭克收藏

瓷杯以黑色琺瑯彩繪有一幢在港口前的古堡，以及正在開炮的船。托盤上則飾三艘正準備出航的船，有一小型徽章紋在波濤中，盤底施兩個釉下藍彩的雙環徽章紋。

157　Chinese porcelain cup and saucer, probably painted in Germany

Qing dynasty, c. 1710 - 30; probably painted soon after

Diameter (saucer) 12.7 cm, height (cup) 5.8 cm

Franks collection, F. 1441

The cup is unusually shaped, with a high splayed foot and flared rim; both cup and saucer have underglaze - blue double rings on the base.

The cup has been painted *en grisaille* with a continuous scene of a castle on the waterfront and a ship firing her cannon. The saucer is similarly painted with a three - masted ship under sail, with a high stern and two rows of cannon along her side, and with a castle in the background and a small armorial emblem among the waves. On the base of the saucer are two coats of arms, also painted *en grisaille*, within the blue rings. The left - hand one shows three fish, with a feathered hat as crest, the shield on the right contains three heads and three cups divided by a palm tree, with a palm tree crest.

The cup and saucer were made at Jingdezhen in Jiangxi province; the enamel decoration was probably added in Germany.

346

清　德國或荷蘭塡彩中國瓷杯和托盤
Chinese porcelain cup and saucer, probably painted in Germany

158. 清　英國塡彩中國茶具一組十件

1740－55，1756－70上彩

（茶壺）高13.5公分　（咖啡杯）高6.5公分　（茶杯）高4公分

（茶盤）直徑13公分　（托盤）直徑12公分

法蘭克收藏

茶具，包括茶壺、茶盤、三個咖啡杯、二個茶杯以及三個托盤。繪有意大利喜劇情節，取材於流行版畫插圖。這組瓷器可能是在倫敦坎地序鎮詹姆斯‧吉爾工作室由傑佛利‧歐尼爾描繪完成。

158 Ten pieces of a Chinese porcelain service, painted in England

Qing dynasty, c. 1740 - 55, painted c. 1756 - 70

Height (teapoy) 13.5 cm, (coffee cup) 6.5 cm, (tea cup) 4 cm; diameter (teapot stand) 13 cm, (saucers) 12 cm

Franks collection, F.654

This group consists of a teapoy, teapot stand, three coffee cups, two tea cups and three saucers.

The painted scenes, which are different on each piece, derive from theatrical characters of the Italian *commedia dell'arte*. They include Harlequin, in the multi - coloured chequered costume and mask, generally holding a club; Columbine in a long pink dress; and her lover. In one scene Harlequin's arm reaches out from a coffin. All the porcelains have toothed golden rim borders.

These characters of the *commedia dell'arte* were depicted in numerous popular prints (Allardyce, 1963).

This porcelain set was made at Jingdezhen, Jiangxi province, and the decoration was added to the plain white pieces in England, in the workshop of James Giles, possibly at Kentish Town, London, where his business was located from 1756. The work may have been executed by the miniature painter, illustrator and porcelain decorator Jeffrey Hamet O'Neale (1734 - 1801), whose painting is said to be characterized by "slender tufted trees and the spikey, 'starfish' hands of the figures, and a group of red-brown rocks in the foreground". (Honey, 1977 [1932], pp. 109 - 10).

A matching teapot is in the Royal Museum of Scotland, Edinburgh (no. 450.47). These designs appear on Chinese porcelain only (private communication of Dr. Bernard Watney).

清　英國塡彩中國茶具一組十件

Ten pieces of a Chinese porcelain service, painted in England

159. 清　英國填彩中國咖啡杯及托盤

1723—35，1756—70上彩

（杯）高6.1公分　（托盤）直徑10.8公分

法蘭克收藏

瓷杯及托盤上的細緻花卉、蝴蝶及昆蟲等圖案是在倫敦坎地序鎮詹姆斯‧吉爾工作室所繪。托盤底部有釉下藍彩雍正年號銘款，中國皇帝年款在歐洲填彩作品上出現是十分罕見。

fig. 159a

159 Chinese porcelain coffee cup and saucer, painted in England

Qing dynasty, c. 1723 - 35, painted c. 1756 - 70

Diameter (saucer) 10.8 cm, Height (cup) 6.1 cm

Franks collection, F.1448

The base of the saucer is inscribed with the reign mark of the Emperor Yongzheng (1723 - 35) in underglaze blue within a double ring.

Both cup and saucer are decorated in enamels with delicate, sparsely arranged multi - coloured butterflies, beetles and other insects and with sprays of rose, lily - of - the - valley and bluebells, and inside the cup are two further flowers.

The cup and saucer were produced at Jingdezhen, Jiangxi province, and were decorated in England, in the workshop of James Giles (1718-80; see also cat.no. 158). Giles acted as a retailer as well as a decorator and had a considerable number of employees. English decoration of Chinese porcelain is generally confined to smaller pieces, possibly due to the prohibitive cost of ornamenting larger pieces of dinner services which could have been more cheaply purchased fully decorated in China (Godden, 1979, p. 358), or due to the fact that few large plain white pieces were available.

It is extremely unusual to find a Chinese reign mark on a piece later decorated in Europe. A similarly marked bowl is in the Watney collection (fig. 159; courtesy of Dr. Watney). Another unmarked plate of this design is in the British Museum (F.1448 b); and a vase with moulded decoration overpainted in this way is in a private collection (Godden, 1979, no.285). This design also occurs on English porcelain.

清　英國塡彩中國咖啡杯及托盤
Chinese porcelain coffee cup and saucer, painted in England

160. 清　英國填彩中國瓷杯及托盤

1740－55，1756－70上彩

（杯）高6公分　（托盤）直徑12.2公分

法蘭克收藏

以黑色琺瑯彩勾勒中國山水，施以綠彩；施釉與描繪法十分特別，是典型的詹姆斯·吉爾工作室風格。這種在中國瓷胎上施英國琺瑯彩的技法始於1750年代。景德鎮素瓷。

160 Chinese porcelain cup and saucer, painted in England

Qing dynasty, c. 1740 - 55; painted c. 1756 - 70

Height (cup) 6 cm, Diameter (saucer) 12.2 cm

Franks collection, F.651

The coffee cup and saucer are painted with chinoiserie landscape scenes in black enamel outlines and a green wash. The saucer shows two boys, one with a bird perched on his hand and the other seated on a wooden platform, with a wooden house and a landscape in the background. The decoration on the cup is similar but here one boy shades the other with an Oriental parasol in front of a wooden house built on a raised platform. The rim of the saucer and lip of the cup have traces of a gilt border.

The cup and saucer were produced at Jingdezhen in Jiangxi province. They were decorated in the workshop of James Giles (1718 - 80), an English porcelain painter who managed a business in Kentish Town, London, from 1756 to 1763, and in Soho, London, from 1763 to 1776 (Coke, 1983, p.4). In his workshop both European and Chinese porcelains were decorated with original designs as well as with copies of prints and oil paintings.

The scenes are an Englishman's interpretation of Chinese figures in a Chinese landscape. Little accurate information about China was available during this period and images of China were a fanciful mixture of the architecture, flora and fauna of different distant countries.

These particular scenes are very rare and do not occur on English porcelain (private communication of Dr. Bernard Watney). However, English and Chinese porcelains decorated by Giles with other monochrome green landscape scenes are well known (Coke, 1983, p. 150). Chinese porcelains decorated in this style include a tea cup and saucer with a factory scene, also in the British Museum (F.652); a saucer and a covered bowl both with an obelisk and ruins of a classical building in a landscape, one in the Victoria and Albert Museum, London, the other in the Museum of Fine Arts, Boston, U.S.A. (Godden, 1979, no. 286; Hervouet and Bruneau, 1986, no. 16.133); and a teapot with a riverscape in a private collection (Coke, 1983, pl. 31 b).

清　英國填彩中國瓷杯及托盤
Chinese porcelain cup and saucer, painted in England

161. 清　歐洲剔花中國瓷碗

1700－1722，隨後不久即上繪彩

高7.8公分　直徑17.3公分

法蘭克收藏

施以紫色單色釉，其上描繪花、鳥、彩緞等物，並以深雕露
出胎底。這種高難度之技法似乎傳承於荷蘭或德國歐洲玻璃
雕刻師。

161　Chinese porcelain bowl, carved in Europe

Qing dynasty, c. 1700 - 1722; decorated soon after

Height 7.8 cm, diameter 17.3 cm

Franks collection, F.59

The bowl has a monochrome aubergine glaze.

A design of a bird with fruiting and flowering plants and ribbon bows
has been carved through the glaze to reveal the white porcelain body.

While the bowl was made at Jingdezhen in Jiangxi province, the
carved decoration was added in Europe. Such decoration was popular
in the 18th century and the British Museum has similarly decorated
brown and blue - glazed cups and saucers.

It has been suggested that the decoration may have been executed at
Dresden, Germany, early in the 18th century, by Tschirnhausen who
also engraved red stonewares and glass vessels (Hobson, 1977 [1932],
p. 107). The work is very skilful since porcelain - being very hard - is
extremely difficult to carve. Similarly decorated stoneware from
Fulham, London, is also known (ibid.)

清　歐洲剔花中國瓷碗
Chinese porcelain bowl, carved in Europe

GLOSSARY

Arabesque
Scrolling leaf motif

Armillary sphere
Celestial globe composed of rings

Armorial
Referring to a family's coat of arms

Arms
see: Coat of arms

Baroque
An exuberant artistic style flourishing in 17th and early 18th century Europe

Bookplate
Label pasted inside a book to identify the owner, bearing his name, coat of arms, crest or other emblems

Caddy
Box and cover for keeping tea leaves

Cherub
Angel of the second order, represented by a winged chubby infant, or the winged head of a child

Chinoiserie
Western adaptation of Chinese designs

Cipher
Decoratively interlaced initials of a name

Coat of arms
Emblems of a family displayed on a shield, originally to identify a man in battle

Coronet
Small crown

Crest
Emblem of a family, placed on top of a helmet

Crown of thorns
Mock crown wound from thorny branches, placed on Jesus' head for the crucifixion to ridicule his claim to be King of the Jews

Doublet
Close fitting vest-like garment

East Indiaman
European merchant ship used for trade between Europe and the Far East

En grisaille
In shades of grey

Faience
European glazed earthenware

Famille rose
A polychrome palette dominated by rose - pink enamel

Famille verte
A polychrome palette dominated by green enamel

Fleur - de - lis
Stylized flower based on a lily or iris, formerly royal arms of France

Freemasons
A non-political, non-religious, semi-secret international fraternity whose internal organisation involves an elaborate system of symbolic rituals, often derived from the work of stonemasons

Frock coat
A man's long-skirted coat

Griffin
Winged creature with the foreparts of an eagle and the hindparts of a lion, with beard and ears

Grisaille
Shades of grey

Helmet
Metal head armour, placed above a coat of arms, bearing the crest and often adorned with lavish plumes

Heraldic
Referring to a family's coat of arms and other symbols of rank and descent

Hydra
Water - monster with many heads

IHS
Monogram of Christ, or Sacred Monogram, representing the initial letters of the name Jesus in Greek transcription as well as an abbreviation of the Latin expression 'Jesus Hominum Salvator' (Jesus, Saviour of Mankind) .

Imari
A type of Japanese porcelain typically decorated in underglaze - blue, overglaze - red enamel and gilding

Impaled
An armorial shield devided in half, showing two coats of arms side by side, usually those of a man and his wife

In pretence
Superimposition of a smaller coat of arms, often that of a wife, on another

Jesuits
Christian order, also called 'Society of Jesus', founded in 1534 by Ignatius of Loyola, particularly active as missionaries

Kerchief
Scarf worn over the head

Kilt
Skirt worn by Scottish men

Knee breeches
Trousers which reach just below the knee

Kraak
Blue - and - white export ware of the Ming dynasty, typically with thin body and panelled decoration

Lodge
Association of Freemasons

Mantling
Ornamental cloth draped around a shield underneath the helmet

Masonic
Of the Freemasons

Monogram
Decoratively interlaced letters, especially initials of a name

Monogram of Christ
See: IHS

Motto
Phrase expressing a principle adopted as a rule of conduct

Ogee
S - shaped curve

Orb
Golden globe as emblem of sovereignty, forming part of royal insignia

Pattipan
Stand for a teapot, usually with fluted edges

Plume
Ornamental feather

Putto
Angel - like figure derived from images of Cupid, the Roman god of love

Quarterly
Division of an armorial shield into four quarters bearing four coats of arms

Rampant
An animal standing on one hind leg

Rocaille
18th century European ornament resembling shells

Rococo
An ornate decorative style derived from Baroque, popular in 18th-century Europe

Sacred Monogram
See: IHS

Sceptre
A staff borne as an emblem of sovereignty, forming part of royal insignia

Sepia
Brown pigment, originally made from the ink of a cuttlefish

Shield
A piece of defensive armour carried on the arm to protect the body, painted with the coat of arms

Supercargo
European merchant working for an East India Company

Supporters
A pair of figures, human or animal, standing on either side of a coat of arms

Tam o'shanter
Woolen cloth cap with bulging top, tightly fitting on the forehead

Tartan
Woolen cloth with horizontal and vertical stripes in distinctive colours, emblematic of different families, worn by Scottish men

Teapoy
Container for tea leaves

Transitional
Refers to the period of stylistic transition from the Ming to the Qing dynasty, c. 1620 - 83

Tricorne hat
Three-cornered hat

Triton
Sea god with fish tail

Unicorn
A mythological animal resembling a horse with a single horn on its forehead

BIBLIOGRAPHY

In the catalogue bibliographical references have been abbreviated to surname of author, or place of exhibition, and publication date.

de Albuquerque, M., 'A Loica Brasonada Portuguesa', *Oceanos*, no. 14, 1993, pp. 58 - 66

Allardyce, N., *The World of Harlequin. A Critical Study of the Commedia dell'Arte*, Cambridge, 1963

Amsterdam, *De Chinese porseleinkast*, exhibition catalogue by D.F. Lunsingh Scheurleer, Amsterdam, 1968

Arapova, T.B., 'The double - headed eagle on Chinese porcelain. Export wares for imperial Russia', *Apollo*, January 1992, pp. 21-6

Arnhem, Gemeentemuseum Arnhem, *Pronken met Oosters Porselein*, exhibition catalogue by S. Hartog, Arnhem, 1990

Bath, Holburne of Menstrie Museum, *The Winds of the Dragon*, exhibition catalogue by P. Hardie, Bath, 1985

Berlin, Martin-Gropius-Bau, *Europa und die Kaiser von China*, exhibition catalogue, Frankfurt am Main, 1985

Berlin, Schloss Charlottenburg, *China und Europa: Chinaverständnis und Chinamode im 17. und 18. Jahrhundert*, exhibition catalogue, Berlin, 1973

Beurdeley, M., *Porcelain of the East India Companies*, London, 1962

Beurdeley, M. and Raindre, G., *Qing Porcelain. Famille Verte, Famille Rose*, London, 1987

Brancante, E. da Fonseca, *O Brasil e a Louca da India*, Sao Paolo, 1950

Brighton, The Royal Pavillion, Art Gallery and Museums, *The China Trade 1600-1860*, exhibition catalogue by P. Conner, Brighton, 1986

de Castro, N., *Chinese Porcelain and the Heraldry of the Empire*, Oporto, 1988

de Castro, N., 'Alguns Brasoes Ineditos', *Oceanos*, no. 14, 1993, pp. 68 - 75

Charleston, R.J. and Ayers, J., *The James A. de Rothschild Collection at Waddesdon Manor. Meissen and Other European Porcelain, Oriental Porcelain*, Fribourg, 1971

Chicago, The David and Alfred Smart Gallery, The University of Chicago, *Blue and White. Chinese Porcelain and Its Impact on the Western World*, exhibition catalogue by J. Carswell, Chicago, 1985

Chompret, M.M. le Docteur, Bloch, J., Guérin, J. and Alfassa, P., *Répertoire de la Faïence Française*, Paris, 1933

Chinese Ceramics in the Idemitsu Collection, Tokyo, 1987

Clunas, C. (ed.) , *Chinese Export Art and Design*, London, 1987

Coke, G., *In Search of James Giles (1718-1780)*, Wingham, Kent, 1983

Conner, 1986, see Brighton, 1986

Crossman, C.L., *The Decorative Arts of the China Trade*, Woodbridge, Suffolk, 1991

Curtis, J.B., '17th and 18th - Century Chinese Export Ware in Southeastern Virginia', *Transactions of the Oriental Ceramic Society*, vol. 53, 1988 - 9, pp. 47 -64

Detweiler, S.G., *George Washington's Chinaware*, New York, 1982

Donnelly, P.J., *Blanc de Chine. The Porcelain of Tehua in Fukien*, London, 1969

Franks, A.W., *Catalogue of a Collection of Oriental Pottery and Porcelain Lent for Exhibition and Described by Augustus W. Franks F.R.S., F.S.A.*, London, 1879

George, D., *Catalogue of Political and Personal Satires preserved in the Department of Prints and Drawings in the British Museum, vol. V, 1771 - 1783*, London, 1935

Godden, G.A., *Oriental Export Market Porcelain and its Influence on European Wares*, London, 1979

Gordon, E. (ed.), *Chinese Export Porcelain. An Historical Survey*, New York, 1977

Graves, R., *The Greek Myths*, London, 1992 (1955)

Gray, B., 'A Chinese Blue and White Bowl with Western Emblems', *British Museum Quarterly*, vol. XXII, 1960, pp. 81 - 3

Gray, B., 'The Export of Chinese Porcelain to India', *Transactions of the Oriental Ceramic Society*, vol. 36, 1964 - 6, pp. 21 - 37

Groningen, Groninger Museum, *Pronk Porcelain: Porcelain after Designs by Cornelis Pronk*, exhibition catalogue by C.J.A. Jörg, Groningen, 1980

Harrisson, B., *Keramiek uit Azie*, Museum het Princessehof, Leeuwarden, 1985

Harrisson, 1986, see Leeuwarden, 1986

Hervouet, F. and N., and Bruneau, Y., *La Porcelaine des Compagnies des Indes a Décor Occidental*, Paris, 1986

Hobson, R.L., 'On Some Armorial Porcelain in the Franks Collection', *Connoisseur*, vol. 21, May - August 1908, pp. 181 - 5

Hobson, R.L., *A Guide to the Pottery and Porcelain of the Far East in the Department of Ceramics and Ethnography, British Museum*, London, 1924

Hobson, R.L., *The Later Ceramic Wares of China*, London, 1925

Holmes, M.T., *Nicolas Lancret 1690 - 1743*, ed. Joseph Focarino, The Frick Collection, New York, 1991

Honey, W.B., *The Victoria and Albert Museum, Department of Ceramics. Guide to the Later Chinese Porcelain. Periods of K'ang Hsi, Yung Cheng and Ch'ien Lung*, London, 1927

Honey, W.B., 'Dutch Decorators of Chinese Porcelain', *Chinese Export Porcelain. An Historical Survey*, ed. E. Gordon, New York, 1977, pp. 101 - 6 (first published, *Antiques*, February 1932)

Honey, W.B., 'German and English Decorators of Chinese Porcelain', *Chinese Export Porcelain. An Historical Survey*, ed. E. Gordon, New York, 1977, pp. 107 - 11 (first published, *Antiques*, March 1932)

Hong Kong, Hong Kong Museum of Art, *Interaction in Ceramics: Oriental Porcelain and Delftware*, exhibition catalogue by C.J.A. Jörg, Hong Kong, 1984

Hong Kong, Flagstaff House Museum of Tea Ware, *Chinese Export Porcelain: Chine de Commande from the Royal Museums of Art and History in Brussels*, exhibition catalogue by C.J.A. Jörg, Hong Kong, 1989

Howard, D.S., *Chinese Armorial Porcelain*, London, 1974

Howard, D. and Ayers, J., *China for the West. Chinese Porcelain and other Decorative Arts for Export Illustrated from the Mottahedeh Collection*, II vols., London and New York, 1978

Hudig, F.W., *Delfter Fayence*, Berlin, 1929

Impey, O., *Chinoiserie. The Impact of Oriental Styles on Western Art and Decoration*, London, 1977

Jacquemart, A. and Le Blant, E., *Histoire Artistique, Industrielle et Commerciale de la Porcelaine*, Paris, 1862

Johns, C., 'The Corbridge Lanx: An Important Acquisition by the British Museum', forthcoming (1994)

Jones, E.A., 'Old Chinese Porcelain made from English Silver Models', *Burlington Magazine*, vol. XX, October 1911 - March 1912, pp. 26 - 33

Jörg, 1980, see Groningen, 1980

Jörg, C.J.A., *Porcelain and the Dutch China Trade*, The Hague, 1982

Jörg, C.J.A., *The Geldermalsen: History and Porcelain*, Groningen, 1986

Jörg, 1989, see Hong Kong, 1989

Jourdain, M. and Jenyns, R.S., *Chinese Export Art in the Eighteenth Century*, London, 1967

Kassel, Staatliche Kunstsammlungen, *Porzellan aus China und Japan: Die Porzellangalerie der Landgrafen von Hessen - Kassel*, exhibition catalogue, Berlin, 1990

Kjellberg, S.T., *Svenska Ostindiska Compagnierna*, Malmö, 1975

Krahl, R., *Chinese Ceramics in the Topkapi Saray Museum, Istanbul*, ed. John Ayers, 3 vols, London, 1986

Landon, C.P., *Vies et Oeuvres des Peintres le Plus Célèbres de Toutes les Ecoles*, Paris, 1803 - 17

Lane, A., *Later Islamic Pottery*, London, 1957

Lane, A., 'Queen Mary II's Porcelain Collection at Hampton Court', *Transactions of the Oriental Ceramic Society*, vol. 25, 1949 - 50, pp. 21- 31

Le Corbeiller, C., *China Trade Porcelain - Patterns of Exchange*, New York, 1974

Leeuwarden, The Princesseh of Museum, *Asian Ceramics*, exhibition catalogue by B. Harrison, Leeuwarden, 1986

Lincoln, Massachusetts, De Cordova Museum, *The China Trade: Romance and Reality*, exhibition catalogue, Lincoln, Mass., 1979

Little, 1983, see New York, 1983

Lion - Goldschmidt, D., 'Ming Porcelain in the Santos Palace, Lisbon', *Transactions of the Oriental Ceramic Society*, vol. 49, 1984 - 5, pp. 78 -93

London, The British Museum, *Fake? The Art of Deception*, exhibition catalogue ed. by M. Jones with P. Craddock and N. Barker, London, 1990

London, The British Museum, *Porcelain for Palaces. The Fashion for Japan in Europe 1650 - 1750*, exhibition catalogue by J. Ayers, O. Impey, J.V.G. Mallet, London, 1990

Lunsingh Scheurleer, D.F., *Chine de Commande*, Hilversum, 1966 (translated as *Chinese Export Porcelain: Chine de Commande*, London, 1974)

Lunsingh Scheurleer, 1978, see Amsterdam, 1978

Lunsingh Scheurleer, D.F., *Chinesisches und Japanisches Porzellan in Europäischen Fassungen*, Braunschweig, 1980

Macintosh, D., *Chinese Blue and White Porcelain*, Newton Abbot, London, Vancouver, 1977

Mez-Mangold, L., *Apotheken-Keramik-Sammlung 'Roche'. Katalog*, ed. M. Schneider, Basel, 1990

Milton, Massachusetts, China Trade Museum, *Yang - ts'ai. The Foreign Colors, Rose Porcelains of the Ch'ing Dynasty*, exhibition catalogue by H.A. Crosby Forbes, Milton, Mass., 1982

Mudge, J.C., *Chinese Export Porcelain for the American Trade, 1785 - 1835*, New Jersey, 1981 (1962)

Mudge, J.C., *Chinese Export Porcelain in North America*, New York, 1986

Münster, Stadtmuseum Münster, *Die Wiedertäufer in Münster*, exhibition catalogue, Münster, 1982

New York, China House Gallery, *China Trade Porcelain. A Study in Double Reflections*, exhibition catalogue by C. Le Corbeiller, New York, 1973

New York, China House Gallery, *Chinese Porcelains in European Mounts*, exhibition catalogue by Sir F. Watson, New York, 1980

New York, China House Gallery, *Chinese Ceramics of the Transitional Period: 1620 - 1683,* exhibition catalogue by S. Little, New York, 1983

New York, New York Historical Society, *New York and the China Trade,* exhibition catalogue by D.S. Howard, New York, 1984

Newman, H., *An Illustrated Dictionary of Silverware,* London, 1987

Oriental Ceramics. The World's Great Collections, 11 vols., Tokyo, New York, San Francisco, 1980 - 82

Oxford, Ashmolean Museum, *Eastern Ceramics and Other Works of Art from the Collection of Gerald Reitlinger,* exhibition catalogue, London, 1981

Palmer, A.M., *A Winterthur Guide to Chinese Export Porcelain,* New York, 1976

Paris, The Musée Guimet, *Le Jardin des Porcelaines,* exhibition catalogue by J.P. Desroches, Paris, 1987

Paris, The Musée Guimet, *Du Tage à la Mer de Chine. Une épopée portugaise,* Paris, 1992

Pearce, N.J., 'Chinese Export Porcelain for the European Market: The Years of Decline 1770 - 1820' *Transactions of the Oriental Ceramic Society,* vol. 52, 1978 - 8, pp. 22 - 38

Pelliot, P., *Les Influences Européennes sur L'Art Chinois au XVIIe et au XVIIIe Siècle,* Paris, 1927

Phillips, J.G., *China-Trade Porcelain,* Cambridge, Mass., 1956

Pijl-Ketel, C.L. van der, *The Ceramic Load of the 'Witte Leeuw' (1613),* Amsterdam, 1982

Pinto de Matos, M.A., 'Porcelanas de Endomenda', *Oceanos,* no. 14, 1993, pp. 40 - 56

Reichel, F., *Die Porzellansammlung Augustus des Starken.*

Porzellankunst aus China: Die Rosa Familie, Dresden, 1993

Rietstap, J.B., *L'Armorial Général,* vol. A-B, Paris, 1903

Rinaldi, M., *Kraak Porcelain: A Moment in the History of Trade,* London, 1989

Rawson, J. (ed.), *The British Museum Book of Chinese Art,* London, 1992

Roth, S., *Chinese Porcelain Imported by the Swedish East India Company,* Gothenburg Historical Museum, Göteborg, 1965

Rouen, Musée des Beaux-Arts et de la Céramique, et. al., *L'Armoire Hollandaise aux Porcelaines de Chine,* exhibition catalogue by D.F. Lunsingh Scheurleer, Paris, 1971

Sargent, W.R., *The Copeland Collection: Chinese and Japanese Ceramic Figures,* Salem, Mass., 1991

Sargent, W.R., 'China, a Great Variety'. Documenting Porcelains for the American Market', *The Porcelains of Jingdezhen,* ed. R.E. Scott, *Colloquies on Art and Archaeology in Asia no. 16,* London, 1993, pp.206 - 31

Schiffer, H., P. and N., *Chinese Export Porcelain. Standard Patterns and Forms, 1780 to 1880,* Exton, Penn., 1975

Scholten, J., *The Coins of the Dutch Overseas Territories 1601-1948,* Amsterdam, 1953

Scott, R.E., 'Jesuit Missionaries and the Porcelains of Jingdezhen', *The Porcelains of Jingdezhen,* ed. R.E. Scott, *Colloquies on Art and Archaeology in Asia no. 16,* London, 1993, pp. 232 - 56

Sekai Tōji Zenshu / Ceramic Art of the World, vol. 15, Tokyo, 1983

Setterwall A., Fogelmarck S. and Gyllensvärd B., *The Chinese Pavilion at Drottningholm,* Malmö, 1974

Sheaf, C. and Kilburn, R., *The Hatcher Porcelain Cargoes: The Complete Record*, Oxford, 1988

Spriggs, A.I., 'Oriental Porcelain in Western Paintings', *Transactions of the Oriental Ceramic Society*, vol. 36, 1964-6, pp. 73 - 87

Stanford, Lincolnshire, Burghley House, *The Wrestling Boys. An Exhibition of Chinese and Japanese Ceramics from the 16th to the 18th Century in the Collection at Burghley House*, exhibition catalogue by G. Lang, Stanford, 1983

Stukeley, W., *An Account of a Large Silver Plate of Antique Basso Relievo, Roman Workmanship, Found in Derbyshire, 1729. Read Before the Antiquarian Society of London, 8 April 1736*, London, 1736

Sun-Bailey, S., 'The E.S. Thornhill Bequest of Chinese Ceramics at the North Staffordshire Polytechnic', *Transactions of the Oriental Ceramic Society*, vol. 48, 1983-4, pp. 63-85

Taipei, National Museum of History, *Ancient Chinese Trade Ceramics* exhibition catalogue, 2 vols, Taipei, 1992

Tietzel, B., *Kunstgewerbemuseum der Stadt Köln. Fayence I: Niederlande, Frankreich, England*, Köln, 1980

Tokyo, Idemitsu Museum of Arts, *Inter-Influence of Ceramic Art in East and West*, exhibition catalogue, Tokyo, 1984

Toppin, A.J., 'The Origin of Some Ceramic Designs', *Transactions of the English Ceramic Circle*, vol. 2, no. 10, 1948, pp. 266 - 76

Vainker, S.J., *Chinese Pottery and Porcelain from Prehistory to the Present*, London, 1991

Van Dam, J.D., *Gedateerd Delfts Aardewerk - Dated Dutch Delftware*, Amsterdam, 1991

Veiga, J.G., *Chinese Export Porcelain in Private Brazilian Collections*, London, 1989

Volker, T., 'Porcelain and the Dutch East India Company as Recorded in the Dagh - Registers of Batavia Castle, Those of Hirado and Deshima and other Contemporary Papers 1602 - 1682', *Mededelingen van het Rijksmuseum voor Volkenkunde*, no. 11, Leiden, 1971

Wästfelt, B., Gyllensvärd, B. and Weibull, J., *Porcelain from the East Indiaman Götheborg*, n.p., 1991

Watney, B., 'The King, the Nun and Other Figures', *Transactions of the English Ceramic Circle*, vol. VII, part I, 1968, pp. 48 - 58

Watson, F.J.B., and Wilson, G., *Mounted Oriental Porcelain in the J. Paul Getty Museum*, Malibu, California, 1982

Williamson, G.C., *The Book of a Famille Rose*, London, 1927

Wilmington, The Wilmington Society of the Fine Arts, *Chinese Export Porcelain and Enamels*, exhibition catalogue by J.A. Lloyd Hyde, Wilmington, U.S.A., 1957

Wilson, D.M., *The Forgotten Collector: Augustus Wollaston Franks of the British Museum*, Wisbech, 1984

Wirgin, J., 'Some Chinese porcelain services ordered by the Swedish Court in the 18th Century', *Nationalmuseum Bulletin*, vol. III, no. 4, Stockholm, 1979, pp. 215 - 24

Woodcock, T. and Robinson, J.M., *The Oxford Guide to Heraldry*, London, 1990

Woodward, C.S., *Oriental Ceramics at the Cape of Good Hope 1652-1795*, Cape Town and Rotterdam, 1974

Yeo, S.T. and Martin, J., *Chinese Blue and White Ceramics*, exhibition catalogue, National Museum, Singapore, 1978

Zick, G., *Berliner Porzellan der Manufaktur von Wilhelm Caspar Wegely 1751-1757*, Berlin, 1978

中國古代貿易瓷特展
大英博物館館藏

發 行 人	陳康順
出 版 者	國立歷史博物館
	台北市南海路49號
	（02）361－0270
借 展 者	英國大英博物館
編　　輯	國立歷史博物館編輯委員會
解說撰文	大英博物館東方部研究員　康蕊君
	大英博物館東方部研究員　霍吉淑
翻　　譯	國立歷史博物館　蔡琳、成耆仁
審　　稿	國立歷史博物館　林淑心、黃永川
執行編輯	成耆仁、楊式昭
美術編輯	王行恭
印　　刷	沈氏藝術印刷股份有限公司
電腦排版	文弘企業有限公司
中華民國八十三年五月出版	
ISBN	957－00－3623－0（精裝）
統一編號	006309830030